MARTIN LUTHER KING, JR.
AND THE CIVIL RIGHTS MOVEMENT

Edited by David J. Garrow

A CARLSON PUBLISHING SERIES

Brooklyn, N.Y.

Chicago 1966:

OPEN HOUSING MARCHES, SUMMIT NEGOTIATIONS, AND OPERATION BREADBASKET

Edited with a Preface by David J. Garrow

CARLSON
Publishing Inc

BROOKLYN, NEW YORK, 1989

Library of Congress Cataloging-in Publication Data

Chicago 1966 : open housing marches, summit negotiations, and
    operation breadbasket / edited with a preface by David J. Garrow.
        p.   cm. — (Martin Luther King, Jr. and the Civil Rights
    Movement ; 11)
    Includes bibliographies and index.
    1. Afro-Americans—Civil rights—Illinois—Chicago—History—20th
century. 2. Civil rights movements—Illinois—Chicago–
–History—20th century. 3. Chicago (Ill.)—Race relations.
I. Garrow, David J., 1953-   . II. Series.
F548.9.N4C46 1989   89-15798
977.3'1100496073—dc20
ISBN 0-926019-07-4

Typographic design: Julian Waters

Typeface: Bitstream ITC Galliard

The index to this book was created using NL Cindex, a scholarly indexing program
from the Newberry Library.

For a complete listing of the volumes in this series, please see the back of this book.

Printed on acid-free, 250-year-life paper.

Manufactured in the United States of America.

Contents

Editor's Preface

The Chicago Freedom Movement of 1966 was as significant a campaign as any that was mounted during the black freedom struggle of the 1950s and 1960s, but now, almost twenty-five years later, it is neither among the best remembered or the most celebrated. Aside from the small community of scholars of the civil rights movement, relatively few members of any wider national public, even ones who could readily identify the meaning of the Montgomery bus boycott or the 1963 Birmingham protests, would be able to identify or locate in time the Chicago Freedom Movement. Additionally, given the Chicago movement's ambiguous conclusion and relatively subtle aftereffects, its anniversaries have only rarely been noted, nevermind celebrated in the style of the 1963 March on Washington or the 1965 Selma to Montgomery march.

Such relative lack of fame and glory, however, does not and should not detract from the tremendous historical significance of the 1966 events in Chicago, a significance that reaches well beyond the consequences they had for Dr. Martin Luther King, Jr., for his organization, the Southern Christian Leadership Conference (SCLC), for Chicago's Mayor, Richard J. Daley, and his political machine, and for the black citizens of Chicago. The significance of the Chicago Freedom Movement reached well beyond the city and the immediate participants because of how the 1966 events there signalled the tremendous obstacles, if not insuperable barriers, that would confront efforts to transfer and expand the basic strategies and tactics of the southern black freedom struggle to the big cities of the north.

The Chicago movement, which formally got underway in the fall of 1965, drew its instigation and inspiration from two main sources: the energy and success that had been generated by the city's local coalition of civil rights groups, the Coordinating Council of Community Organizations (CCCO), and the desire of Dr. King and the SCLC to undertake a major initial challenge against the *de facto* injustices of the urban north, injustices that were most often manifest in the forms of inferior housing, inferior schools, and inferior jobs. The interplay between those two arms of the Chicago Freedom Movement—the indigenous activists whose organizational affiliations ranged across a wide gamut of groups, and the new-to-Chicago staffers of King's SCLC—is almost as significant a part of the Chicago movement's history as is the more publicly visible interplay between the movement itself and Mayor Daley's city government.

To date only one significant volume, Alan B. Anderson and George W. Pickering's *Confronting the Color Line: The Broken Promise of the Civil Rights Movement in Chicago* (University of Georgia Press, 1987), has focused totally upon Chicago's 1960s civil rights scene. In this valuable but oftentimes dry and abstract study, Anderson and Pickering devoted considerable attention to events in the years before 1965-1966 as well as to the occurrences of that more notable period. Other volumes, such as my own *Bearing the Cross: Martin Luther King, Jr., and the Southern Christian Leadership Conference*, have devoted extensive attention to the Chicago movement in the course of treating broader periods and subjects, but to date the Chicago Freedom Movement and the entire family of strategic questions involved in the effort to "bring the movement north" have received far less careful and thoughtful scholarly attention than they should have.

The five major pieces of contemporary or almost-contemporary participant-observer analysis of the 1965-1966 Chicago movement and its immediate aftermath presented in this volume ought to go a good ways toward encouraging the expanded scholarship that the Chicago story very much deserves. All five of the studies are previously unpublished pieces of work, and each was authored by someone who either directly participated in the Chicago movement or sympathized and worked closely with it. Mary Lou Finley's 1967 paper, "The Open Housing Marches, Chicago, Summer '66," supplies an excellent, broad-gauged overview of the Chicago Freedom Movement, an overview that offers a nicely detailed history of the early stages of the effort and a well-informed depiction of the movement's tactical evolution from an initial focus upon organizing slum dwellers into the dramatic, violence-evoking protest marches through all-white neighborhoods of Chicago that represented the movement's climax in the summer of 1966. In 1965 and 1966 Professor Finley, now a sociologist, worked as principal administrative assistant to SCLC's most significant and mercurial Chicago staffer, James L. Bevel, and her study provides an extremely important picture of the internal dynamics that existed between the movement's staff-constituted "Action Committee" and its policy-making parent body, the "Agenda Committee," composed of Dr. King and other significant organizational leaders. Wholly apart from its excellent portrayal of the behind-the-scenes relationships within the Chicago Freedom Movement, Professor Finley's paper offers an insightful treatment of the leadership problems encountered by a social protest movement built upon a multi-organization coalition and featuring fluid—and hence often conflictual—decision-making roles and responsibilities.

Professor Finley's essay provides important portraits of two of the Chicago movement's most significant activists, Bevel and CCCO convener Albert A. Raby, and it also offers a valuable sketch of the internal tensions that were generated by the onset of direct negotiations between movement and city leaders in August of 1966. Those negotiations themselves are the subject of Kathleen Connolly's solid and valuable 1967 paper, "The Chicago Open Housing Conference," which provides a background overview of the period leading up to the negotiations as well as a useful analysis of the "summit conference" and the resulting "summit agreement" that movement leaders and city officials formally adopted.

The two major summit negotiating sessions, on August 17 and August 26, 1966 are the subject of this volume's third and perhaps most remarkable piece, John McKnight's careful and complete observer's transcription of the very rich and very detailed extended discussions that characterized both of these important occasions. Although more than a score of participants from the movement and the city took part in each session, the leading figures—Dr. King and Al Raby for the movement, and Mayor Daley and Chicago Real Estate Board chairman Ross Beatty on the city's side—undeniably dominated the crucial exchanges at both sessions. No other document on the Chicago movement offers such a remarkably rich and informative portrait of the struggle's leading actors, and few, if any, other original source documents provide such fascinating and extended pictures of both the combative, short-tempered Chicago mayor and the smoothly mellifluous, yet cagily careful Dr. King. McKnight's invaluable observer's transcription also offers important perspectives on other significant participants, such as the tired and frustrated Raby and the gently compromising presiding officer, liberal railroad president Ben W. Heineman. All in all, the McKnight transcription is a truly timeless document, and one that each and every serious student of Dr. King should read and reflect upon with care. Bracketing the McKnight manuscript in this volume are both the initial set of demands with which the Freedom Movement entered the negotiations and the full text of the official Summit Agreement that was ratified at the August 26th session.

Chicago divinity professor Alvin Pitcher was, somewhat like SCLC's Mary Lou Finley, one of the crucially important behind-the-scenes figures who played significant roles in the Chicago Freedom Movement without ever becoming a widely-familiar name. Pitcher served as principal administrative deputy to the CCCO's Raby (much as Finley did to SCLC's Bevel), and his important organizational position, together with his analytical skills and academic bent, allowed Pitcher to glean significant critical insights about the way in which the complicated, coalitional Freedom Movement developed and functioned. Both with regard to his paper's analysis of the Freedom Movement's structural pluses and minuses—some of it articulated in question and answer format—and with regard to the essay's treatment of CCCO's own evolution and weaknesses, Pitcher's frank, contemporaneous (November 1966) analysis offers yet another important and insightful participant-observer's account of 1965-1966 from inside the Freedom Movement itself.

Professor Pitcher's influence was important not only within the CCCO/CFM organizational structure, but also upon one of his divinity students, Jesse L. Jackson, who took a role in SCLC's early Chicago neighborhood organizing efforts in the fall and winter of 1965-1966 and then shifted into a significant role in the summer "Action Committee" protest decisions while simultaneously playing an important role in encouraging black Chicago clergy to actively support the Freedom Movement. Jackson's active but limited involvement in the summit negotiation sessions can be witnessed in John McKnight's observer transcriptions, but as the protest phase of the Chicago struggle came to an end with that August, 1966, accord, Jackson's most significant work blossomed in the form of Chicago's Operation Breadbasket chapter. Breadbasket had for six years been an SCLC program modelled on the Philadelphia efforts of ministers such as Leon Sullivan, but only when Jackson, in conjunction with local Chicago ministers such as Clay Evans, began applying its strategy—firms whose products were purchased by black consumers were asked by black ministers to provide significant job opportunities to black workers, or face a consumer boycott—on the Chicago scene did Breadbasket begin to approach its true potential.

Throughout the period from 1966 into the early 1970s, one of Jackson's two closest colleagues and assistants was Gary Massoni, a one-time fellow divinity student whose 1971 master's thesis on Operation Breadbasket has stood for almost twenty years as both far and away the most important and detailed study of Breadbasket's development and evolution in Chicago and as a rich but little-used source of insights on a crucial but little-appreciated period in the life of Reverend Jackson. Like the Chicago movement of 1965-1966, the Chicago Breadbasket operation of the late 1960s and early 1970s has received far, far less scholarly attention and strategic reflection than ought to have been the case. Like Finley and Pitcher, Massoni's invaluable work on Breadbasket and Jackson is another significant example of the best sort of participant-observer history and reflection, a document that will be important to any student of consumer boycott strategies and that increasingly will be appreciated as an indispensable source for anyone who seeks to come to a dispassionate and well-informed understanding of the significant life of Jesse Louis Jackson.

I am very pleased that Carlson Publishing's series of volumes on *Martin Luther King, Jr., and the Civil Rights Movement* is able to bring all five of these significant but previously unpublished studies of civil rights activism in Chicago to a broad audience of scholars and interested students. The McKnight, Finley, and Pitcher papers are indispensable sources for any serious student of Dr. King's move north and the 1966 Chicago movement, and Massoni's important study ought to be widely read both by movement historians and those interested in the life history and political background of Jesse Jackson. The publication of these previously all-but-unavailable analyses will, I hope, stimulate greater appreciation of the 1960s black freedom struggle in Chicago, and more explicit analysis of the linkages between the activism of those years and the significant 1983 election of Harold Washington as Chicago's first black mayor.

David J. Garrow

Chicago 1966

The Open Housing Marches Chicago Summer '66

MARY LOU FINLEY

Prelude to the Summer

The marches for open housing which left Chicago deeply shaken after the summer of 1966 did not, like Athena, spring full-blown from the head of Zeus. Much preliminary work had gone on quietly during the winter, spring, and early summer, preparing those who became the leaders and participants in the marches. Though the open housing marches *per se* were not conceived until rather late, the general groundwork laid earlier made possible their execution.

During the summer of 1965 Dr. Martin Luther King had decided that he wanted to begin work in a northern city. A summer tour of several northern cities gave him the opportunity to talk with leaders, and to assess the nature and strength of the civil rights movement in these important urban centers. He chose Chicago, and announced in September, 1965, that he would soon be coming to lead his first major drive in the North.

This paper was written in the Spring of 1967. It is published here for the first time.

1

Three considerations seem to have been important in making this decision. First, the Coordinating Council of Community Organizations, the umbrella group of Chicago civil rights organizations had been able to bring together some kind of coalition and to carry out a summer-long direct action program in 1965, a rare accomplishment for Northern civil rights groups. The CCCO, which had been functioning for several years, had invited Dr. King to come to Chicago to help them oust Benjamin Willis, the Superintendent of Schools; thus King could be certain of a warm reception. Secondly, power in Chicago is extremely centralized in Mayor Daley, who not only controls the city but also has a significant influence in national politics. Pressure on the mayor would be quickly felt at the national level. And finally, James Bevel, one of King's chief lieutenants, had already located himself in Chicago, taking a job as Program Director of the West Side Christian Parish. His talents would be extremely useful—perhaps necessary—in carrying out a nonviolent movement. (The emphasis placed on these considerations varies, according to the informant; Chicago leaders tend to believe his chief reason was the first, while those familiar with the way in which Bevel and King work together tend to think that it was Bevel's presence in Chicago which was the deciding factor.)

Preparations for a movement, presumably to include direct action, began on two different levels in September. Bevel began to work with staff persons, both local community organization staff and the dozen SCLC field staff sent from the South to work under his direction. At the same time, Andrew Young, executive director of SCLC, and Dr. King began meeting and planning with the recognized and established leadership—chiefly CCCO. (There was some overlap in these two processes; Bevel occasionally went to the meetings with CCCO, and Young and King attended some of the staff activities. However, this was usually more just to make an appearance than to actually become involved in the process of developing cooperation.)

Bevel's work with the staff had two distinct aspects: getting the staff of the various organizations to work together toward common goals, and providing education for the staff about the nature of the problems in the urban ghetto. It began with a week-long workshop for nearly one hundred staff persons, chiefly from organizations on the West Side. At the conclusion of the week the group decided to continue to meet twice weekly; one meeting would be devoted to a presentation by an outside speaker on some aspect of the problem of life in the slums, the second to discussing programs which groups were doing, and to develop projects which all would work on together. These meetings continued through January, 1966.

The attempt to get the community groups to cooperate on a common project was only of limited success. Bevel's original idea had been that with each group working on a different aspect of the problem, it would never be possible to garner enough resources to get anywhere on any one problem; he proposed that the group decide on which problem they wanted to begin, and then when that had been resolved, go on to something else. This proved to be difficult, however; some groups wanted to work on welfare, while others were concerned about housing or urban renewal. In addition, no one had a clear plan upon which the group could begin working. The community groups tended to feel that SCLC should be helping them out on the projects which they had designed, and when it became clear that this was not what Bevel intended to do, there were hard feelings. The failure of the SCLC staff to develop and maintain a good relationship with these groups had its consequences in the summer direct action program when the time came for mobilization of the participants; this will be discussed in greater detail at a later point.

Some forms of cooperation did emerge out of these meetings; JOIN and the West Side Organization realized that they had a common interest in welfare problems and cooperated on developing techniques for organizing welfare recipients. These meetings provided a foundation for the cooperation which developed in February and March among the groups in East Garfield Park as they banded together to form the East Garfield Park Union to End Slums. In addition, the very fact of having gotten acquainted with the staff persons of the other community organizations made informal cooperation easier in the future.

The most significant aspect of the Wider Community Staff meetings (as the twice-weekly meetings were called) was the process of education undergone by the staff. The "outside experts" brought to the group the information which led to an understanding of the "forces that create slums." It was Bevel who led the group in putting together these bits and pieces of information into a coherent whole—centered around the idea that a slum is an exploited community, created and maintained by "forces" in the larger community which drain the resources from the community. These "forces" were chiefly institutions, either private or public; they included the slum landlords, who overcharge for bad housing; the banks, which will not loan money for purchase or repair of housing in the ghetto; the school system, which does not provide an adequate education for Negro children; the welfare system, which provides a below-subsistence income and robs recipients of their dignity; the political machine, which obtains votes by bribery and coercion and thus does not have to serve the real needs of the Negro community; and the board of realtors, who keep Negroes "locked in" the ghetto by refusing to rent or sell them housing elsewhere. These institutions should be the targets of the civil rights movement; if slums were to end, these "forces" would have to change. The decision of where to break into "the cycle," as the problem is often phrased, was for Bevel a tactical decision; one point would be as good as the other, providing that one could gain successes which would encourage the Negro community to take up the next battle.

During these Wider Community Staff meetings Bevel lectured often on nonviolence: the power of nonviolent direct action which cannot be stopped by the conventional tools at the disposal of those who wield power, the necessity of putting the issue in its simplest terms so that all can understand the problem, the necessity of standing firm on your position, and of developing people who understood the problem and were committed to solving it enough to give up the smaller projects in which they were then involved. Out of this group there began to develop a smaller core who began to understand what had to be done.

At the "executive" level plans were also being laid. By December Dr. King had decided that a nonviolent action program would be on the agenda for Chicago the following summer. Early in January he met with a group of about forty leaders of the Coordinating Council of Community Organizations in a two-day long session at Sahara Inn, during which time SCLC's plan (prepared by Dr. King and Reverend Andrew Young, the executive director of SCLC) was presented for the consideration of this group. The plan envisioned a 'Movement to End Slums,' directed at all of the "forces that create slums." Proposed was a tentative timetable which included beginning some kind of direct action as early as May. The plan was, in general, accepted by the group, and the initial preparation for the Movement was under way.

Shortly thereafter the Freedom Assembly and the Agenda Committee were set up as the formal structure of the Chicago Freedom Movement. The Freedom Assembly was to be a group of about 100 persons representing community organizations, civil rights groups, church organizations with civil rights interests, some labor unions, and other groups which wished to be a part of the Movement. It provided an umbrella, a means by which those who were not members of CCCO could be a part of the Freedom Movement. The Agenda Committee, consisting of about twelve persons, was to plan the agenda for this group, and to carry on its business between meetings. It met weekly, and informally assumed the major policy-making responsibility for the Freedom Movement.

In early February Dr. King moved into an apartment just off 16th Street in Lawndale. Arriving with great fanfare, he made the point that he was going to live with "the people" in Chicago. (Though the landlord did a speedy clean up, paint-up job when he learned that Dr. King was to move in, the fresh paint did not long endure, the smell of pine oil soon wore off, and the apartment suffered the usual ills of slum buildings—plumbing that works only half the time, heat problems, etc.)

The mechanism for carrying out these plans was to be the organization of a community base in East Garfield Park, and to a lesser extent, in Lawndale, where the SCLC staff had settled down to work. The staff began organizing the Union to End Slums, envisioned as a block-by-block organization of people who *understood* the source of their problems and would be willing to work together on a number of issues. Slum housing conditions were to be used as the focus for organizing, which was to be done on a building basis; organizing to get the landlord to fix up the buildings would be a means by which people could work toward immediate, concrete results.

Work in organizing the Union to End Slums progressed more slowly than had been anticipated. There were a number of reasons for this. The staff were all novices in community organization, and thus had to experiment with various techniques as they went along; more supervision would probably have helped in overcoming more quickly the problems which they encountered. In addition, expectations had been set excessively high. I doubt if even top notch professional organizers could have organized this community of 70,000 people in just a few months. As it became clear that they were not going to accomplish as much as they thought they could, the staff became very discouraged, feeling that it was their fault that things were not going well. This discouragement slowed them down even more.

During May and June there was some revival of interest with the campaign of rent strikes and picketing directed against the Condor and Costalis Realty Company, managers of about fifty buildings in the community. The protests finally culminated in the Company agreeing to sign a collective bargaining agreement with the Union, giving them the right of bargaining for the tenants and guaranteeing certain rights for the tenants. Though this victory was important for the organizing effort in the community, it did not really affect the SCLC staff very much; they still felt they had been unable to do what they had started out to do—organize a community-wide Union to End Slums.

The Direct Action Program

By late spring it had become apparent that the Union to End Slums would not be able to provide a very large base for a summer direct action program. Some other form of involving the Negro community would be needed if an action program was to be carried out.

Dr. King suggested a gigantic rally to be held on a Sunday afternoon for the purpose of setting forth the summer program. It was eventually decided to hold such a rally, and immediately following it, those in attendance would march to City Hall; Dr. King would lead the march, and would post the "Demands" of the Freedom Movement on the door of City Hall.

The rally, originally planned for early June, was postponed first because of interference with the June election in which a number of independent candidates were running, supported chiefly by the volunteer campaign work of groups sympathetic to the Movement. The second postponement occurred because Dr. King and a number of other civil rights leaders were completing James Meredith's march to Jackson, Mississippi, and would not be able to return to Chicago in time. July 10 was finally set as the day for the rally.

There were two differences of opinion which arose over the rally; the nature of the "Demands," and, in Bevel's words, whether the rally was to be a "war dance or a freedom picnic." The "Demands" consisted first of a series of papers prepared on various issues by "experts" in the fields. Later community groups working directly with these problems were brought in to draw up the final form of the demands. The housing demands, in particular, received special attention, chiefly from the staff members of the American Friends Service Committee and SCLC, who were working toward housing integration and the end of slum housing conditions. As the "Demands" were clarified and refined, it was finally decided to center them around the demand for an "Open City."

About the first of July the Action Committee was appointed, under the chairmanship of Bevel. This group was given the responsibility of planning and executing a summer action program, based around the demand for an "Open City." It was this group that was concerned that the rally be not just a "freedom picnic," but a kick-off for an action program; it would be important, then, to spend time at the rally explaining the rationale behind the action program and urging all those present to come back and participate in it. A compromise was finally reached regarding the rally program; there would still be the list of "important speakers" who would speak generally about the problem, and Bevel would give his speech exhorting the people to action and detailing what they should do next.

Attendance at the rally was smaller than had been anticipated (estimates varied from 25,000 to 50,000), but the attendance was nonetheless quite significant as it was almost all Negro. It was announced at the rally that those who wanted to participate in the action program should come to mass meetings to be held the following week at churches, one on the South Side and one on the West Side.

Selection of Open Housing as the Central Issue

I am not certain of the exact pathway along which this decision passed before it became the official program of the Chicago Freedom Movement for the summer. I do know, however, that Bevel had become convinced by late spring that open housing would be the best issue around which to organize a summer action program.[1] It is very likely that he convinced Dr. King, and that Andrew Young and Dr. King helped to sell the idea to CCCO. At any rate, it was presented as a suggestion at an ad hoc CCCO meeting on the "Demands" shortly before the July 10 rally, and was agreed upon by that group; the program would be an "Open City," with open housing as the first step.

Since Bevel was very likely the key person in choosing open housing, a discussion of his reasoning behind this decision seems relevant.

Open housing was *not* selected because it was believed to be the key problem facing the Negro community. Bevel realized that the lack of good jobs, for instance, had a much more profound effect upon the nature of life in the slums. It was chosen because it offered the best opportunity for the Negro to "stand up and be a man, to declare that he was a human being and would henceforth expect to be treated like one."

Bevel recognized that the chief problem of the poor ghetto Negro was his own hopelessness; this sense of futility, this acceptance of the white man's definition of him as somehow less than a man incapacitated the Negro. He could not organize himself, he could not work for change as long as he did not accept his own manhood, if the Negro could just rise up and recognize himself as a man, he would no longer tolerate the multitude of oppressive forces which governed his life; "*men* do not tolerate being forced to live in rat-infested slums, to work at a wage so low they cannot support their families, to sit by while their children go through school without becoming educated." Bevel believes that Negroes could become men if they would just, for once, stand up to "the man" and declare that they could not be turned back. He declares that this is what the Movement did for the South—provided Negroes with the sense of being somebody important, who did not have to bow and scrape and do as they were told. Once hope is rekindled, organizing can be done, and work can progress much faster toward the solution of the rest of the problem.

The open housing issue had many advantages as a means of reaching this goal. The housing market is the most clear-cut form of discrimination which exists in the North; a Negro walking into a real estate office in a white neighborhood is told that nothing is available for him, simply because he is a Negro. The affront to his dignity is sharp, direct, insulting. This situation provides an ideal framework for the Negro to stand up and say that he too is human and demands to be treated the same as are other human beings seeking a place to live.

In addition, the problem of housing discrimination has an easy solution, compared to other types of problems. It would take only an administrative order—from the mayor, the governor, Congress, or the President—to end discrimination in housing. Since realtors are licensed both by the city and the state, these organs of government have a readily available sanction—confiscation of licenses. Other problems, such as job discrimination and school segregation, have much more complex solutions; it would thus be harder to win a concrete, measurable victory—so necessary for the rekindling of hope—in these areas.

Finally, an open housing campaign had certain tactical advantages. The source of discrimination could be easily located, and was highly visible—the real estate office. Direct action could thus be centered around Negroes trying to get service at real estate offices. The education of the city as to the nature of the problem would be graphic: Negroes were not treated like men when they went to real estate offices. Demonstrations around real estate offices had great dramatic potential; they would probably not be ignored by the community. If violence should erupt, it would only strengthen the Negro's position and clarify his moral righteousness, as white teenagers attacking the Negro students during the sit-ins had done. The goal of a direct action program is to so dramatize a problem so that the injustice is vivid for everyone to see, and so that the community can no longer ignore it. Demonstrations around real estate offices seemed to have that potential.

Bevel and other leaders of the Movement were well aware at that time of the relationship between slums and the closed housing market: Negroes could be charged high rents for abominable housing only because they had no alternatives. Careful analysis of census data had revealed that rents were in fact cheaper in a number of communities outside the ghetto; thus open housing would be helpful not only to the middle class Negro, as had been traditionally assumed, but to the poorest as well.

The real estate system, which kept Negroes "locked in" the ghetto, was only one of the "forces which create slums." Nonetheless, it was as good a place to start as any; breaking down the bars which keep Negroes imprisoned in the ghetto would be an important victory in itself, and should have a profound psychological effect on the Negro community.

Bevel was aware that slum-dwelling Negroes were far from understanding the closed housing market as one of their key problems. Yet, some did. He hoped that those who did would be ready to join in the action immediately, and that others would begin to understand as the educational processes of the Movement progressed, as mass meetings and radio programs brought critical information to the masses of people in the slums.

The Action Committee

The Action Committee, appointed by Dr. King and Al Raby about the first of July, was given the responsibility of planning and executing a direct action program around the open housing issue. The committee was originally composed of about fifteen staff persons from several organizations; others, some of which represented community organizations, and some of which were persons with specific responsibilities for the action program, were added later. The key people on the committee—i.e., those who spoke for it and those who represented its point of view—were:

9

James Bevel, Jesse Jackson, Bernard Lafayette—These men were all veterans of nonviolent movements in the South and were the chief strategists.

Bill Moyer, Bert Ransom, and (to a lesser extent) Jerry Davis—These men were the staff members of the housing program of the American Friends Service Committee; they contributed their rather extensive experience with organizing direct action at real estate offices, and carried a large part of the burden of the detailed work and planning required to see that the marches actually came off as planned.

Al Pitcher—the CCCO administrator, who served the committee as an administrative assistant and provided a link to the Agenda Committee.

(For a complete list of the members of the action committee, see Appendix A.)

The group was strongly dominated by Bevel, who was aided and abetted by Lafayette and Jackson. Bevel was occasionally overruled, but it was usually his suggestions that the group ended up adopting, though often only after much heated discussion.

Since the action program was carried almost to its conclusion by the Action Committee alone, the following discussion of nonviolent theory, goals, and strategy will be presented as viewed by the Action Committee. The tensions between this group and the Agenda Committee, including their different ideas concerning strategy, will be discussed later; it was not until the end of the program that the will of the Agenda Committee dominated. Until that time, they gave their blessing, more or less, to the plans of the Action Committee. (Though they sometimes were not too happy about what was being done, they made only one serious attempt to change the course of events.)

Theory of a Nonviolent Movement

The purpose of nonviolent action is to so dramatize injustice that the conscience of the community is aroused, and responds to make right the wrong. The problem must first be reduced to its simplest terms, then dramatized through action.

In reducing the problem to its simplest terms, one should state it as something which is very plainly unjust. In Selma, the problem was the right to vote; in Chicago, it was the fact that Negroes were not treated as men by real estate offices. This serves two purposes; it helps mobilization, as the oppressed themselves have not always understood the cause of their oppression, and can rally to support a Movement only when it is pointed out to them very clearly. In addition, it is the chief device for educating the rest of the community, for helping them to realize the injustice which is being perpetrated. This educational technique is based on the premise that if people can really understand the problem and have to face it, they will recognize the justice of the protesters' cause.

The demand made by the movement should also be very simple; it should go to the heart of the problem, and should not be debatable.

The action itself must be carried out nonviolently, with dignity; this is necessary because one does not achieve just ends by using unjust means. Hatred and violence can only make the situation worse. In addition, it is recognized that when a demonstration is carried out in a dignified manner, with participants enduring abuse if necessary, spectators will gain more respect for the protesters, thus seeing more clearly that their cause is just.

Tension may erupt during nonviolent action; but this is necessary if injustice is to be ended. As Dr. King wrote in his "Letter from a Birmingham Jail" to the clergymen of Birmingham during the massive demonstrations there:

> Actually, we who engage in nonviolent direct action are not the creators of tension. We merely bring to the surface the hidden tension that is already alive. We bring it out in the open where it can be seen and dealt with. Like a boil that can never be cured as long as it is covered up but must be opened with all its pus-flowing ugliness to the natural medicine of light and air, injustice must likewise be exposed, with all of the tension its exposing creates, to the light of human conscience and the air of national opinion before it can be cured.

In addition to gaining public support through the exposure of injustice, nonviolent direct action is a source of power. This power to disrupt, and by so doing to demand attention, is especially important to groups without more conventional kinds of power—economic or political. It provides a bargaining position for the group that is protesting, a position perhaps unattainable any other way. Bevel often stated during the year previous to the demonstrations that it might be necessary to "close down the town and set the rules straight." King, in his "Letter from a Birmingham Jail," further clarifies this power dimension of nonviolence.

11

Nonviolent direct action seeks to create such a crisis and establish such creative tension that a community that has constantly refused to negotiate is forced to confront the issue. It seeks so to dramatize the issue that it can no longer be ignored.

Furthermore, nonviolent action is to be carried out without malice toward the oppressor, fully recognizing the forces which cause him to oppress and continually trying to win him over, to help him see the light and join the fight for justice.

These were the basic principles which Bevel and the others working with him on the Action Committee were trying to apply to the problem of housing segregation in Chicago. They had been successful in Birmingham and in Selma, as Bevel often recalled; now, could they work in Chicago? (King was also acting on these premises, but he did not participate very much in the day-to-day planning; this he left to Bevel, primarily.)

Goals of the Open Housing Movement

The goal of the direct action program, as it finally took shape after the July 10 rally, was simply that, "All housing should be available to all people." More specifically this was a demand that no realtor accept a discriminatory listing, that Negroes seeking service in real estate offices be treated like whites, i.e., shown all the available listings, and then be allowed to choose whatever housing they were interested in.

Though recognizing that all housing does not pass through real estate offices, the movement leadership chose to emphasize these offices for several reasons. The offices are open to the public and licensed by the state, and, thus, as public businesses, should not be allowed to discriminate. Sanctions could be easily applied, as licenses could be taken away from noncomplying realtors. In addition, the Board of Realtors is a strong, fraternal, professional organization which exerts control over its members; it has a policy of housing segregation, opposing fair housing laws. It *could* be an organ for change, if it wished; thus it provided a centralized source of power to which demands could be made. Also, one could anticipate that, were realtors forbidden to discriminate, they themselves would push for an open housing law including individual homeowners, to avoid their losing the business of individuals who wished to discriminate.

It is not quite clear what kind of a response the Movement leaders hoped to get to their demand for open housing. There was some hope that the Board of Realtors might agree to open the housing market, if they were sufficiently pressured by public opinion which the Movement hoped to awaken. It was more likely, though, that change would have to come through legislation of some kind. Though he did not often say so directly, Bevel seems to have anticipated a national response from Congress and the President, akin to the response to Birmingham and Selma, which produced the Civil Rights Bills of 1964 and 1965. It was decided to concentrate first in the city, not because the wish for change was limited to the city, but because of Mayor Daley's power at the national level and the recognition that pressure he felt would be quickly felt in Washington also.

I really do not think the leaders of the Movement—either Bevel or King or the Chicago leaders—had decided beforehand at what level they wished to negotiate, what kind of settlement would have been acceptable. There is a kind of working philosophy in nonviolence which says that one never knows what will happen next, what responses one's actions will bring; therefore one can only act, and wait for the response, then decide what is best in that situation. Perhaps this was governing the thinking about the kind of settlement which could occur. (I should emphasize that this is only a personal judgment, based on the information available to me; it could well be that some persons had decided this beforehand, but they chose not to speak about it, not to make it explicit.)

In addition to the goal of equal services for Negroes at real estate offices, several other aspects of the housing problem were discussed by the Action Committee, and tentative plans were made to incorporate them into the program. They tended to be shunted aside, however, as it became necessary to sharpen the focus and concentrate upon one goal, in order to make at least that one point very clearly.

Bevel had hoped that tenants in slum buildings who were being organized during the spring would be ready to go on a rent strike during the summer, while the demonstrations were going on. This coordinated effort would have provided a means of saying to the community at large that, "We refuse to pay rent any longer for slum housing; we demand the right to move out of the ghetto." Though some rent strikes were going on during the summer, the coordination envisioned never was enacted.

The West Side Organization with its welfare union was interested in raising the question of the public aid department placing recipients in slum housing;

13

they expressed some interest in getting the welfare union to protest this, as the direct action program aimed at the realtors was going on. Though specific action was never organized around this issue by the welfare union, the raising of the question at this time insured its being brought in at the time of the negotiations.

Strategy for the Direct Action Program

According to Dr. King,[2] there are four basic steps in any nonviolent campaign. These are: 1) Collection of the facts to determine whether injustices are alive, 2) Negotiation, 3) Self-purification, and 4) Direct Action. These were the framework around which the summer action program was planned.

As soon as open housing had been agreed upon as the chief target for the summer, testing of real estate offices began. Though it was well-known that discrimination existed, the Movement wished to have concrete facts about this before taking further action. About fifty cases of discrimination were documented previous to the July 10 rally.

On the basis of this evidence, plus past documentation of discrimination, Dr. King and Al Raby requested a meeting with the Board of Realtors to ask them to change their policies. After several telegrams and letters passed back and forth, the Board of Realtors stated that they would meet only if the Freedom Movement accepted their basic premise—that they were the agents of the homeseller, and thus could not be nondiscriminatory. This the Movement could not accept, for it was functioning upon the premise that the real estate office was a business open to the public and licensed by the state and thus could not offer discriminatory service. Thus, it was declared at the July 10 rally that the Board of Realtors had refused to meet with the Movement to discuss the problem. Thus other methods would have to be used to call the problem to their attention. (This was merely a formal step; there was no real hope that the Board of Realtors would offer any kind of concession at that point.)

In addition the posting of the "Demands" on the door of City Hall, and Dr. King's meeting with the Mayor the following day, were additional steps to offer to the city the opportunity to negotiate a settlement, to respond to the stated needs of the Negro community without waiting for the pressure of direct action. This meeting, too, brought no change. (Again, none had been anticipated. But it was necessary to give the city a chance to respond, so that they could not come back later charging that they had never been consulted, never been asked to implement changes, etc.)

With these steps out of the way, having proven that there was no alternative but direct action, the action program itself went into motion.

White communities where the cost of housing was comparable to the cost of slum housing were chosen as the target areas. These were to be neighborhoods not adjacent to the existing ghetto; it was important that people not think the Movement just wanted to move these people from their homes more quickly, but wanted Negroes to be free to disperse themselves anywhere in the city. Using census data, the Action Committee chose a number of neighborhoods which fit this criteria; Gage Park was chosen as the first neighborhood primarily because of its accessibility from the large South Side Negro community.

The first step in one of these white communities would be to send Negroes and whites in to test the real estate offices, to establish which ones discriminated. Then activities to acquaint the Negroes with the community—and to give the white inhabitants a chance to "get used to" having Negroes in their community would follow. Picnics, shopping excursions, and visits to the local churches' services would take place. Prayer vigils led by Negro preachers would be held Sunday afternoon on the steps of churches in the community, as "prayers that the people of the community might be moved to act with justice and to recognize their brotherhood with all men" were offered. Finally, prayer vigils, picketing, and marches would be held around the real estate offices. These would be demonstrations in support of Negro families who were seeking service at the real estate offices. As soon as feasible (i.e., whenever the staff felt able to undertake broadened responsibilities), this process would begin in a second community, a third, and so on.

In addition contacts would be made with sympathetic persons in the target communities. These persons would be encouraged to call meetings of people from their community at which the leaders of the Movement would interpret the ongoing activities, answer questions, and attempt to enlist the support of the people who lived in that neighborhood.

The Action Centers

The Action Committee was charged not only with planning the action program, but with carrying it out also. In order to facilitate these organizational tasks, two action centers were established, one on the South Side and one on the West Side. Mass meetings would be held at the centers (which were located in churches) once a week. Marches and other activities would depart from there; anyone who wanted to work or participate in any of the activities would report there. Also staff would have office space there to use for contacting people and for working out the logistics of the marches.

The South Side Action Center was under the direction of Bert Ransom, staff member of the housing program of the AFSC. He had several full-time volunteers, and quite a few other volunteers who came in to help, particularly with the extensive clerical work involved with testing the real estate offices, keeping records of the cases of discrimination, etc. In addition, Ransom recruited a neighborhood gang to help; they canvassed the community to get people to come to mass meetings and to the marches, and trained themselves as the marshals for the marches.

The Center was located in the New Friendship Baptist Church, 71st and Halsted. The pastor of the church, Reverend Strom Freeman, had been one of the leaders in Operation Breadbasket, the organization of ministers which negotiated with companies in the ghetto for more jobs for Negroes. It was because of this connection with the Movement that he was willing to let his church be used. During the first week in August, though, he asked that the action center be moved from the church. He had received a number of threatening phone calls which were frightening his family, and a homemade "bomb" had been thrown at the church. This was just more than his family and congregation could take.

So the action center picked up and moved to Greater Mount Hope Baptist Church, 60th and Princeton. The minister there had been with Dr. King in the civil rights movement in the South, and said that he would stick by the Movement, even if it meant that his church was blown up. The center remained there for the rest of the summer.

The West Side Action Center did not fare quite as well. It was not only moved twice; it also failed to get a staff organized to carry out the work of the center consistently. The Action Center was first established at Stone Temple, headquarters of the Lawndale Union to End Slums. It was moved from there, partly because the poor acoustics made it a bad place for mass meetings, and partly because the loyalty of the pastor did not seem particularly secure. (At a funeral held here for a young girl killed by a stray police bullet during the riots, the pastor invited both Dr. King and Alderman Collins to speak. Dr. King was unable to attend at the last minute.) The Action Center was moved to Warren Avenue Congregational Church, 3101 Warren, the headquarters of the SCLC field staff.

Jerry Davis of the AFSC housing staff served as the first director. After two weeks his job was taken over by William Hollins and Mark Harrington of the SCLC staff. Neither of the directors, however, managed to get a staff together to do the work of the center. Though they managed to get the essential things done, such as planning the logistics for the marches and setting up the program for the mass meetings, they did less work in the community than the South Side Center. As a result the mass meetings and the marches departing from the West Side Center were usually smaller. (The SCLC staff contributed some to the efforts of the Action Center. Most were too discouraged at this point to take on major responsibilities and follow through with them, with the exception of the center directors and Claudia King, who was press secretary.)

In spite of these difficulties the action centers did organize people, hold mass meetings, plan logistics for the marches, etc.

Mobilization of Participants

The Action Committee's plan for mobilization was developed by Bernard Lafayette, and presented at a Committee meeting preceding the July 10 rally. Mobilization was to focus around community organizations, each of which would be asked to ready a platoon of 50 to 100 persons and prepare to take responsibility for the demonstrations in one white community. As escalation began, other groups would be brought in, with action—picketing, marching, vigiling, etc.—taking place in several communities at a time. Each community organization would still have responsibility for one community.

The plan was aimed at spreading out the task of mobilization, and, more important, involving community organizations in the direct action program. Community groups were asked not to give up the programs they were currently involved in but to spend two days a week working to mobilize people for the open housing program and to continue their own work

17

during the other five days. Lafayette also expressed the hope that this would help to strengthen the community organizations, as they served as the focus in their community for recruiting the persons who wanted to participate in the direct action program. Any community organization participating in the program would be invited to send a representative to the Action Committee, and thus to participate in the planning and decision-making.

The plan was tried at the beginning of the marches, though it never really got off the ground. The first march in Belmont-Cragin, for instance, was to have been the responsibility of the Lawndale Union to End Slums. The West Side Organization was also asked to take responsibility for one of the marches. The plan did not work chiefly because escalation occurred much faster than had been originally anticipated. After the two marches in Gage Park, July 30 and 31, which received such a hostile reception, anticipated marches brought forth hundreds of people, without relying on the community organizations. The platoon plan was obsolete before it was really tried.

Efforts were made, nonetheless, to involve community organizations. The directors of the Action Centers were constantly instructed by the Action Committee to spend more time contacting community groups and getting them to mobilize their members. In addition, a number of groups were contacted by the Action Committee and asked to participate in its planning. Representatives from some did come to some of the meetings. (See Appendix B for a list of the groups contacted and information about the extent of their participation.)

The involvement of community organizations was not very successful in spite of these efforts. The time required to explain the program to them, deal with all of their questions, and really incorporate them into the planning was just not taken. Relationships with these groups had not been cultivated as assiduously as they should have been in order to insure full cooperation at this point. Some of them had long-standing suspicions and complaints with CCCO and SCLC; the time needed to iron out these difficulties was simply not spent in that way. I think the importance of their involvement was understood. The lack of energy expended on involving them was due more to inefficiency than lack of comprehension of the importance of doing so.

If the people of the marches did not come from the community organizations, where did they come from? The data on the participants has not yet been tabulated; therefore a detailed, statistical answer cannot be given. Some tentative hypotheses, based chiefly on observation, are possible, though.

Some of the people came because they had been contacted directly, either by the canvassers from the action centers, a community group they were affiliated with, or friends. Others—I would guess the large majority—came after hearing about the marches through the mass media. Some of these were activists with long-standing commitments; others just responded to the requests for supporters which they heard or read about.

About half of the marchers were white. Among these were many who had been involved in suburban open housing projects, city civil rights activities. Some "new recruits" even came from the target areas. There were also significant numbers of clergymen and nuns—perhaps encouraged to express their convictions in this way because high level representatives of the three major faiths had all given their blessing to Dr. King's project at the July 10 rally.

There seemed to be quite a large proportion of middle class Negroes present—perhaps because they understood more clearly how the housing market affected them. Poor Negroes were also represented; among them were a number of gang members, chiefly from the South Side. Quite a few of the Negroes mentioned that they came because they had seen the marches on television, or had heard Dr. King speaking on WVON. (Several mass meetings were broadcast live.)

The Direct Action Program

Based chiefly on the premises and strategy outlined above, the following events occurred, making up the heart of the action program. Following this calendar of events, the rationale behind some of the specific actions will be given, as a means of illustrating how this strategy worked in day-to-day decision-making.

CALENDAR OF EVENTS

July 2-9   Attempts to arrange negotiating meeting with the Board of Realtors.

Thurs. July 7   Meeting of representatives of community organizations to explain the action program and to enlist their support (200 people).

July 8-9   Testing of real estate offices in Gage Park. Obtained thirty cases of discrimination.

Fri. July 8   Meeting with a sympathetic pastor in Gage Park. Said he couldn't do anything openly to help.

Sun. July 10   Rally at Soldier's Field and March to City Hall. Posting of the demands on door of City Hall (25-50,000 people).

Mon. July 11   Mass meeting at New Friendship Baptist Church, South Side. Announced plans for action; asked people to report to action center.

Tues. July 12   Mass meeting at Shiloh Baptist Church, West Side. (The West Side riots broke out just a few blocks from the church just as the meeting was to begin. Some staff persons went out to attempt to stop the riot. They hoped to calm the rioters down enough to bring them into the church for the meeting, but they refused to come as long as there were white people there. The white people were asked to leave and hold their own meeting at Warren Avenue Church, which they did.)

Wed. July 13   Meeting with Negro ministers to discuss the action program.

Thurs. July 14   "Mass testing." About 100 people went to 2 real estate offices together to ask for service. The offices were closed when they arrived.

Mass meeting, New Friendship Church, South Side.

Sat. July 16   Picnic in Marquette Park, Gage Park area. About 200 people, half of them Negroes, spent the day in the park. No violence; only curious onlookers.

Shopping in Gage Park. About 25 Negro women went grocery shopping, comparing prices, etc.

Sun. July 17   Church visits. About 60 Negroes attended church services in Gage Park.

Prayer vigil. About 150 persons, led by a Negro pastor, walked several blocks from a small park to St. Gall's Catholic Church, and conducted a prayer service "for the people of Gage Park" on the front steps of the church beneath a cross towering twenty feet above the church. Jeering from onlookers.

Mon. July 18   Mass meeting at Stone Temple, West Side.

Testing of real estate offices began in the Belmont-Cragin area.

Thurs. July 21   Mass meeting at New Friendship Baptist Church, South Side.

Sat. July 23   Picnic in Gage Park. Jeering.

"Mass testing" at real estate offices in Belmont-Cragin; office closed shortly before the group arrived. Picnic in Riis Park, Belmont-Cragin area, following the testing. Swimming pool closed down, ostensibly because of glass in the bottom of the pool.

Sun. July 24   Church visits in Gage Park. About 60 Negroes attended services.

Prayer vigil. About 200 persons, led by a Negro pastor, returned to St. Gall's Catholic Church to pray on the steps. Jeering from onlookers.

Mon. July 25   Mass meeting at Stone Temple, West Side.

Thurs. July 28   Mass meeting at New Friendship Baptist Church, South Side. Dr. King spoke, urging people to come on Friday for the all-night vigil to be held outside a real estate office in Gage Park.

Fri. July 29   All night vigil in front of Halvorsen Real Estate office in Gage Park. Began in mid-afternoon; called off at 10 p.m. because the large crowd of onlookers was threatening to attack the vigilers. At midnight the Action Committee told the people still waiting at the church to return at 10 a.m. on Saturday for a march to Gage Park.

Meeting in Belmont-Cragin at St. Genevieve's Catholic Church, to explain the activities and concerns of the civil rights movement to interested people in the community. About 500 people present. Bernard Lafayette spoke for a short while, but had to stop when he could no longer be heard. Priest unable to quiet crowd. Meeting dispersed in chaos.

Sat. July 30   March from New Friendship Baptist Church to real estate offices in Gage Park, carrying picket signs. Onlookers became hostile near end of march and began to throw bottles. When marchers arrived in Marquette Park, still 3 miles from the church, the leaders decided that the group would not walk back. Cars sent from the church, and, at the insistence of the police, police vans carried the marchers back to the church (450 persons).

Sun. July 31   Prayer vigil, planned for Methodist Church in Chicago Lawn. About 500 persons walked from Marquette Park to the church. Hostile crowd prevented stopping at the church. Onlookers began to throw bottles and bricks. When the marchers returned to the park, they found that the cars parked there under police guard had been set on fire, overturned, etc. Marched back to New Friendship Baptist Church, accompanied by rock-throwing onlookers. About 50 people injured, 40 cars damaged or destroyed.

Mon. Aug. 1   Mass meeting, Warren Avenue Congregational Church, West Side.

Wed. Aug 3   Vigil at real estate office, Belmont-Cragin. About 300 people.

Thurs. Aug. 4 Mass meeting, New Friendship, South Side. Broadcast on WVON.

Dr. King and Al Raby: meeting with Archbishop Cody, Chandler, Conference on Religion and Race, and other religious officials.

Fri. Aug. 5   March to real estate offices in Gage Park, led by Dr. King. About 800 people. Dr. King hit by rock. Others also injured.

Testing began in Jefferson Park and Avondale, on the North Side.

Sun. Aug. 7   Prayer vigil in Belmont-Cragin. Stopped to pray at one Catholic Church, one Protestant Church, and one real estate office. About 700 people. Angry onlookers; little throwing of bricks and bottles.

Mon. Aug. 8   Mass meeting, Warren Avenue Congregational Church, West Side. Jesse Jackson announced marches to Bogan and Cicero.

Tues. Aug. 9   Student mass meeting, Fellowship Baptist Church, South Side.

Wed. Aug. 10 Vigil at the Board of Realtors office in the Loop. About 150 people (March to Bogan cancelled).

Thurs. Aug.11 Mass meeting, Greater Mount Hope Baptist Church, South Side.

Fri. Aug. 12   March to real estate offices in Bogan. About 700 marchers, 1000 policemen, 5000 spectators. Almost no violence.

Sun. Aug. 14 Marches to real estate offices in Gage Park, Bogan, and Jefferson Park. Total of 1160 marchers. Some hostility.

Mon. Aug. 15 Mass meeting, Warren Avenue Congregational Church, West Side.

Tues. Aug. 16 Picketing in the Loop at the offices of the Board of Realtors, Department of Public Aid, City Hall, Chicago Housing Authority, and First Federal Savings and Loan, during the afternoon. Some picket lines joined by sympathetic onlookers.

               Picketing at six real estate offices in Jefferson Park, 7 p.m. to midnight. About 150 people. Some early hostility, but quiet most of evening.

Wed. Aug. 17 Negotiating meeting with city officials, called by Conference on Religion and Race.

Thurs. Aug.18 Mass meeting at Greater Mount Hope Baptist Church, South Side. Dr. King spoke; broadcast on WVON.

               City issues injunction, limiting nature of marches.

Fri. Aug. 19   "Mass testing"; 100 real estate offices tested.

Sun. Aug. 21 Marches to real estate offices in South Deering (in the city) and Evergreen Park and Chicago Heights (suburbs). Some hostility in South Deering and Evergreen Park. About 1500 marchers, marched in heavy rain.

Tues. Aug. 23   March to real estate office in South Deering. About 300 people.

Thurs. Aug.25   March to real estate office in Belmont-Cragin after dark. About 125 marchers, 700 police. No violence.

Fri. Aug. 26   Summit agreement.

The decision to hold the all-night vigil in Gage Park on July 29 was chiefly Dr. King's; he felt that it was time to escalate. Though the sorties into the white communities had begun to draw some public attention, confronting those living in the communities with the fact that Negroes could and should be sharing their communities with them, there had not been a real confrontation. Such a confrontation was necessary for several reasons. First, it would be an educational tool—to make it clear to all that Negroes were being denied access to these communities. Many—including city officials—have long refused to recognize this reality; they have chosen to deny the existence of the problem, pointing to the city fair housing ordinance as evidence that there was no discrimination. Before any kind of change could occur, the "authorities" and the public had to acknowledge that the problem existed. A violent response of some sort was anticipated; this would serve two functions: first, as a means of exposing the "sickness of racism" which pervades the white society, and which could only be "cured" if it was brought out into the open, and, secondly, a means for Negroes to "stand up and be men," to demand that they be treated as human beings. Through courage and redemptive suffering the Negro could begin to gain back his lost manhood. Finally, a confrontation creates power for those who are causing it. It means that one has a position of power from which to bargain.

The all-night vigil was to be the beginning of the confrontation; it almost escalated things too fast. When violence became imminent, leaders decided to pull back. Though they did not fear violence *per se*, they felt that one should not send people into such a situation unless they were aware of what might happen and would be able to face a possible attack. The people on the vigil were not sufficiently aware of what they might be getting themselves into—and thus were probably not very well-prepared. Also, if a fray broke out on the street, it was very likely that the only kind of publicity would have been about a fight; the question of open housing still would not have been raised into public attention. So the Action Committee leaders present decided to send everyone home, and to ask that they return at 10:00 a.m. to march back to Gage Park. Picket signs would be made during the night so that the march would be an "educational experience" for the people of Gage Park. Signs such as "Negroes are people. People need houses," "All men are brothers," "All God's children need a place to live," etc. were carried on the march on Saturday.

The decision not to return to Gage Park on Monday—after the violence-ridden marches on Saturday and Sunday—was made for several reasons. First, it was clear that violence could be expected again. If the marchers returned, the only thing which they would be able to "educate the city" about was the existence of violence in Gage Park; the question of the closed housing market would be further obscured. In addition, it was important to make the point that it was not only Gage Park which was a closed community, but that all of the white areas in the city were the same. Also, if the group returned to Gage Park, they would have to go "in full force," a show of strength, not weakness and fear. Such a march would take more time to mobilize. So it was decided to go to Belmont-Cragin on Wednesday, and then return to Gage Park on Friday, with Dr. King leading the march. Friday's march would follow the Thursday night mass meeting, to be broadcast, which would be a means of recruiting people.

On the Wednesday march, drivers were asked to leave their cars in a parking lot in Belmont-Cragin, or if they chose, to drive them back to the church. All of the cars were left in the lot—though the memory of Sunday's destruction of most of the cars left in Gage Park was still fresh in everyone's mind. This was often cited later as proof that people who were really committed were not afraid to take risks; that the planners need not fear asking people to make sacrifices.

Immediately following the Gage Park march discussion began about holding marches in several communities simultaneously; this was envisioned as a technique of "educating the city" to the fact that Negroes were denied housing all over the city (not as a means of harassing the police, as Orlando Wilson later charged). The Action Committee agreed that such action could be taken only when there was sufficient leadership trained, and sufficient marshals available to make sure that all of the marches could be kept under control. Discipline must be kept tight. Plans for this had to be secure before marches could be scheduled.

The decision to cancel the Bogan march, originally planned for August 10, and replace it with a vigil at the Board of Realtors was a multi-faceted affair. Bevel first suggested the postponement, chiefly because he felt the "press is planning strategy for us" and because the community was so prepared—the precinct captains having been out quieting people, the security tight—that the value of surprise would be lost. He was also concerned that the issue of the closed housing market was not being raised well enough, that perhaps it was necessary to focus attention on the seat of the problem—the Board of Realtors. After much discussion, it was generally agreed that this would be a good strategy; however, its effectiveness would be greatest if it was a surprise move. Therefore, several tentative plans would be made, and the final decision would be made the next day immediately preceding the march; if information leaked out, another strategy might be chosen at the last minute. This march became the point at which a major power play was made by the Agenda Committee—especially Al Raby—to exert control over the planning of the action.

The meeting described above ended at 2:00 a.m. In the first editions of the early morning papers were headlines that the Bogan march had been cancelled. Quoted were a secretary of CCCO and Al Raby. Bevel regarded this as a breach of trust on the part of someone present at the previous night's meeting; quite perturbed, he decided that the Bogan march should go on anyway, and attempted to convince those Action Committee members who arrived to make the final decision before the march of this plan. The decision to go on to Bogan was agreed upon before Al Raby arrived. (He seldom came to Action Committee meetings, and so was not really expected.) Raby stated that he and Dr. King had final authority on all matters and cited a memorandum which Dr. King reputedly had agreed to. Bevel tried to convince him that this was a "group decision," and that no one could have veto power. The decision was finally made to march to the Board of Realtors to avoid bringing these internal disputes to public attention. (The implications of this will be further discussed in the section on decision-making structure.)

After the injunction was issued on August 18, the Agenda Committee ruled that all decisions regarding action had now become 'strategy' instead of 'tactics' and thus under their jurisdiction. They made all further decisions. The key question was whether or not to break the injunction. Some felt that the Freedom Movement should be willing to go to jail, and should thus not fear breaking the injunction. Others felt that the followers were not ready for jail, that breaking the injunction would be too much an act of defiance. It was decided by the Agenda Committee not to break it but to begin holding marches in the suburbs, outside of the Mayor's jurisdiction.

The announcement of a march to Cicero for August 28 was made by the Agenda Committee. The reasoning behind this is not entirely clear. Some think it was a very militant thing to plan; others say that the Agenda Committee never intended to go to Cicero; that they had planned to come to some kind of an agreement when the Summit meeting was reconvened on August 26.

The Question of Police Protection

How and when to notify the police and how much to worry about adequate police protection were questions which were continually injected into tactics discussions. The police were constantly complaining publicly that they had not received adequate notice; Bevel articulated a general feeling of the Action Committee when he said, "We are conducting nonviolent psychological warfare. The matter of protection isn't our problem." Strategists felt that flexibility was essential—and that they could not always tell 24 hours in advance precisely what they would be doing. However, Dr. King had promised Orlando Wilson several months earlier that 24 hour notice would be given—and it generally was, whenever possible. Some worried about the "bad image" the Movement would get if it did not give adequate notice and thus seemed to be reneging on its promises. This concern was generally quieted when it was pointed out that the police had been given adequate notice on the 31st of July, but had later announced publicly that they had not. Thus the 'public image' could not be salvaged by giving adequate notice. The police department could not be relied upon to tell the truth.

Concern for adequate police protection varied among Movement leadership. Bevel and the others with experience in nonviolence were adamant that no mention be made of the question; it would only sidetrack discussion from the central issue, the closed housing market. They led the way in quelling discussions of police protection at rallies and press conferences. A nonviolent army should be ready to accept any injury inflicted upon it by onlookers; it fact this was the source of much of the moral suasion of the Movement, as evidenced in the South. If the police wanted to provide protection, that was their decision—and their business. Those with less experience in nonviolence did not always readily accept this point of view.

There was, of course, concern privately for the well-being of the marchers. Bevel felt, though, that participants were willing to take risks, and should do so.

At the far end of the nonviolent spectrum were some Quakers who felt that it was not right to *allow* the police to protect marchers, when that entailed beating the onlookers, as it did under Orlando Wilson's crowd control tactics. Those demonstrating are supposed to be taking the suffering of an unjust society upon themselves, not watching it be inflicted on others, even if it is by the police. This question was discussed by the Action Committee but never satisfactorily resolved. Nonetheless it raises an important question regarding the nonviolent nature of the demonstrations.

White Communities Project

From the beginning of the direct action program attempts were made to reach the white people of the target areas. This project scarcely got off the ground during the summer, but is important, I think, as an indication of the concern of the Freedom Movement—often accused of only trying to create conflict.

The original plan had been to hold mass meetings in the white areas to explain the nature of the closed housing system and the goals of the Freedom Movement to the people. Based on the premise that much good will existed in these communities, the meetings were an attempt to bring change through education. At the first meeting of this kind, held in Belmont-Cragin on July 29, Bernard Lafayette, who was to give the main address, was out-shouted and booed until the meeting ended in chaos. After that the meetings in the white community were private, arranged for a small group of known sympathizers.

Meetings were held with Catholic liberals in Bogan and with ministers on the Northwest Side. In late July "The Concerned Citizens for an Open City" was formed. This group sponsored ads in the Southwest Side papers entitled, "How Can We Save Our Community?" explaining the reasons why open occupancy would benefit white homeowners by removing the threat of the advancing ghetto. From this group sprang several others which have continued through the winter, one in Gage Park and one in Albany Park. The latter one has been active in working with the Lawndale Union to End Slums in finding housing for Negroes on the North Side.

SOUL, a high school student group organized by the American Friends Service Committee in East Garfield Park met in mid-August with teenagers from Chicago Lawn, in an attempt to create bridges of communication.

Other contacts with the white communities were being planned when the marches were halted by the Summit Agreement. Some of these have gone on under other auspices.

The Decision-Making Processes

The formal structure of the Chicago Freedom Movement as it related to the open housing direct action consisted of three groups: the Freedom Assembly, the Agenda Committee, and the Action Committee.

The Freedom Assembly was formed in mid-winter from the groups within CCCO and other community organizations, churches, labor groups, etc. It was the official body behind the action, but it had virtually nothing to say about what happened. It met only infrequently, and Al Raby cancelled its August meeting; thus it was only an organization on paper. Some of these people were later vociferous with their complaints that they had been given no role in decision-making during the summer; this conflict, however, did not arise until fall.

The Agenda Committee was—and is—the focus of policy-making within the Freedom Movement; it consists of twelve of the key people from the Freedom Assembly, chosen by Al Raby and Dr. King on the basis of their power, in terms of either money or followers. Though it maintains the seat of authority, the Agenda Committee generally does not initiate programs; rather, it sanctions and supports those begun by other groups, usually by staff persons. It functioned primarily this way during the open housing campaign.

For the summer the Agenda Committee delegated to the Action Committee, appointed by them July 1, the authority to plan tactics for open housing, but reserved the right to resume control any time a decision involved policy. The distinction between tactics and policy decisions is not a clear one, and was a constant source of tension. Bevel proclaimed that the policy was "open housing" and that everything else fell into the category of tactics. This was a little hard for the Agenda Committee to swallow, as evidenced by their attempted interference about the August 10 march to Bogan.

The situation was further complicated by the fact that most of the members of the Action Committee were staff members of organizations headed by the members of the Agenda Committee. Staff persons were never allowed to forget their subordinate status. Even those who represented the Action Committee on the Agenda Committee—Bevel, Jackson, and Pitcher—were often referred to as "just staff," and there is evidence that their comments and positions were not respected as much as were those of the other Committee members.

The immediate issue of contention during the summer was control over the direct action. Deeper than that, though, were differences in a philosophy of leadership, in the degree of conflict tolerance, and in the understanding of goals which could not be compromised. The gulf between these two groups had been developing since the earliest activities in the fall, when preparations on the staff level were almost entirely separate from these among the "executives." Two styles of coordination were functioning. On the one hand was the more traditional approach, represented by Andrew Young, which consisted of getting powerful people together to form the nucleus of decision-making. Based upon the premise that bringing powerful persons into the group gains for the coordinated effort resources these persons have to offer, this technique worked well with CCCO and the other organizational heads. These people made up the Agenda Committee. Pulling them together was a natural job for Andrew Young, a middle class Congregational minister with a background of work within the national bureaucracy of the National Council of Churches. Al Raby worked closely with Young; the organization-types which Young wanted to organize were partially in CCCO already; others were friendly.

Bevel was the moving spirit behind the second style of organizing. With his background in the Student Nonviolent Coordinating Committee, which he helped to found in 1960, he preferred to work with more "grass roots" oriented community groups. He strongly believed that the people who are doing the work should make the decisions, and often referred to the Nashville Student Movement as a classic example of this. He tried to mold the Action Committee in the image of the Nashville students, announcing that decisions were *collective* decisions and responsibility for them lies with the group, not any one individual. (In fact, Bevel himself was the dominant influence in the group. However, it did function, more or less, as a group of people who were both doing the work and making the decisions.)

The experience with nonviolent direct action varied enormously between the Agenda Committee and the Action Committee. The Action Committee contained the veterans from the South—Bevel, Jackson, and Lafayette—and the staff persons to whom they had been teaching nonviolence all year. On the Agenda Committee were some who had had experience with the Willis marches in the summer of 1965, but none of the Southern veterans; previous experiences in Chicago had not really brought confrontations comparable to those in the South and to those created by the open housing marches. This difference in past experience may account for the Action Committee's higher tolerance for tension. The marches infuriated the Mayor and alarmed other segments of the power structure; all sorts of pressures were applied to stop them. Bevel was totally unaffected by this; he anticipated such a response and was able to carry on, undistracted, toward the goal of an open city. It seems very likely that the members of the Agenda Committee may not have expected so much pressure, so much withdrawal of support from some of the moderates, like the newspapers and the archbishop. This may well have influenced the decisions made at the negotiating table. It certainly was reflected in the questions they raised to the Action Committee during the course of the action—such things as, "We shouldn't march into Catholic neighborhoods until we've consulted with the priests;" or "We should be sure to give Orlando Wilson his 24-hour notice."

The Agenda Committee had been further removed from the details of the discussion on what action would be necessary to guarantee open housing. It was clear to the Action Committee that "All realtors should serve all people" and that anything short of that was no victory. This does not seem to have been as clear to the Agenda Committee.

The questions raised concerning the decision-making process usually were such things as, should the Agenda Committee review each action planned before it was carried out, or should they review the week's action in retrospect, issuing policy directives for the next week's action if they did not approve of the way things were being carried on; who would make the decision about the next community to be chosen as target area; or what should be the timing of the marches. In most cases the Action Committee had its own way; these questions were left up to it.

Though questions were raised about the relative authority of the Agenda and Action Committees, no question was ever raised about the seat of ultimate authority, which was assumed by both groups to reside in Dr. King. Though some may have disagreed with him and tried to influence him privately, no one questioned his final authority. Like a tribal chief, he was called upon to give guidance, settle disputes, and to participate in crucial decisions. But his lieutenants were expected to carry out the routine business of the day-to-day battles. Dr. King was in the city only part of the time, and thus not always available for arbitration; it was during his absence that conflicts were most likely to flare up.

Andrew Young had an important, but somewhat ambiguous position in these processes. He was formally a part of the Agenda Committee, and functioned comfortably within it. Like Dr. King, however, Young was in the city only part of the time; thus his influence on the Agenda Committee was limited. Had he been present more often he might have been able to serve as a stabilizing force as the tension grew. He had both experience in the South—lacked by the other members of the Agenda Committee—and rapport with Agenda Committee members, lacked by Bevel and Jackson.

Al Raby, while formally a member of both committees, rarely participated in Action Committee meetings. He functioned as an integral part of the Agenda Committee; he spoke for it and represented its point of view. However, he was also (officially, at least) a co-holder of ultimate authority with Dr. King. This authority was not recognized by everyone, though; whenever he tried to assert it, he got into difficulties, particularly with Bevel.

Negotiation and the Summit Agreement

The direct action program was drawn to a halt after a series of negotiation meetings with a wide array of dignitaries and powerful people, representing both the city government and private interests in the city. It is not the purpose of this paper to try to explain in detail the processes which went on during these deliberations. Rather I shall concentrate on the Freedom Movement's participation; who made the decisions for the movement, and why were those particular decisions made?

The first meeting, called for August 17 by the Conference on Religion and Race, brought together in a ten hour meeting representatives of the city's interests and the Freedom Movement. It became clear quite early that the Mayor's passion was to end the marches; he was really little interested in even discussing the problem of open housing. As the meeting wore on, he seemed to become aware that settlement would not come so easily; he began to do more of his own talking, instead of relying on his lieutenants. In mid-afternoon the meeting recessed so that the representatives of the Board of Realtors, which had a full meeting of their membership scheduled for that afternoon, could take the requests of the Freedom Movement to the Board, and see if an agreement could be reached. When the meeting reconvened, the representatives of the realtors returned to report that the Board had agreed to "withdraw all opposition to the philosophy of open occupancy on the state level—provided it is applicable to owners as well as brokers."[3] When questioned by a Freedom Movement spokesman if this meant that Negroes could "live anywhere in the city tomorrow," the spokesman for the realtors hedged, admitting that it did not mean that, really. On that note the meeting broke up, the Movement stating that the marches would be stopped only when Negroes were free to move anywhere. Though both sides agreed to report that the meeting had been "fruitful," and that they hoped there could still be found grounds for agreement, neither side had actually budged from its original position.

The following day, August 18, Mayor Daley issued an injunction against the Freedom Movement, limiting the size and timing, and further regulating the marches. This came as a shock to the CFM; some felt it would interfere with the progress of the negotiations. Others were concerned about what course the direct action should take. The restrictions were so extensive that many felt *no* demonstrations could take place without violating the injunction at some point. It was at this point that the Agenda Committee took over the planning of the direct action. They obviously did not want the delicate process of negotiation to be overturned by the action.

At the close of the meeting on August 17, a subcommittee had been appointed to work out some suggestions for an agreement. This group met almost continuously until August 25, drawing up an agreement. When the full committee reconvened on August 26, the result seems to have been a foregone conclusion; the statement was agreed upon by both sides, hailed as a "great victory" by all. The marches stopped.

It was clear to almost everyone that the Freedom Movement had seriously compromised its position. The *Daily News* stated in an editorial on August 27 that, ". . . in the end Dr. King's group dropped its emphasis on demands that no agency—not the city, not the real estate industry, not the churches—could promise in good faith to deliver."[4] Though hailed by Dr. King as a "significant victory," the agreement was far from that which he and other Freedom Movement spokesmen had said only days earlier that they would demand. The critical question for the Freedom Movement then becomes, who made the decision to settle for this agreement, and why was it made?

The Agenda Committee was the representative of the Freedom Movement during the negotiations. Even those staff members who were a part of the committee were not fully included in the negotiations. At first only Bevel and Bert Ransom were included. Bevel insisted that Jackson be included, which he finally was. Pitcher was not included until much later. This composition of the negotiating team meant that Bevel and Jackson, those most likely to refuse to compromise, were in the minority. Others who would have been a support to them—Pitcher, and Bernard Lafayette and Bill Moyer from the Action Committee—were not invited to attend. Why Bert Ransom was singled out of the Action Committee for participation is not at all clear. He is somewhat less forthright in taking a stand against a roomful of people than the others which were not included, and thus was probably less help to Jackson and Bevel than others might have been. None of the community organization representatives from the Action Committee were invited to attend.

Those who represented the Freedom Movement came primarily from its more conservative faction. They had never been overenthused about the action program, had encouraged caution throughout its execution, and were probably anxious to have it ended. As the heads of large human relations agencies, some of these men were undoubtedly under pressure from their peers and associates, who were the heads of city and private agencies, all urging the Freedom Movement to come to a speedy agreement.

The subcommittee which in effect wrote the agreement contained five representatives from the Freedom Movement; they had a major part in its writing, and thus cannot claim that it was foisted upon them. Why the agreement was not stronger is not really clear. (There are indications, in fact, that the Mayor was prepared to make more concessions than were asked of him in the agreement.) It may be that those who wrote it believed that the things they were including would in fact bring open housing; this would indicate a naivete on the part of those who did the writing. This seems highly unlikely, however. The chief demand, asked of real estate boards and brokers, that "All listings (be) immediately available on a nondiscriminatory basis,"[5] was left out. The significance of including such a point had been repeatedly pointed out by the Action Committee members familiar with the workings of the real estate system. It is also possible that those who wrote the agreement realized the necessity of such a change, but felt that the Board of Realtors would not be likely to make such a promise, and that enforcement of the city ordinance would serve the same end. It seems to me quite likely that the Board would not have been agreeable. Though they were feeling some pressure—i.e., houses being withdrawn from the market in areas where the marches were being held,—it was certainly not enough to encourage major concessions. It was the city government which wanted desperately to stop the marches. Thus it seems likely that only pressure by the city on the Board of Realtors—in the form of some kind of legal sanction—could possibly bring the desired change. If this does reflect the thinking of the subcommittee, then their agreement could be explained as having been reached in haste, without adequate time to think through the legal procedures necessary to bring about actual open housing.

In addition, the agreement was weak because of its failure to include a timetable of change and specific details of changes to be made. This could be attributed to a lack of foresight. Later some of those who participated in the writing of the agreement (the CFM representatives) recognized this, and attributed it to haste.

There are a number of reasons which probably justified the acceptance of the agreement by the Freedom Movement representatives. Dr. Alvin Pitcher, in a recent paper[6] has listed some of the possible arguments which could have been made for accepting it. Some felt that open housing could not be won, and thus the Movement should accept whatever victory they could and move on to more realizable goals. Others felt that the injunction so hampered the demonstrations that they were virtually ineffective, and that there were not enough troops to challenge the legality of the injunction. Still others believed that the threat to the "power structure" was at its height, and that the Movement should take advantage of its position before it was lost. Finally, there were those who believed that there was a need for victory, and that "the summit agreement did represent the achievement of accommodation and adjustment on the part of the power structure of the city."

It is quite certain that these kinds of things were in fact on the minds of the CFM leaders who made the decision to accept the pact. Most felt that this was a victory—if not a total victory, yet an important one—and that the time had come to end the marches before tensions in the city got higher or before the marches lost their effectiveness.

There were others, unmentioned by the press, but most likely Bevel and Jackson, who felt that the time had not yet come, that a much better agreement could have been reached after two or three more weeks of demonstrations. Others on the Action Committee—and possibly Bevel—felt that an effort should be made to stimulate action in other cities and raise the issue to a national level. This was, evidently, a minority view, however.

The final responsibility for acceptance of the agreement lies with Dr. King. Though often heavily dependent on his advisors, he himself has the final authority. It is not really possible to tell which of the above arguments were most convincing to him—or if there were others which were really the deciding factor. This is not altogether inconsistent with his decisions in similar situations, though. After the direct action campaign in Birmingham in the spring of 1963, King and the local SCLC leaders concluded an agreement with the city which really gave only minor concessions. It was the effect of the Birmingham demonstrations nationally, leading to the passage of the Civil Rights Bill of 1964, which was the real triumph. Perhaps King felt that the appeal to the national government would not be necessary in the North, where the "power structure" seemed to be unusually responsive.

Evaluation

The key problem unresolved by the Chicago Freedom Movement was—and is—a theory of leadership. Key persons were unable to agree on a structure of leadership for the organization.

Martin Luther King was accepted as commander-in-chief. Though his authority was derived somewhat from his position as president of the Southern Christian Leadership Conference, its chief source was charismatic. Dr. King's ability to articulate the problems others feel, his dynamism and personal attraction, are the basis for his widespread support—and those confidence-inspiring qualities, coupled with the popular support which backs him, led the Chicago leaders to accept the final authority of King.

King only partially fulfills the role of a charismatic leader, however. He mobilizes mass support and serves as the symbolic leader of the Freedom Movement. He serves as a spokesman for this mass of followers, and inspires them to act. But he does not really lead the deliberations and the planning which detail the action into which his followers will be led. This he leaves to his aides—chiefly James Bevel and Andrew Young. The problem of "succession" of the charismatic leader thus is posed while he is still present. The delegation of authority is not made clear by the leader himself, and thus must be decided among his lieutenants. The problem is further complicated by King's active schedule, taking him outside the city for a large part of the time. Decisions made in his absence must be made by the lieutenants—in whatever way they can arrange among themselves.

There were three different principles of leadership operating during the open housing campaign last summer. The Chicago Freedom Movement as a whole never agreed on any one of them; the resulting tension was the cause of many of the internal problems.

Al Raby wanted to participate in the authority derived by Dr. King from his charisma. When questions of authority came up, he often emphasized that he and Dr. King were "co-partners" in the leadership of the Movement, and that if Dr. King were not present the mantle of leadership fell to him. This approach was not very effective. Raby simply does not possess the personal qualities which are the prerequisites of charismatic leadership—personal magnetism, clarity of thought, a bearing which inspires confidence. He could not wear well the mantle of charismatic leadership. By insisting upon this means of legitimating his authority, he sometimes made himself appear foolish, thus further decreasing the possibility of his being accepted as the bearer of Dr. King's charisma. He was much more successful when he sought authority as an organizational leader.

Bevel believes in a kind of "conspiratorial model" of leadership. He wanted a cadre of highly disciplined persons, agreed in ideology and uncompromising in the pursuit of their goals, to make the major decisions. It was around such a model that he fashioned the Action Committee; it would be open to anyone who represented a group ready to commit itself to the program—but only those who agreed to participate in the project as it was then under way. Bevel encouraged Raby to participate in the Action Committee, to be a part of this group making the plans, but Raby refused to submit himself to the authority of such a group. Bevel believed that the leadership group should be exclusive—limited to those committed to its ideology and strategy.

The Agenda Committee, organized according to Andrew Young's principles of leadership, represented a third kind of authority. This group was a broad-based coalition, made up of people chosen not so much because of agreement to a common ideology, but because of the resources which they could contribute—or, more bluntly, because of their power. Young preferred to include anyone with major resources, and was willing to make compromises to those persons, if necessary. Al Raby participated in the Agenda Committee; however, it was not the chief means by which he attempted to gain his authority.

A fourth group should also be mentioned; though it did not enter into the conflicts during the summer, it did raise its voice in the fall. The Coordinating Council of Community Organizations is a coalition group which admits to membership virtually any group interested in some way in civil rights, from CORE to the Lincoln Dental Association and the National Association of Social Workers. During the summer of 1965, when the CCCO ran the direct action campaign against School Superintendent Benjamin Willis, delegates from all of these groups sat on the committee which planned the action. Because of the lack of consensus on basic issues, meetings were long and drawn out, as attempts were made to satisfy the various points of view represented. This group was an extremely broad-based coalition, used to functioning in a manner in which each delegate had one vote, regardless of the power of his organization. In the fall of 1966 when the group began meeting regularly again, they became incensed that their principle of leadership—i.e., a vote for everyone—had not been used.

The serious conflicts caused by these basic differences in understanding of leadership have seriously weakened the Freedom Movement, and have not yet been resolved.

Effectiveness of the Direct Action Program

Nonviolent direct action has two different forms, distinguished from each other by the mechanisms through which change is to be effected. Though most concrete acts include elements of each, an important analytical distinction can be made. Each form produces its own results; to the extent that one is present it affects the results of the total action program.

The first, which Gandhi called *duragraha*, makes the system of domination embarrassing to its rulers. It includes forms of disruption, which are embarrassing to those responsible for keeping law and order. The means chosen are not especially significant in themselves, but are chosen because they are believed to be the most *effective* in a particular situation; they take into account the nature of the economic relationships in the society, the number of recruits and potential recruits, the use of force by the rulers, and other contingencies. The success of this form of nonviolence usually depends on the extent of mass participation and the consequent embarrassment of the rulers.

The second, *satyagraha*, results in the conversion of rulers through a change of heart. The techniques for this kind of nonviolent action are similar to those of the first type, and may include demonstrations, strikes, etc. But the crucial element distinguishing it from the first is the acceptance of suffering by the protesters. Gandhi's fasting was probably the most pure form of *satyagraha*. It does not really depend upon mass participation, but upon the effect of voluntary suffering upon the conscience of the rulers.

The first, which relies upon embarrassment of the rulers, creates only temporary power—probably power to get the ruler to negotiate and perhaps arrive at a settlement; but whether or not he carries out that settlement depends upon the existence of a constant threat of continued action, which may be difficult to maintain.[7]

The Chicago open housing marches were an attempt to use both of these mechanisms of change. Though the thinking of the planners aimed them toward the second, they were much more effective in "embarrassing the rulers." The marches proved to be a political threat to the Mayor—much more so than had been anticipated by the planners. Thus they gained a rather speedy political advantage for negotiations. There has been little, however, to insure that the promises made in the summit agreement would be kept.

The marches were aimed chiefly at a "change of heart" among the rulers. "Change of heart" might be accomplished either by an appeal to reason—by "telling the truth" about the situation, or by an appeal to the values of the rulers through redemptive suffering. An appeal to reason was made by the educational campaign, carried out by the use of picket signs, leaflets, and press statements. Because of its heavy reliance on the mass media, the educational campaign was only a partial success; the press often chose to write about the violence encountered rather than the issue of open housing. The general public was probably not able to clarify its understanding of the injustice of the dual housing system to a very large degree.

The response of the business community indicates that the educational campaign was at least partially successful, however. There is little indication that their "conversion" was a moral one. However, the marches did seem to bring to the attention of the business community a problem which they had previously been able to ignore; some leading businessmen began to realize that the solution of the housing problem was crucial to the health of the city—and hence to their own best interests. Thus their support was recruited for the battle.

The power to mobilize support which lies in the acceptance of suffering at the hands of an oppressor was not really available to the housing direct action program. The first two major marches into Gage Park did begin to mount this kind of support; a number of people were injured by the onlookers; the hate of the opponents, and the willingness to suffer to protest injustice won the CFM praise and support—from some of the more moderate quarters at least. However, Chicago's Police Chief Orlando Wilson does not run an oppressive state, as do the state troopers of Mississippi, and the sheriffs of Alabama. After the first two marches in Gage Park, during which the police did indeed let their personal prejudices against the marchers interfere with their work, the police force functioned as an efficient protective force for the marchers. Injuries were few after that time. Marchers were not permitted to "suffer for righteousness' sake." One of their major weapons was thus taken from them.

It is important to remember that the nonviolent technique was devised for use in oppressive states—colonial India, South Africa, Alabama, and Mississippi—where rulers used force against any who protested. Chicago may well have been its first major testing ground in an area where the police are nonrepressive. The results are considerably different. (This does not mean to imply that "redemptive suffering" would be impossible in Chicago; it simply means that techniques would have to be much more sophisticated. Large numbers would have to be willing not only to get beaten but to go to jail, for instance.)

The response of the police is one of the major differences between North and South. The Bull Connors and the Jim Clarks allowed the Negro protest movement to mount to heights of heroism and to attract enormous public sympathy for those who suffered for the cause of justice. This did not happen in Chicago.

In addition, the Movement in the South did not rely upon changes which could be wrought in the George Wallaces and Ross Barnetts. It is likely that no amount of suffering would have brought a "change of heart" to these men. However, the suffering in the South reached above the heads of Southerners to the rest of the nation; there it found sympathetic persons, and the laws enacted at the national level were not the result of a change of heart in Alabama, but of a nationwide change which put enough political pressure in Washington to see that bills were passed.

The appeal to the national level was not made in Chicago. Open housing is a controversial subject throughout the country; there is no residue of supporters ready to emerge as there was for the right to vote movement in Alabama. In addition, the decision to negotiate with the mayor instead of raising the issue to the national level precluded such an effort.

In summary, the direct action program did provide an important means of embarrassing the mayor, and causing the "power structure" in the city to negotiate seriously with the Freedom Movement. It enlisted the support of some influential men in the city who began to see that open housing would serve their own interests. However, it was not successful in bringing about any basis for solid lasting change. No new laws were instituted; no legal pressures from without (i.e., from Washington) were created. There is little indication that the mayor has had a serious change of heart. The promised changes can be insured only by the constant threat of more demonstrations, more disruption; whether or not this can be realistically maintained is questionable.

Effect on the Negro Community

We cannot overlook one of the most important aspects of the program, according to its framers. They anticipated that the direct action program would give a new kind of strength and hope to the Negro community. After once having stood up and demanded to be treated as men, Negroes would no longer be willing to suffer indignities.

There is no clear answer explaining the psychological effect of the marches on the Negro community; it would be an interesting subject for further study. There are indications that some of those who participated were changed by that experience; some are now working with the Freedom Movement. The Movement's effectiveness in bringing psychological change seems to have been dampened somewhat by the fact that some called the agreement a sell-out from the beginning, others have become disillusioned as it became clear that the promises were not being faithfully kept, that no significant changes had really occurred. The results of any mobilization attempts made this summer may be to some degree a reflection of changes—or lack of them—wrought by the open housing marches.

APPENDIX A

MEMBERS OF THE ACTION COMMITTEE

SCLC STAFF

James Bevel
Jesse Jackson
Stony Cooks
Bill Hollins
Al Sampson
Claudia King
Mary Lou Finley

CCCO STAFF

Alvin Pitcher
Sol Ice
David Wallace
Sara Wallace

AFSC STAFF

Bernard Lafayette
Bill Moyer
Bert Ransom
Jerry Davis

COMMUNITY ORGANIZATION REPRESENTATIVES (*=rarely attended)

*Bill Briggs—East Garfield Park Community Organization
Bill Darden—West Side Organization
*Rennie Davis—JOIN
Bill Griffen/Preston Harwell—Kenwood-Oakland Community Organization
Bob Hoover—West Side Federation
Mike Lawson—Catholic Interracial Council
*Andrew Ransom—Tenants Action Committee, Old Town Gardens
George Vickers—North Shore Suburban Organization for Fair Housing, Direct
Action Committee
Addie Wyatt—United Packinghouse Workers
representative from the Student Union for Better Education
representative from Chicago Heights group SOCCA

APPENDIX A, cont.

OTHERS

Charlie Brown—chief marshall
Leo Holt—legal advisor
Don Rose—public relations advisor
Dick Murray—ecology advisor

NOTE: Martin Luther King, Jr., Andrew Young, and Albert Raby were also official members of the Action Committee. They rarely attended its meetings, however. For practical purposes they were much more a part of the Agenda Committee, and thus have not been included in the above list.

APPENDIX B

COMMUNITY ORGANIZATIONS CONTACTED THROUGH THE ACTION COMMITTEE

MEMBERS OF ACTION COMMITTEE

East Garfield Park Community Organization
Bill Briggs represented this group on the action committee. He did not feel that open housing was a particularly salient issue in his community; the group was also occupied during the summer with the negotiations on their collective bargaining contract with a slum landlord, and chose to devote little time to the open housing marches. The group did send marchers, however.

West Side Organization
Bill Darden was a member of the Action Committee. He was interested in trying to mobilize welfare recipients, with whom WSO primarily works, to pressure the welfare department to find good housing outside the ghetto for recipients. The group sent participants to some of the marches.

JOIN
Rennie Davis was involved in the first meetings of the Action Committee, but when it became clear that the issue would be open housing, he ceased coming, feeling this to be an issue of little interest to the Appalachian whites with which JOIN works.

Kenwood-Oakland Community Organization
KOCO sent representatives to the Action Committee frequently. They were chiefly interested in using the committee as a forum for promoting activity in their own community, such as organizing a mass meeting at which Dr. King could speak. They sent participants to the marches but did not participate actively in the planning.

West Side Federation
Robert Hoover and Lew Kreinberg participated actively in the action committee meetings.

Catholic Interracial Council
Though not originally a member of the committee, Mike Lawson came representing the CIC. He worked chiefly with the white communities project.

Tenants Action Committee, Old Town Gardens
TAC sought the support of the committee for its picketing during the August rent strike. Though tentative plans were made by the action committee to participate, the plans never really got off the ground.

APPENDIX B, page 2

North Shore Organization for Fair Housing, Direct Action Committee
This group was included with the hope that they might be able to stimulate direct action projects in their communities. This never was done, but perhaps could have been if the action had not terminated so quickly.

Student Union for Better Education
A number of rallies for students were held during the summer, attempting to involve them in the direct action program, and to organize them for activities around school problems.

Chicago Heights Civil Rights Organization—SOCCA
Representatives from SOCCA came to the action committee requesting assistance in setting up a center and developing an action program for their own community. Jerry Davis spent two weeks there, helping to organize an action-oriented group. They "hosted" the Chicago Heights marches held on Sunday, August 21, and mobilized about 100 people for the march. They were planning to begin marches on real estate offices in Chicago Heights, but this did not get off the ground before the summit agreement.

OTHER PARTICIPANTS IN THE ACTION COMMITTEE

Oakland Committee for Community Improvement
Frank Ditto was invited to the action committee meetings and came to several. He had long-standing problems with CCCO which had not been worked out, and which probably prevented his full participation.

Lawndale Union to End Slums
This group, founded by SCLC, was not officially represented, but often sent a representative to Action Committee meetings; quite a few marchers were mobilized.

Medical Committee for Human Rights
This group provided first aid during all of the marches after July 31. Representatives occasionally came to Action Committee meetings to straighten out their cooperation, though most was arranged outside meetings.

Urban League
Near the end of the campaign, the Urban League began sending representatives from their staff to the Action Committee meetings. They did not volunteer their services for anything.

Chatham Community Organization
Georgia English came to some of the early Action Committee meetings representing this group. She did not have time to come to the meetings but seems to have mobilized marchers. She conducted the shopping trip to Gage Park on July 16.

45

APPENDIX B, page 3

Project Open Communities—Oak Park
> This group had been holding marches at a real estate office in Oak Park during the spring. They discontinued their project—which involved fair housing people from all of the western suburbs—to participate in the CFM program. They were invited to the Action Committee and came several times, but their representatives were too busy to attend often.

GROUPS ALSO CONTACTED

> Englewood Civic Organization—Rev. John Porter
> Near North Side Union to End Slums—Jerry Herman
> Christian Action Ministry (West Garfield Park)—Rev. Doss
> Austin Community Organization
> CHAIN (Chicago Housing Authority tenants group)

These groups expressed interest and probably sent some marchers. With more effort they probably could have been recruited for full participation.

NOTES

1. Bevel, in turn, had learned from Bill Moyer, of the American Friends Service Committee housing staff, the relationship between slums and open housing. Moyer, drawing on his own experience in organizing direct action programs around suburban real estate offices in the summer of 1965 and spring of 1966 also suggested the form such protest might take and further helped to develop plans and strategy later presented as the summer action program.
2. Martin Luther King, *"Untimely and Unwise?" A Letter from Eight Alabama Clergymen to Martin Luther King and His Reply to them on Order and Common Sense, the Law and Justice, Nonviolence and Love*, pamphlet, published by Fellowship of Reconciliation, New York, 1963, p. 4.
3. "5 Point Statement by Realtors" *Chicago Daily News*, August 18, 1966.
4. "Respite for Chicago", (an editorial), *Chicago Daily News*, August 27, 1966, p. 14.
5. From the *Program of the Chicago Freedom Movement*, July, 1966.
6. Alvin Pitcher, "The Politics of Coalition," unpublished paper, Spring, 1967, p. 3.
7. For this discussion of nonviolence I am indebted to Leo Kuper, Chapter 3, "The Sociological Nature of Passive Resistance," *Passive Resistance in South Africa*, New Haven: Yale University Press, 1957, pp. 72-96.

The Chicago Open-Housing Conference

KATHLEEN CONNOLLY

Preface

On Friday, August 26th, as the temperature registered 91 degrees at noon in Chicago, some seventy-five men filed out of the Walnut Room of the Palmer House Hotel. While nothing visibly distinguished this group from any other, participants and observers acknowledged that this was a historic meeting of the "power elite" of Chicago. "The only other meeting which brought together under one roof so many powerful men from government, business, politics, religion and labor in Chicago was when there was a school crisis in 1946, and I know of no other before then," observed Dr. Stanley Hallett, researcher and planner.

In 1966, the crisis which forced this elite to come together face to face had been stated by a subcommittee of this group:

> This subcommittee has been discussing a problem that exists in every metropolitan area in America. It has been earnestly seeking immediate practical and effective steps which can be taken to create a fair housing market in metropolitan Chicago.

This paper was written in January of 1967. It is published here for the first time.

Or, as the *New Republic* analyzed: "The Daley machine is reaping the bitter harvest of years of civil neglect in the area of race relations."

Negro and white citizens and civic officials of these other metropolitan areas had more than a casual interest in the nature of the open-housing agreements reached in Chicago—a city in crisis during the summer. Sensing this national attention, Mayor Richard J. Daley announced as he emerged from the meeting, "This is a great historical day in the City of Chicago—Chicago as usual is leading the way for all other cities."

These cities knew that Chicago had been picked in the fall of 1965 by Dr. Martin Luther King, Nobel Prize Winner, as the new target for his Southern Christian Leadership Conference.

> I chose Chicago because conditions here typify slum conditions that prevail throughout the nation. Because it is big, it seemed an ideal place in which to dramatize the deplorable situation and to mobilize the public into action.

Now, months later, King announced as he emerged from the meeting:

> Never before have such far-reaching commitments been made and programs adopted and pledged to achieve open housing in a community. The Chicago Freedom Movement takes great pride in providing a nonviolent vehicle through which the total eradication of segregated housing can be made possible.

While King reaffirmed his position supporting the nonviolent theory and Mayor Daley announced a "historic day," the nation knew it had been spectator to one of the most violent summers Chicago had ever seen. The violence had begun in an unexpected quarter: the Puerto Rican ghetto where in June an angry minority protested their subtle segregation from the good life in Chicago, the nation's wealthiest city. July was the month of Negro riots within the teeming black ghetto on the west side. In August, Chicago again became a national focal point when the fears and hostilities seething within the middle-class white ghetto of the northwest and southwest communities were communicated and articulated with violence.

In the case of the embarrassing Puerto Rican riot, calm came about through the promise of a redress of grievances; the Negro riot was put down with 4,000 National Guard troops; the white riot was quelled by means of a conference table.

This paper will attempt to analyze the nature of the conference table around which sat Chicago's leaders. It will attempt to discuss the history and issues which brought them together and the divergent attitudes which interpreted the problem. It will discuss the subcommittee report which was accepted and called by the press "the Summit Agreement."

This Agreement was seen by some as a necessary price paid to stop three weeks of white violence, violence which was seriously threatening the eleven-year-old political administration. Many have chosen not to pass a premature judgment but only witness its outcome. Others see this Agreement as just a beginning step by men of good-will desirous of implementing its open-housing goals in order to break through one city's many ghettos. Of unknown number are those who feel that they were participants around the conference table where their goals were discussed and promises and commitments made which would influence their lives.

I. *Events Leading up to the Open-Housing Marches and Agreement*

It sounded like a declaration of war: "I want the unconditional surrender of forces dedicated to the creation and maintenance of slums." On entering Chicago, Dr. Martin Luther King had ten years of direct action in the South as his credentials.

> When the SCLC went to Birmingham in 1963, we said that if this capital of segregation suffered even a single defeat, the effects would radiate across the South. Birmingham met a succession of defeats and is influencing not only the South but the North as well. Chicago is the capital of segregation in the North, and transformation of its slums will make no Northern city secure with its own.[1]

In the fall of 1965, when Dr. King announced his plans to extend his SCLC staff operations to Chicago, the Southern Christian Leadership Conference was still fresh from its triumph in Selma and the passage of the Kennedy Civil Rights Legislation. It had pushed the Federal Government to its logical limit in the South and was looking for a new challenge. One of King's success levers, besides his bouncing-back ability, was his timing. In St. Augustine, Florida, while King was making "creative tension," Congress was drawing up and passing the 1964 Civil Rights Law. The goal of King's marching was the desegregation of public accommodations which Congress handed over to him. Later, in the spring of 1965, King organized the Selma-to-Montgomery march, while Congress debated the voting rights bill.

The Chicago which awaited King did not look like Birmingham. A sprawling metropolis of nearly four million, one-half of the population Roman Catholic, Chicago had become a mecca for southern Negroes after World War II. "Going to Chicago—sorry but I can't take you along" they sang. Between 1950 and 1960, the Negro population had increased by 65%. One million Negroes are contained within sixty-five miles of ghetto perimeter along the south and west sides. The ghetto was a product of farsighted city planning by the Chicago Real Estate Board which laid down the basic policies of racial segregation in housing which persisted since 1917:

> The old districts are overflowing and new territory must be furnished. It is desired in the interests of all, that each block shall be filled solidly and that further expansion shall be confined to contiguous blocks, and that the present method of obtaining a single building in scattered blocks be discontinued. Promiscuous sales and leases here and there mean an unwarranted and unjustifiable destruction of values . . .[2]

The systematic bombing of homes, averaging one every twenty days, continued to 1921. Some of the homes belonged to Negroes outside the ghetto and others belonged to whites who had sold to Negroes, or said they would, or helped Negroes buy a home. In 1922, the Chicago Race Relations Commission reported:

> News of threatened bombings in many cases was circulated well in advance of the actual occurrence. Negroes were warned of the exact date on which explosions would occur. They asked for police protection and, in some instances where police were sent beforehand, their homes were bombed, and no arrests were made.[3]

White real estate interests began a new approach in the early 1920s—the racial restrictive covenant. This was a mutual, written agreement among property owners in a given area, by which each signer agreed not to sell or lease his property to a Negro and not to let a Negro live on it except as a "bona fide" servant. In a 1928 speech, a member of the Chicago Real Estate Board, "summarizing the earnest and conscientious work of the Board for the last twelve months," described the "fine network of contracts . . . which the owner of the property signs not to exchange with, sell to, or lease to, any member of a race not Caucasian."

Due to the southern migration at mid-century, the outward expansion of the ghetto was even greater than would be expected. Moreover, during the 1950s and 1960s, tens of thousands of families had to be relocated as a result of urban renewal, expressway construction and slum clearance. An estimated eight out of ten persons relocated were Negro. In spite of those massive transfers of population and destruction of sections of the ghetto, the ghetto pattern was effectively maintained by extending it into new areas.

It was estimated in 1960 by Dr. Karl Taeuber of the University of Wisconsin that, since residential segregation in Chicago had become so intense, in order to achieve integration within the city limits, ninety-three out of every one hundred Negro households would have to move into blocks that were then white occupied. The problem by that time had become metropolitan, affecting the 250 municipal units surrounding the six county Chicago area.

Dr. King knew he was not bringing the Civil Rights Movement to Chicago—he already found it there, organized far beyond any other city.

> I have received requests from several cities, including Washington, and Los Angeles, but I decided to come to Chicago, mainly because of Al Raby. I had been watching Al for some time and I must say that I became enormously impressed with his work and the sincerity of his commitment.[6]

Young Chicago school teacher Al Raby, 33, was the acknowledged head of the Civil Rights Movement in Chicago due largely to his ability to weld together the forty-odd organizations which comprise the Coordinating Council of Community Organizations. Raby's federation embraced both old-line and the more militant groups: NAACP, Negro American Labor Council, Teachers for Integrated Schools, Catholic Interracial Council, American Jewish Congress, CORE, etc. and one of the best Urban League branches in the country. As "convener" of these groups, Raby's authority and power was grounded by the decisions and unanimity to be found among the member organizations.

Forged together by the school segregation fight in 1963, the CCCO had its first success in the school boycott of that year in which 250,000 children were kept home by their mothers. Convener Raby's tactics were direct, impulsive, untheoretical and usually aimed at a specific enemy—Mayor Daley. After the third mass demonstration in three days against the rehiring of School Superintendent Benjamin C. Willis, Daley angrily asked reporters: "Who is this man Raby? He doesn't represent the people of Chicago. I've received almost a thousand phone calls from Negro mothers saying he doesn't represent them."

The King-Raby relationship had been firmed by a three-day King barnstorm of Chicago in July 1965 when he rallied Negroes to the Chicago Movement and anointed its leadership. A year later, King had conducted an anti-Goldwater campaign in Chicago and drew 75,000 to a Soldiers Field rally.

In 1966, King and Raby jointly announced they were "co-chairmen" of the new Chicago Freedom Movement which was to be a marriage of CCCO, SCLC and other organizations. Decisions rested with a Steering Committee (later to be called the Agenda Committee) composed of representatives of the CCCO member-affiliates, SCLC staff and individual leaders in civil rights. The planning of strategy and its implementation lay with the Action Committee which was in turn represented on the ultimate decision-making body, the Agenda Committee. Tactics and strategy were often a cause of debate within the Chicago Freedom Movement on such issues as direct action, political association, the efficacy of marches and black power. But, underlying specific issues were the questions concerning SCLC's long-range efficacy within the Chicago setting.

> . . . some local leaders are not at all happy about the presence of Martin Luther King in Chicago. Once he has attained some or even all of his stated objectives, they argue, it will be the people who were on the scene before who will have to work out the practical implementation of the promised reforms with local authorities.[7]

However, the united front of King and Raby, SCLC-CCCO was diplomatically maintained. Since the arrival of King in Chicago, one civil rights leader observed, "There has been a deeper mutual trust in CCCO than there has ever been."

Now that King was in town to stay (at least two and one-half days a week) he announced his "Chicago Plan." "The problem of Chicago, indeed, the problems of the northern city demand something new," he explained. For several months, King's aides had scouted the urban complex. The SCLC tactics had been successful in small towns in the South: arriving in town and not finding strong leadership among the apathetic, the SCLC would import leadership, identify the issues in hope of arousing the Negro population, confront the establishment through "creative tension" and the lifting up of the truth dramatically, creation of sympathy and a "coalition conscience" in face of injustice, anticipate a strong reaction, reach some agreement, and then leave.

When pressed to describe his Chicago plan, King was vague:

> There are two ways to concentrate on the problems of the slum. One would be to focus on a single issue. But the CCCO and SCLC have chosen to concentrate all our forces and move in concert with a nonviolent army on each and every issue . . . the Chicago problem is simply a matter of economic exploitation. Every condition exists because someone profits by its existence.[8]

The Chicago approach would be "the crystallization and defining of the problem in Chicago in terms which can be communicated to the man in the street," King elucidated. Would there be demonstrations in the "Chicago Plan?" "Yes," he replied, "on a scale so vast that they would dwarf some of the biggest demonstrations we have seen in the history of the Movement."

King's scouts in the Chicago ghetto began with a laboratory approach. They experimented with a variety of ideas and techniques, seeing what would elicit a response from a bewildered Negro community. They first tried listening to the community, being sensitive to what the people were saying. In action, they would try anything to see what would work: organizing teenage gangs, tenant unions, a high school boycott. "From the outside it looked like chaos but inside it was creative . . . this confused city hall and made it more confident," explained John McDermott of the Catholic Interracial Council.

King's presence in the North had caused a financial crisis within the SCLC. Northern white liberals who had contributed 70% of SCLC's budget now reconsidered their pledges. Financial support slipped from $1.6 million in 1965 to less than one million in 1966. "We knew before coming here that contributions would suffer," said a King aide from Atlanta. "There were a lot of people in Chicago who were our financial and moral supporters. But now that we're in Chicago, we've only been getting moral support from these people and when we march into their neighborhoods, the moral support might be withdrawn, too," he observed in the early summer. Nationally, labor unions reaffirmed their pledges which ran into hundreds of thousands of dollars in cash and personnel.

As King diagnosed the political ills in the "City of Clout," he warned: "We are faced in Chicago with the probability of a ready accommodation to many of the issues in some token manner merely to curtail the massing of forces and public opinion around those issues." Awaiting King was Mayor

Richard Daley, the model of enlightened big city bossism. Daley had never encountered anyone like the preacher King. "The city hall attitude," said one Chicago observer, "was that he was just a little nuisance. They couldn't comprehend that he couldn't be bought off . . ." Conversely, Dr. King had never run into anything like Chicago and Daley.

> The city itself is a nest of paradoxes—dynamic, static, ugly, beautiful, outgoing, and inbred. The Daley administration had efficiently, even boldly, helped engineer a transportation, building, and utilities renascence. But the underpinnings remained squalid. Virtually everyone you talk to acknowledges that Chicago remains the crookedest city in the country. The stench rising from hoodlumism permeates vast areas of politics, labor and industry and fosters a cynicism about everything (a civil rights movement, for example) that does not depend on pull, pay-off or raw muscle to achieve its ends.[9]

Guided by expediency and the threatened loss of votes and power, Daley steered his eleven-year course to re-election issues: "better police and fire protection, cleaner alleys and streets, the best lighting in the nation, a tremendous expressway system, purer air . . ." Through his Negro lieutenant Rep. William Dawson, Daley had 90% of the Negro vote in his pocket, ghetto wards accounting for his entire 1960 plurality. Negro bolts were tightened in the machine through control of six Negro aldermen, called the "silent six."

> King was confronted with these complicated facts of political life when he reached Chicago—a metropolis that has usually shrugged off demands for white or black reform, an unresponsive Democratic machine, and Republicans of dubious value as allies. His past record for rousing the nation to demand federal legislation against racial injustice was magnificent, but he has always been able to motivate better than he could consolidate. City after city that had given him stirring national victories—Birmingham, St. Augustine and to a lesser degree Selma—were substantially unchanged in basic areas like jobs and housing after he had left them. The truth was, he had small talent for organizing outside or inside his own group. Now, with growing white national reaction pressing him from one side and Black Power from the other, he could not afford a failure.[10]

Part of the King plan was to heighten the "visibility" of the slum problem. Moving into a typical slum apartment in North Lawndale, King and his family were quickly visited by an anxious white landlord followed by crews of carpenters, painters, plumbers, electricians and exterminators working overtime to increase the "visibility" of the building. Wrote the *Sun-Times* editorial writer: "We don't know the terms of Dr. King's lease, but if possible, once the area of his present apartment is rid of slums, he should then move on to another area, and there, hopefully stimulate the same sort of healthful and helpful shock wave. In time, Chicago might achieve an elimination of blight that would amaze even the most optimistic of city planners."

Still concerned about making slum conditions visible, King decided to risk the legal embarrassment of taking control of a blighted building. When it was brought to his attention that a run-down building overcrowded with six families had been all but abandoned by its owner without heat or janitorial service in dead winter, King announced to the press: "I hereby assume trusteeship of this building to make life more liveable for the tenants." When asked about the legality of his move, King replied that his action was "supralegal." "We aren't dealing with the legality of it. We are dealing with the morality of it." There was no economic exploiter to make an enemy of since the owner was a dying, eighty-one-year-old slum dweller himself. Mayor Daley was not impressed and began injunction proceedings. "There are legal and illegal ways of achieving our objectives. None of us would say we should use illegal ways. We have our courts and our legislation."

Furthermore, Daley had announced his own plan to end the slums by 1967. "In the next two years we will eliminate every slum and blighted building in Chicago," he declared soberly. Certainly the Daley apparatus had conducted anti-slum programs before. But now there would be a beefed-up, block by block building inspection with slumlords facing court action. Bitter and feeling victimized were scores of Negro landlords who had invested their last dollar in worn out fifty-year-old dwellings and whose location did not allow them ready mortgage money for repairs. Mayor Daley boasted the best extermination program in the country using federal poverty funds to kill ghetto rats and roaches. Now teams of white exterminators were sent not to just alleys and porches but inside homes as well. A pragmatic neutralist, Daley kept pace with King's newspaper announcements and demands, only saying he could do the job better and bigger. "In the South," said one of Mayor Daley's aides, "King offered them love and he got back hate. Here he's offering us love and we're giving him love right back."

Speaking of Mayor Daley, an associate remarked: "a measure of his power is that the Mayor is a telephone call away from the President." Daley's open lines included one to Illinois Governor Kerner who, before the summer open-housing marches got under way, issued an Executive Order on open housing thus bypassing a bill stalled in the State Legislature for three years.

Approaching summer, the Daley machine moved into first gear in preparation for an ultimate test of Daley's popularity. An ambitious bond issue for $195 million to finance such brick-and-mortar improvements as rapid transit extensions, street and alley lighting, and sixty-three miles of new sewers faced its test at the polls in June. The entire business community rallied behind Daley pressure, as deals were closed buying support for the bond issue. In 1962, a $66 million city bond issue heavily touted by Daley was ingloriously defeated at the polls. The 1966 campaign was better organized as bank depositors found among their cancelled checks flyers urging a yes vote, police and firemen trod sidewalks distributing literature and wearing buttons, and Chicago's Roman Catholic Archibishop John P. Cody resorted to the pulpit to plug the measure. The result: the bonds passed by a two to one margin. Daley was still King.

Moving into summer, the King-SCLC crusade secured a victory in a collective bargaining agreement between a union of tenants and their slumlord in East Garfield Park. City hall observers noted however that victory came after around-the-clock picketing by United Auto Worker organizers, white college students and behind-the-scenes lawyers at work. The grassroots continued to look on in bewilderment.

Imported from the South was "Operation Breadbasket"—an effort to obtain fair employment for Negroes. Through boycotting and picketing, businesses serving the Negro community agreed to add Negro employees in more lucrative jobs. While a victory, it was also called by some "Operation Drop-in-the-Bucket."

In June, national attention was drawn to the Meredith Mississippi March where the first cries of "Black Power" were heard. King, as acknowledged head of the national civil rights movement, preached moderation. Observed the *Christian Century*: "History has given him (King) the double role of controlling violent Negro extremism with the one hand while attacking blind, bull-headed white racism and injustice with the other. If whites, bemused by King's dilemma, continue thwarting his nonviolent solution of racial injustice, his failure will not be their gain."

Summer in Chicago began early, on June 12th when a Puerto Rican mob was ignited when police brought dogs into their hot tense neighborhood to quiet spectators at an arrest. Acknowledged Puerto Rican leadership was hard to find since community leaders had joined the ranks of payroll public servants and no longer frequented the heartland of the Spanish-speaking ghetto. It was an ominous note on which to begin the summer and the Mayor's statesmanship advised him to respond with concessions or the promise of them.

Events sped toward a Daley-King encounter. Both had steadfastly avoided a personal encounter. Earlier in the year, Daley had invited King to join a delegation of religious leaders to discuss city problems. King had arranged to be out of town. In May, Daley called another meeting of the religious leaders, in his office, to discuss heading-off any possible racial trouble. It was a small summit of religious elite who filed into the Mayor's office, including Archbishop John P. Cody. Rather than raise eyebrows by a second absence, King chose to attend and warn against city problems. King in his campaign had warned his workers against an out-and-out clash with any individual, declaring, "I'm not interested in making this a campaign against any one man. We're against an evil system."

But by July 10th, after several delays, SCLC organized a rally in Soldier's Field—to kick off the massive action phase of the summer campaign.

"We are here today because we are tired," King told a crowd of 40,000 on the hot muggy afternoon. "We are tired of paying more for less. We are tired of having to pay a median rent of $97 a month in Lawndale for four rooms while whites in South Deering pay $73 a month for five . . . this day we must decide that our votes will determine who will be the mayor of Chicago next year." Leading 30,000 in a march on city hall, King, after his namesake, posted "The Program of the Chicago Freedom Movement (for) An Open and Just City" on the door of city hall with scotch tape and withdrew. A ceremonial encounter with the Mayor ensued the next day. Daley agreed with the bulk of the thirty-five demands and insisted that his reforms were already affecting those areas. The CFM demands included open housing, open employment and education. Various institutions in the metropolitan area were singled out: real estate boards and brokers, banks and savings and loan institutions, the Chicago Housing Authority, the Governor of Illinois, the Federal Government, the Mayor and City Council, the advertising media, business, unions and the Board of Education. Prefacing the demands were several pages of Movement prose describing "The Problems of Racism, Ghettoes, and Slums." The document reflected various currents within the Movement, notably the militants:

Negroes for years have been asking, begging, and pleading that white employers, board presidents, bankers, realtors, politicians and government officials correct racial patterns and inequities. The major lesson that the Negro community has learned is that racial change through this process comes only gradually, usually too late, and only in small measures. . . . but the time has now come for Negroes to set up their own instruments that will direct pressure at the institutions that still adhere to racism policies. Negroes must form their own power base from which Negro aspirations and goals can be demanded, a base from which they can make a strong common fight with others that share their problems or their aspirations. Chicago will become an open city only when Negroes develop power in proportion to their numbers.[11]

The Program was not a document of strategy, just purpose. How were these gains to be made? "The Chicago Freedom Movement and its constituent organizations use many means to bring about change. Community organization, education, research, job development, legal redress and political education are all weapons in the arsenal of the Movement. But, its most distinctive and creative tool is that of nonviolent direct action."

Leaving city hall empty-handed, King was grave:

While the Mayor showed warm and sympathetic expressions concerning these demands, no specific commitments were made. For this reason we will move forward to our action program . . . the purpose of the action program is to make the problems so clear that negotiations must be resumed. But we are demanding these things, we are not begging for them.

Discussing political adversaries, King had said: "In the South we faced all-out white resistance from political leaders. Mayors would not meet with us. In the North, you often have the sophisticated granting of minor concessions that may go just far enough to take the steam out of the movement, yet not far enough to solve the problems." He placed Daley's programs in that category, calling them superficial. "His (Daley's) refusal grows out of his inability to grasp the depth and complexity of the problem. We pointed out the massive discontent, the seething desperation in the Negro community."

According to Movement theory, power would come to the Negro community through "the non-violent movement which provides power to participate in decisions which now subjugate rather than elevate, which suppresses man's humanity rather than expresses it."

The next evening, violent rioting broke out on Chicago's West Side, an area described by the *Chicago Daily News* as "the part of Mississippi that got away." For four nights, cries of "Black Power" fell with bricks, bottles and bullets. Three days later, 4,000 men of the 33rd Infantry Division, armed with bayonets, machine guns, tear gas, and crash helmets mobilized in the Sears Roebuck parking lot. This cost the city $100,000 a day. Daley called the violence "a juvenile incident" but the attention was directed to King. On the scene day and night, King was ineffective in quieting the riots and even became the object of youthful jeers and laughter. At the police station the first night he kept saying over and over again, to no one in particular: "I told Mayor Daley, I told Mayor Daley something like this would happen if something wasn't done." The following night he told a press conference, "I want to see the riots end, but the largest job of staying riots is in the hands of the people in power." By Thursday night, King pledged to continue his nonviolent protests. Even if all Negroes favored violence, King declared, "I'm going to stand up as a lone voice and say this is wrong."

> In Chicago's mood of the moment, the role of Dr. Martin Luther King is as hotly debated as the role of the gangs. Once again, as in Selma and Montgomery, he is branded with the now familiar epithet of "outside agitator." None but the most rabid racist, of course, would hold him directly responsible for the riot. There are many in the city, though, including a number of long-time Negro community leaders, who say privately that by placing pressure on the sensitive areas of Negro frustration in the middle of a hot summer, Dr. King is somehow accountable for the explosion. And it is a number of these leaders, too, who mutter about him as an "outsider." Housing and education, they say, cannot be created overnight *a la* voter registration in the South. In short, they question whether the techniques of the Southern Christian Leadership Conference, so successful in the South, can be—or even ought to be—applied to the problems of the urban Negro.[12]

Massive outbursts, such as Chicago witnessed, could only, in King's words, "intensify the fears of the white majority while relieving their guilt."

Pleading for concessions to end the violence, Dr. King seemed outmaneuvered again as Daley bought peace for the price of one portable swimming pool and ten hydrant sprinklers. As the water cooled off West Side youngsters, the Chicago Freedom Movement picked up all the broken pieces and put together the action phase of the Movement. The goal—open housing.

II. *Opening a Closed City*

"Operation Open City" was conceived by Bernard Lafayette of the American Friends Service Committee, one of the most vocal exponents of nonviolence in Chicago. It carefully followed nonviolent strategy: discover a clear and simple issue of injustice—specifically, that Negroes cannot live anywhere in the city; secondly, lift up this truth dramatically and keep focusing on it despite violence and hostility—the truth being that realtors break the law every day in Chicago; third, produce "creative tension" around institutionalized racism in Chicago; fourth, elicit sympathy or a "coalition conscience" around the injustices at hand, putting the responsibility squarely upon all involved . . . realtors, complacent Negroes, homeowners, the City. Through demonstrations and marches, numbers would be drawn to the movement and courage built up to continue to face the issue. Rather than focus on one community, several would be selected as targets in order that all residents would be forced to face the reality together.

Developed by the Action Committee and approved by the Agenda Committee, Operation Open Housing was begun immediately after the King rally. Six steps were involved.

1. "Testing" of realtors by individual white and Negro families would determine the existence of actual discrimination.

2. Mass visits by groups of 50-200 persons, usually on Saturdays, to selected realtors who discriminated were then planned.

3. Picnics were to be held in parks in closed communities by large integrated groups who would make full use of the public accommodations.

4. Worship in churches by individuals and families on Sunday mornings. Negroes select a church of their faith for this action.

5. Mass outdoor prayer vigils on Sunday afternoons in the closed communities.

6. An educational program for whites in the communities visited, to be organized through the local churches and community groups in an effort to gain local support for making housing opportunities available to Negroes.

The Action Committee selected two communities in starting their campaign: the Belmont-Cragin neighborhood on the northwest side and the Gage Park-

Chicago Lawn neighborhood to the southwest. Inhabited by second generation Italian and Polish residents, Belmont-Cragin was tested by sixty-one Negroes and forty-seven whites. Of thirteen realtors, only one had the policy of offering his listings to Negroes. Visits often resulted in realtors locking their doors. At a picnic in the same neighborhood, the swimming pool was closed down upon arrival by the group. Park officials maintained there was glass at the bottom of the pool and rather than cleaning it out, closed it on the hot Saturday afternoon. An attempt to educate the community to the demands of the Movement took place in a Catholic church. Hecklers in a crowd of 250 broke up the meeting and booed the pastor when he attempted to restore order.

Meanwhile, in Chicago Lawn-Gage Park, inhabited by many first generation Lithuanians, Germans, and Poles, similar steps were taken. Realtors refused Negro applications, agencies were closed and exclusive listings by homeowners were withdrawn from the market.

Towards the end of the month of July, Dr. King observed that August was the month of riots within the Negro community, therefore more marches and demonstrations should be held to relieve mounting tensions. Demonstrations ought to be more dramatic, movement strategists analyzed, to begin to highlight the injustices which were found to exist. The first all-night prayer vigil met with loud hootings and jeerings from local white youths so threatening that it was called off. Finally violence broke. Four hundred and fifty marchers arrived in Chicago Lawn's Marquette Park on Sunday, July 31st, for a one-and-a-half hour prayer vigil before a realty office. Leaving their cars in the public parking lot and assured of police protection, the marchers set out.

The scheduled hour-and-a-half march turned into a four-hour nightmare as we wandered haphazardly through the neighborhood, unable to get through the mob and back to our autos. (Before the day was over, at least 40 of our cars, left on public park lots with the promised protection of police, were damaged or destroyed by the mob.) A girl about ten years old and wearing shorts got me with a rock during the frenzied attack. When Sister Mary Angelica, a first grade teacher at Sacred Heart School in suburban Melrose Park, was struck in the head and fell dazed to the ground, a roaring cheer went up from the rabid hecklers on the opposite sidewalk. The cheering continued as other marchers scooped up her limp and unconscious form and shouldered their way to a police car. "We've got another one!" the hecklers screamed. (A man standing in an alley holding the hand of his wide-eyed toddler hefted a large piece of paving stone and put it in his pocket, producing a significant bulge. Boys wearing Catholic high school football jerseys pranced

63

along the curb opposite us carrying an oversized noose and chanting: "I'd love to be an Alabama trooper/That is what I'd really like to be/For if I were an Alabama trooper/Then I could hang a nigger legally.") White persons in the line of march were targets of special abuse as the residents—especially older women—spat at us and called us "traitors, communists, white-niggers" and ranged a long list of sexual perversion charges against us. One man, apparently not yet master of the English language, shouted in fierce German which one marcher translated for me as: "I am an American; you are communists." Many youths cried, "Burn them like Jews," and "White Power." Others yelled, "Polish power." Gallantly, a young man handed a stone to his girl-friend. She threw it at the marchers and then smiled up at her date, who kissed her. Priests and ministers who were moving among the hecklers hoping to be able to restore order were met either by resentful silence or by taunts: "Are you one of those nigger lovers too?" (Some of the missiles aimed at us missed and broke store windows. Several marchers, though adept at ducking, were cut by shattered window glass. Three bottles that missed their mark landed unbroken at the foot of an outdoor shrine to the Blessed Virgin in someone's front yard. Marchers at the end of the line reported the bottles were retrieved as ammunition by still more hecklers. In the gathering dusk, the weary marchers returned to their cars in Marquette Park, intending to drive away from the mob, but a hideous coil of black smoke signalled that new horrors were in store. One marcher shouted: "They're burning the cars!" Incredibly, they were. The next day, the city would see films on television of the cars being ignited, and many would ask, as we had: 'If the television crews could be there, why couldn't the police have been there?' Many of the cars were marked with decals and stickers identifying them with the Chicago Freedom Movement; these were the first to be attacked. Two cars were pushed into a nearby park lagoon, a small foreign car lay on its side like a sleeping dog; others sat on four slashed tires. The next day, city newspapers designated the car burners as "counter-demonstrators.") A soft-spoken Negro lady, who confessed that she and her family had been ready to face the risk of being "first" when realtors' listings finally do become available to her, shook her head sadly and commented: "I'm going to stay where I am, with black folk. I don't want to live with maniacs."[13]

Fifty-six demonstrators including a priest, a nun and five policemen were hurt.

Despite the innocence pleaded by Real Estate Dealers relative to community reaction it must be realized that they were not only aware of the violent reactions in the Gage Park-Chicago Lawn area . . . but since the early 1940s had encouraged the feelings manifested in these reactions.[14]

With 90% of the population of Gage Park Roman Catholic, there were only two Negroes out of the total number of 28,244 residents.

During the week that followed, marchers were dispatched to the Belmont-Cragin neighborhood to demonstrate at realty offices. This time, more than 1,000 crash-helmeted police kept a tight guard around the demonstrators while plain-clothes officers waded in crowds and hurriedly threw the owners of cherry bombs and bottles into nearby patrol wagons. Loud shouts of protest followed the police action and chants of "Wilson Must Go" broke out.

By Friday of the first week of August, tension had built up within the Movement to "Return to Gage Park," this time with Dr. King. The cast of characters was unchanged from the previous Sunday: five hundred demonstrators sat in the middle of Marquette Park, protected from a shouting mob of 8,000 by 1,200 police. As King alighted from his car, the mob rushed and screamed when a rock the size of a man's fist caught him in the head. "Get the Witch Doctor!" "Kill him, Kill him," "Go Back to Africa," "We Want King," "Go Home You Apes," "Wallace for President"—shouts, screams, cries, bottles and bombs that lasted five hours. Described King: "I have never seen such hostility and hatred anywhere in my life, even in Selma." Commented a police official: "This night has to rate as one of the worst in our history. The outrageous cop-fighting we experienced here was about the most vicious I've ever seen in nearly thirty years of service. It was the Negro policemen who took the greatest abuse from the crowds."

Meanwhile, militant Robert Lucas of CORE was urging: "We cannot continue the passive reaction to all that hatred."

As the marches continued, the number of demonstrators for the Movement increased. Reaching its high mark of close to 1,500, the composition of the marchers continued to be 80% middle class, with a ratio of 50% white and 50% Negro.

On the following Sunday, another march brought 1,000 demonstrators to the Belmont-Cragin neighborhood. Along with the usual curses, catcalls and slogans there arose the shout: "Don't vote for the Democrats" and "If Daley can't get rid of the marchers, let's get rid of Daley!" The voices were heard in City Hall.

Both Belmont-Cragin and Chicago Lawn were considered by politicians as "swing neighborhoods" which could go either way in an election. When violence broke out, ward committeemen and aldermen dispatched precinct captains on a door-to-door calming mission, urging parents to restrain youngsters who were identified as the source of the trouble. In most cases, an angry backlasher would not let the politician make it up to their doorstep before angry denunciations of the political system were unleashed. Meanwhile, anti-Daley Republican Alderman John Hoellen of the north side 47th Ward presented a petition of several thousand names demanding that Mayor Daley stop the civil rights marches by enforcing a section of the municipal code which requires parade permits. One Democratic worker analyzed: "We lose white votes every time there's an outburst like this and you can bet that we don't gain any Negro votes either. Whites resent the force used by police while Negroes tend to respect the demonstrators, many of whom oppose Daley politically."

The political question was delicate and crucial. In the balance hung the future of race relations and Negro gains. If the cautiously moderate Daley machine were to be defeated, any new administration could be relied upon to put back racial progress for several decades.

Calling a meeting of Negro politicians, the Movement sought support for its open-city demands. While "substantial agreement" was found, the Democratic chiefs were adamant: credit must be given Mayor Daley for his leadership in the civil rights struggles over the years. Summarizing the then current political scene, the *Chicago Daily News* reported:

> Dr. King and Al Raby have vowed to carry their demonstrations for open housing into as many as 18 other all-white areas. Such a program, politicians say, could create enemies for the Democrats throughout the city. . . . Daley is reportedly working with the city's Negro Aldermen and human relations experts to see whether the rights demonstrations can be halted. Many observers believe that chances to halt the marches are slim because the marchers and their leaders are openly anti-Daley. Political leaders admit privately that the Daley organization was caught unprepared when the violence flared. Once the violence began, the 13th and 36th Ward Democrats were powerless to stop it. This is in sharp contrast to the speed with which the Daley Democratic chieftain for the 11th Ward brought violence to a halt last summer when his own neighbors became angry at Negroes picketing the Daley home. Daley seemed surprised that his boys in the 13th and 36th Wards don't have the influence he has in the 11th Ward, said one source.

Since his office was charged with putting out racial fires, Director Ed Marciniak of the Chicago Commission on Human Relations urged the Movement to "use the city's fair housing ordinance to stop alleged discrimination" instead of carrying protests to the street. Although empowered to revoke licenses, the City had never found a realtor in clear violation of the law. Since 1963, 241 complaints had been filed. "The overwhelming majority of these complaints were settled satisfactorily during a conference between all parties," he reported. Integration, he said, must take place on an area-wide basis which includes cities and suburbs.

Meeting at noon on Tuesday, August 9th, the Commission on Human Relations discussed the city's violent outbursts and anticipated a meeting with the Mayor later that day.

> The commissioners unanimously agreed that some effort should be made to set up a meeting with the Mayor, the civil rights leaders, the Chicago Real Estate Board and other interested organizations and citizens to discuss the problems and try to make some recommendations for solutions to the problem.[15]

Meanwhile, speaking at a press conference, his first in a week, Mayor Daley called for reason to help put an end to the violence touched off by the civil rights marches in the city. "We're hoping people will sit down and confer." The Mayor added that he was hopeful "that some people would try to work out in a conference table way some of these problems." He said, "I'm for anything that will put an end to what is happening to our city." Would there be a halt placed on the marches? Corporation Counsel Raymond Simon restrained the Mayor: "It's the government's duty to protect the marchers as long as they march in a peaceful orderly manner," and he cited the case of Alabama where federal troopers were called in to protect the marchers' rights. Urged Mayor Daley, "we hope Dr. King will reconsider his position—that we can resolve these questions without marches . . . that this would be resolved around the conference table and without violence in the streets." The Mayor said he was convinced that the Chicago Fair Housing Ordinance "will work out if people will cooperate and become convinced that this is the law of our city. We are hopeful some other way or method can be found because of what they are doing to our police department, our community and our neighborhoods. And of course all of us realize it is affecting the name of our city." When questioned about a white backlash, he maintained: "A lot of people are always taking advantage of a situation to inject politics. There are not going to be gains by trying to turn this into a political question. Our people are too intelligent to buy that argument."

Later that day, "at the meeting in the Mayor's office there was general agreement that immediate initiative should be taken to convene the city's top leadership for the purpose of taking issues off the streets and bringing them to the conference table. It was also suggested that the call for such a meeting should not come from the Mayor, but some other agency."[16] Immediately after the meeting, "the Mayor called Ross Beatty of the Chicago Real Estate Board to ask him if he would invite business, financial, civic, religious and civil rights leaders to a meeting to discuss fair housing practices with a view to resolving the issues which were the subject of street demonstrations. Mr. Beatty agreed to do this and said he would call Dr. Martin Luther King, Edwin C. Berry, Executive Director, Chicago Urban League, and Thomas Ayers, President of the Association of Commerce and Industry."

Officers of the Real Estate Board had looked upon their agency as a third party to the conflict. One officer explained the Board's position: "The Real Estate Board does not actively support either segregation or integration in housing. The pattern of housing reflects community attitudes. Brokers do not set these patterns." Or as another official was quoted: "the demonstrations have made it clear that it's not the real estate broker who is at fault. The problem is in the hearts and souls of the property owners."

> Concerned that the Chicago Real Estate Board might not be able to sustain the series of meetings necessary to resolve the issues, two commissioners, William Caples and Hale Nelson (and a business associate, Paul Lund) met to discuss the problem. The next day, Lund and Caples persuaded the Chicago Conference on Religion and Race to assume responsibility for convening a "summit" conference.[17]

With official institutional Church and Synagogue support, the Chicago Conference could send out a call that could be heard. In 1963, Chicago delegates to the National Conference on Religion and Race voted to form a local branch. For three years it had served as a clearinghouse for Catholic, Protestant and Jewish groups, working with Negroes and whites, to "stand together for racial justice." Seen from within, the CCRR was challenged with confronting Chicago's white middle-class religious institutions and denominational leaders with the pressing realities of racial injustice. By summer, however, few remained unconvinced that Chicago had an explosive problem.

Executive Paul Lund of the Illinois Bell Telephone Company and member of the CCRR Board, was now faced with the problem of getting the Chicago Real Estate Board to appear at a summit meeting in the role of a protagonist in a civil rights confrontation. Chairman Ross Beatty resisted encountering the Movement on this basis. Lund hammered: "Look, if you don't show up at that meeting, you're not going to have a city left to build in!" After four hours of debate, the Board consented. Their only stipulation insisted that other private and government agencies be invited to hear the Movement's demands. The presence of the Movement was taken for granted. "Marches have only one purpose and that is to be eventually halted in favor of some kind of an agreement with the power structure," analyzed one Movement strategist.

As spokesman for the CCRR, Bishop James Montgomery of the Episcopal Diocese was careful to state that the purpose of the meeting was not to call off the marches: "Up until this time there was not a favorable climate for a top level meeting of civil rights leaders and realtors. The injustices of housing discrimination and the shocking lawless reaction to the marches require a meeting to begin negotiations as soon as possible. Our concern for the redress of grievances and the reconciliation of peoples lead us as religious leaders to issue this invitation."

Earlier Archbishop John Cody of the Roman Catholic Archdiocese had lent his ecclesiastical support to the Mayor's plea to end the marches. Observing the one-year anniversary of his appointment to the Chicago Archdiocese in August, Bishop Cody brought with him from New Orleans a "get-tough" reputation in the field of racial justice. Chicago had waited until the summer to see how he would react to a northern city's brand of injustice. At the July 10th rally, a strong and accurate statement of the Archbishop officially put him behind Movement goals and singled out a list of public and private agencies which were derelict in their responsibilities. It was, according to the *New York Times*, the most forceful statement on race ever issued by a Catholic Archbishop. The Movement accepted his stand, leaving him to face a barrage of phone calls and letters from white Catholics. On the scene during the white violence, Bishop Cody conferred constantly with priests who reported back that his flock was carrying signs such as "Archbishop Cody and his commie coons." By August 10th official statements asking for a cessation of marches and an immediate conference table were being issued from high Protestant and Jewish officials, but the Cody statement made the front pages. In three pages, the Archbishop defended the rights of the marchers ("They have not been guilty of violence and lawlessness, others have.") but called upon the Movement to reconsider its strategy, or "the result will very likely be serious injury to many persons and perhaps even the loss of lives." Only in the last paragraph did the Archbishop call for solutions to the problems caused by a closed city. The

Archbishop's position was interpreted as a pro-Daley stance for peace-for-the-sake-of-peace.

A "strong-man," mediator-type Chairman was necessary to keep order at the meeting and make the sessions productive. From the several names suggested, that of Ben Heineman was selected by the CCRR Board. President of the Chicago and Northwestern Railroad, Heineman had moderated the 1966 White House Conference on Civil Rights at the request of President Johnson. One obstacle arose: Heineman and his family were then on vacation in Sister Bay, Wisconsin and not accessible. "The only person who could call him back was Mayor Daley," recalled Gene Callahan. Daley was then asked to get Heineman. "The Mayor called Heineman on his yacht. Then Daley called me back from his car to tell me Heineman would be our chairman." Early next week, the Northwestern Railroad jet plane flew to Wisconsin to transport Heineman to Chicago.

Telegrams were sent to the list of names agreed upon by the Conference, particularly those who had an interest in open housing. Many names had to be omitted. "When word got out that this was going to be a meeting of Chicago's 'power group,' I started getting calls from everybody asking to be included," recalled Callahan.

Concern within the Movement for the continued safety of the marchers was spoken of. "If some of us have to die to achieve integrated housing in Chicago then we will die," remarked King in an interview. In the marches lay the Movement's only source of bargaining power. The Movement threatened to increase them to five or eight daily, using 1,000 to 5,000 marchers during the coming two months. Within the Movement itself there was anxiety. "We knew we had only two or three weeks more if we were to get anything from the marches," a civil rights leader admitted. "Past labor day we were dead. After the kids go back to school, things would quiet down and we all knew it."

King analyzed: "The marches have not only aroused consciences, but are threatening existing political alliances." To protect his "vested interest," Daley will eventually "choose to negotiate civil rights issues rather than face a complete collapse of the alliance," King analyzed.

Indeed for several months the city had attempted to negotiate civil rights issues with Dr. King. Individuals acting unilaterally had tried to find Dr. King's price. Stories of such attempts abound within the Movement. Particularly active was Charles Swibel, president of the Marina Management Corporation and Chairman of the Board of the Chicago Housing Authority.

By late spring, Swibel felt Dr. King had gotten in over his head and needed a "victory." In return, King would leave Chicago and carry his crusade to other cities. The victory statement would have read:

Mayor Richard J. Daley and Dr. Martin Luther King today issued a joint statement of cooperation to achieve the common objective of opening the doors of opportunity to all people.

Mayor Daley and Dr. King stated that the challenge of the urban areas throughout our nation can only be met by programs that root out poverty, rid the community of slums, eliminate discrimination and segregation wherever they may exist, improve the quality of health and education, and provide every able person with the opportunity for meaningful work at decent wages.

Dr. King said, "Those of us in the Civil Rights Movement are deeply aware that the goals we seek must solidly be founded on goodwill and understanding among all people. We do not urge the building of programs that are recklessly put together overnight. We have enumerated long-range goals to which Negroes and Puerto Ricans and other minorities rightfully aspire. We seek immediate measures that strengthen the economic foundation of families that still do not share in the affluence of American life. We are concerned with programs that protect the health and safety of all urban communities. Our commitment is to those programs that bring greatly improved education to youth. We demand measures that open job opportunities without discrimination.

We have seen the people of Chicago respond to the urgent problems confronting urban society. Under the leadership of Mayor Daley, this city has invested great human and material resources in the fight against poverty, against slums, against ill health, against conditions of deprivation that stem from out of slavery, segregation, economic exploitation, and social discrimination. Throughout our nation the burden of accumulated human neglect has fallen upon the present generation of municipal leadership.

Chicago has been fortunate that under Mayor Daley's wise administration it has programs underway which seek to attack the causes of poverty—to provide jobs and job training, to advance merit employment, to open apprenticeship opportunities, to compensate for cultural deficiencies and to open more recreational facilities. Chicago's poverty program is considered one of the best in the country and it has launched health care programs which are the most far reaching in the nation.

Today Mayor Daley has again demonstrated his leadership by acting upon our request to institute programs in the Chicago Housing Authority which are urgently needed."

Mayor Daley said that programs recommended by Dr. King would help make the Chicago Housing Authority the finest institution of its kind in the nation and had received the full support of the Commissioners.

The Mayor said that the following programs will be adopted:

1. Installing a guard system with elevator operators in all high-rise Chicago Housing Authority installations.

2. That recruitment for the guards should be from among project tenants. The pay should be pegged around $2.30 an hour. This will provide not only security but employment for between 300 and 400 men. The initial guard project should be set up between the hours of 4:00 p.m. and 12:00 p.m. Mr. Swibel has already talked to retired Commander Kinsey Bluitt of the Chicago Police Department about heading and training and supervising such a crew.

3. There will be established a flat rent schedule for Chicago Housing Authority. This means that leases would be signed for a one-year period and there would be no snooping on the part of Chicago Housing Authority personnel relative to the change of income status with any tenant other than at the time of renewal of the lease.

4. There will be installed a bell and buzzer system in all three- and four-story walk-ups.

5. A Negro journeyman glazer will be hired by the Housing Authority.

6. An integrated committee will be appointed. This committee will examine admission sources in all locations. Integration of the buildings should be sought even if this means keeping certain apartments vacant until integration can be achieved in existing buildings. The conservation of buildings, rent supplements and subsidies will be started in Lawndale with which 150 new units on scattered sites will be constructed and 150 rehabilitated units in existing buildings. One hundred and eight new houses are to go up at Hermitage and Maple Streets.

"This is a great occasion," Mayor Daley said. "The programs of opening the doors of opportunity to all people cannot be accomplished by government alone. There must be the cooperation and support of every segment of the community, business, labor, the clergy and civil rights groups, and most important—the cooperation and support of the residents of the city and the metropolitan area."

Mayor Daley and Dr. King said:

"There may be differences of opinion concerning methods and procedures but there can be no difference regarding our mutual support for those programs which seek to open the doors of economic and social opportunity to all people."

Dr. King said that he pledged his cooperation to Mayor Daley in implementing the positive programs the city has underway.

The Movement had rejected this and similar concessions, calling them "pretty small potatoes." The Movement would have to generate greater power to produce satisfactory terms for an agreement. Now as the summer progressed, that "temporary" power grew. On Tuesday, August 16th, Police Superintendent Wilson held a press conference to announce that 7,000 policemen were on alert because of simultaneous civil rights demonstrations that "eat into our manpower." Wilson reported that crime had increased 25% during the period beginning July 18th. "The demonstrations are knocking our fight on the crime rate into a cocked hat." Wilson reported that police morale was high and that he saw nothing alarming in the record number of resignations.

Movement leaders expected little to come from the negotiations the next day. Besides the usual statement of fixed positions and strong pressure to cease marching, little more could be anticipated since the Mayor had assembled forces to put pressures on the Movement. Hastily, the Movement put nine points together, rather than to appear at the Wednesday session empty-handed. Remarking on the meeting to be held the next day, Rev. Bevel mused: "But that is nothing more than a bull session. It's not a negotiating session. It's simply to get a negotiation session started." Representatives for the Movement were drawn from the Agenda Committee. From SCLC, there was Dr. King, and staff aides, James Bevel, Jesse Jackson, Andy Young; from CCCO, Al Raby, Edwin Berry, Arthur Brazier, Arthur Griffin, Kale Williams and John McDermott; from the Unions, James Wright of UAW and Charles Hayes of the Packinghouse Workers. By mid-August, the unions supporting Dr. King's efforts had felt pressures from national offices and City Hall concerning repercussions of the marches. Especially effected was the campaign of Senator Paul Douglas for the Senate. Following a strong liberal platform, Douglas and his campaigners heard the loud rumblings of a growing backlash. At the negotiations, SCLC staff would follow the direction of Dr. King. Finally, local civil rights leaders were seriously reconsidering the long-range implications of the marches. "By the end of the summer we were all worn out," explains one leader. "The violence had come so suddenly that we had no time to reflect on what we were doing."

Anticipating the next day, Realtor Ross Beatty reaffirmed the Board's position: "We do not plan to enter into a debate with Dr. King. All I can do is to discuss the problem with them and try to make them understand the problem facing real estate members."

On Tuesday, a spokesman for the American Nazi Party announced that his members would conduct a march into a Negro neighborhood: "I want to see if the Negroes get the same rough treatment from the police that the white kids got when the Negroes invaded white neighborhoods. The Negroes got the white cops—whom I'm sure hate the Negroes as much as the white kids do—to fight for them. We want to see if there's a double standard of law enforcement." The Nazi Party, he informed the press, numbered fifty Chicago members, thirty "storm troopers" and 1,500 national members. "Buy yourselves guns and teach your wives to use them too," Chicago Lawn residents were urged. "We won't wear our Nazi uniforms, but we will probably carry placards. We'll have quite a few preachers with us too. We'll stop every once in a while and we will pray that the Negroes will all go back to Africa peacefully."

The stage was set for Summit I.

III. *The Summit Conference and Decisions*

The City officials had come to deal on the issue of open housing. But only late in the afternoon did the Movement realize how seriously the leaders viewed the situation. Close to seventy men filled the hot stuffy parish hall at St. James Episcopal Cathedral where they were to remain, relieved only by a floor fan, for nearly eleven hours. After a prayer by Bishop Montgomery, Ben Heineman quickly shifted the burden of the city's immediate problem away from the marches conducted by the Movement, to the need for opening the entire metropolitan area. Although coming to deal, Mayor Daley's introductory statement reflected the consistent stance taken by the City and the pressures being undergone. He reviewed the progress in jobs and housing in the City and pointed out that the problem was a metropolitan one. The City of Chicago in fact, he stated, had done more than any other city in these areas and therefore marches must stop.

Following Mayor Daley, Dr. King reminded the leaders of the reality of the ghetto of race, poverty and misery within the City. He implored the men to face it and deal creatively with it. He was followed by Ely Aaron of the Commission on Human Relations.

> I want to thank the Chicago Conference on Religion and Race for taking the initiative in convening this conference. I believe I express the appreciation of the entire community in thanking the civic, business, labor, religious and civil rights leaders who are present today around the conference table to resolve grave issues that confront us.
>
> To assist in the constructive resolution of these issues, I personally wish to recommend that we conscientiously consider and seek to agree on the following matters. I wish to emphasize that these are proposals aimed at uniting us in a common purpose. We seek to open up opportunities throughout the entire metropolis, city and suburb, opportunities for freedom of residence and for all the other rights which are every man's inheritance under our law.

His eleven-point program covered compliance by real estate brokers in letter and spirit to the Chicago Fair Housing Ordinance, nondiscriminatory mortgage loans, suburban "summit" conferences, and better enforcement by the Human Relations Commission of the Ordinance.

Faced with an audience of the City's leaders, Al Raby hammered for factual change and not mere verbal assurances. To Raby, the only man who could do this was the Mayor himself, who should immediately launch a new program to enforce the Chicago fair housing ordinance effectively and vigorously in the City. His nine-point program had been hastily drawn up during the previous days by the Movement in the event that negotiations should reach that point. Several were taken from the "Demands for Open Housing" made at the July 10th rally. While demanding concessions from various city agencies and the Real Estate Board, the Movement's demands pointed the finger at the City for foot-dragging.

> Specifically we ask (of the City) as first steps of such a good faith program:
>
> a) that the city policy of equal housing opportunity and a copy of the fair housing ordinance be posted on the windows of all real estate offices in the city.
>
> b) that the city test real estate offices to comply with the law all over the city and on a year round basis.

c) that the city launch a program of initiating complaints against violators of the ordinance all over the city and on a year round basis.

d) that the city hire additional people to enforce the law and act upon complaints within 48 hours as is done by other city agencies when inspections reveal violations of liquor and food laws.

e) that the licenses of real estate brokers found in clear violation of the law be immediately suspended.

f) that the city seek authority for a more powerful fair housing ordinance, one which would apply to property owners as well as real estate brokers.

Agency heads were then given the opportunity to reply to the Movement's demands and explain the concessions they were prepared to make. Movement leaders observed with amusement Mayor Daley's "concession" that "yes, we can enforce the (open housing) law better . . . that's no problem," when days previously the Commission on Human Relations maintained that they could not be more effective. From the east side of the parish hall, where city leaders were seated together on both sides of a long table, there came encouraging words of concern and reform: the Chicago Housing Authority would try to reverse its traditional policy of building high-rise public housing in dense ghetto areas; the Urban Renewal Department's relocation office would now endeavor to look for apartments for Negroes outside of the ghetto; the Federal Government expressed its concern for more fully utilizing Federal power to break discriminatory patterns followed by savings and loan associations; Chicago mortgage bankers would begin to enforce its formal policy of nondiscrimination in lending money to any qualified family.

By noon, the only hold-out was Ross Beatty, who had not been empowered by his Real Estate Board to make any concessions in its name. He maintained that the realtors' position was fixed and there was nothing he could do. In the silence that followed, Callahan leaned over to Heineman: "Look, their Executive Board is meeting today . . . why not adjourn for a few hours until they can come back with some kind of concession." Knowing that if there would be a refusal from the realtors, the Movement would walk out on the entire Conference, Heineman then drew himself to his full height and addressed Beatty and Arthur Mohl: "Gentlemen it would seem to be the consensus of all in this room that the monkey's on your back. . . . I'd suggest you do something about it!"

The meeting was adjourned until four o'clock. Reporters buzzed the halls of the Episcopal Parish House looking for the story which was being withheld from them by common consensus: publication of the frank exchanges could jeopardize the delicate deliberations. Almost assured of obtaining his cessation of the marches Mayor Daley remained through the entire lunch break and after. "It was very fruitful," remarked the Mayor to the press. They noted he looked drawn and harassed. The discussions were "fruitful" remarked Heineman. The deliberations were "fruitful," commented King. Wrote Gruenberg of the *Daily News* on the climate at the lunch break:

> Daley, the strongest mayor in America, seemed backed into a corner for the first time in his political career. Only the Summerdale police scandal—when Daley had to go to California to seek a new police superintendent outside of Chicago's Irish culture—was a comparable crisis. And that, by its nature, was much smaller. Now there seemed to be something almost to be pitied about the mayor, as he sat perspiring in the shabby parish house lunchroom. He was not, as is usual for him, sitting at the center of the tables arranged in U-form. He was, instead, shunted off to a side table. It was hot, dim and stuffy. A single floor fan provided little breeze for some 60 perspiring men, and it was, after all, a far cry from the plush, carpeted, fifth-floor air conditioned office, where he was used to hearing little, if any rebuttal from anyone. Every prelate and participant, of high and low stature, tried to paint the best possible picture for reporters in the corridors outside. They were talking amicably inside, the reporters were told. They were friendly; there was good spirit. One city official even detailed in great self-pride all the "concessions" the city, and especially his agency, had granted to Dr. King and his followers. Talk of pessimism and rigid positions and stubborn attitudes was just plain nonsense they all said.

After lunch, the Mayor placed a call through to Beatty at the Real Estate Board offices. "In the interest of the City of Chicago you cannot come back here this afternoon with a negative answer," he insisted.

In the morning session, Beatty had read a three-page statement making it clear that the Board could not drop its traditional position against open occupancy. Instead, he suggested market-research studies on property-owners' attitudes and another community-level "summit conference."

At four in the afternoon, Beatty returned with an additional statement containing the key paragraph: "We have reflected carefully and have decided we will—as a Chicago organization—withdraw all opposition to the philosophy of open occupancy legislation at the state level, provided it is applicable to owners as well as brokers. We reserve the right to criticize detail as distinguished from philosophy and we will require that the State Association of Real Estate Boards do likewise but we cannot dictate to them." Further, he promised the Chicago Realty Board "will effectively remind our members that it is their duty to obey the Chicago Fair Housing Ordinance as their lawyers interpret its meaning."

Although the monolith had been moved a couple of inches, the Movement wanted to see more. "This is nothing," King whispered to another. During the next three hours, the Movement reconsidered its position. Both sides had come with their demands and concessions. Those skilled in negotiating knew that these had become the limits within which they could move. Faced with the willingness of the City leaders to make an immediate deal, the Movement sought time. By the afternoon, they were sold on the idea of seeking support of the power structure in a joint program of desegregation. "The movement's leaders," wrote the *Daily News*, "didn't want its followers to feel they had settled for too little, but didn't want to appear unreasonable, unwilling to bargain, and unappreciative of the good will and good faith shown at the meeting." As the afternoon wore on, King insisted that the concessions were not "massive enough." Rev. Bevel arose and announced that the marches could not stop until the concessions were actually "put into effect." Wrote the *Daily News*, "Mayor Richard J. Daley angrily denounced the movement's caucus decision, it was learned, and countered by saying he was withdrawing his agreement to enforce the city's fair housing ordinance vigorously. To which the Rev. Dr. Martin Luther King and rights leader Albert Raby replied with words to this effect: "We haven't got much but we do have people who are willing to take risks for what they believe is right. You cannot ask us to abandon them for mere promises." Analyzed another writer: "The Mayor—used to the give-and-take of politics—was angered because he thought he had struck a deal. This was a solid declaration to work for an 'open city' by himself and his department heads, plus the real estate board's concession, in exchange for a 'no-march' pledge."

However, the Movement would agree to meet in a subcommittee to work further on the commitments. A nineteen-man committee was then created to work under the chairmanship of Thomas G. Ayers, president of the Chicago Association of Commerce and Industry. By Friday, August 26th, they would try to untangle the problem. "The charge I gave this subcommittee was to come back with recommendations on how white Americans and Negro Americans, with respect to housing in Chicago, can live together in peace," observed Heineman.

Leaving the conference, obviously exhausted and disappointed, the Mayor bristled when newsmen fired a string of questions at him as he sought to get into his limousine. "Will the civil rights marches end now?" "Ask Dr. Martin Luther King . . . don't ask me." "Would the realtors end their opposition to open-occupancy legislation?" "Ask the real estate people." "Are you disappointed with the results of the meeting?" "Yes, I am, because there does not seem to be a cessation to the marches."

Observed an aide of Daley: "The Mayor worked like a Trojan in there for a peaceful and quick solution, but the civil rights people kept pulling away from him whenever it seemed there could be a stop to the marches. They were apparently teasing him . . . and the mayor is not used to being teased."

After adjourning, Heineman remarked: "The biggest stumbling block was to pin everything down in two hot hours . . . I personally think there is an attitude of determination on the part of all participants to get this very unworthy problem behind us."

The first official meeting of the subcommittee was set for Friday, August 18th. Appointed representatives were:

Conference on Religion and Race:Eugene J. Callahan; Rev. Robert Christ; George Jones, Dr. Robert Spike

Commission on Human Relations: Ely Aaron; William Caples; Edward Marciniak; William R. Ming

Real Estate Board: Ross Beatty; Arthur Mohl

Commercial Club: Leonard Spacek

Movement: Edwin Barry (Urban League); Rev. James Bevel (SCLC); John McDermott (Catholic Interracial Council); Albert Raby (CCCO); Kale Williams (American Friends)

City Representatives: Thomas Paul (Chicago Federation of Labor); William Lee; Charles Swibel (Chicago Housing Authority)

To Swibel's mind, negotiations could better take place among a few key persons, informally gathered to hammer out differences. "For months I had been getting closer to the leaders in the Movement and I think they trusted me." Swibel arranged for an all-night meeting at the O'Hare Inn. By the end of the joking, drinking, negotiating session, the Movement leaders had themselves consented to several agreements. Swibel reminded that they had to keep within the limits of the original concessions and not introduce new points. A late morning meeting of representatives of member-organizations of the Chicago Freedom Movement was scheduled for Thursday to discuss the lately thrashed-out agreement and the whole position of the Movement to date. Swibel himself headed home, showered, and proceeded to the Mayor's Office where he waited for a telephone call from CFM leaders. By noon, both the Mayor and Swibel had received no call. Meanwhile, at the Urban League, the at-large membership had decided: the agreements were not massive enough . . . more should be obtained from the subcommittee sessions.

"We have to keep on marching," Dr. King told a rally Thursday evening. "The Chicago Freedom Movement will not stop until Negroes can move anywhere they want to in the City of Chicago." Leaving the Wednesday meeting, a Daley aide had said: "The thing Mayor Daley wants more than anything else for the city now, is for the marches to stop." By Thursday evening, the late-editions of the *Chicago Daily News* tipped-off that the Mayor had indeed found a way: Daley would lower an injunction on the civil rights marches on Friday. At the first meeting of the subcommittee the next day, formal announcement of the injunction created a crisis. It took the Freedom Movement by surprise and two members of the city's human relations commission said they had been unaware of the move. Churchmen at the meeting were furious. Dr. Robert Spike made a scathing speech questioning the "good faith" of the city negotiators.

From a noon meeting at City Hall with the Mayor, Police Superintendent Wilson and Corporation Counsel Raymond Simon, details of the injunction were released: a twenty-four-hour notice must be given to the police superintendent concerning any demonstration, there must be only one demonstration per day, there would be a limit on the marchers at 500, and marches were limited to daylight hours alone.

Sources close to the Mayor revealed that the injunction was not as strong as he would have wanted. To prohibit marches altogether, the Mayor was willing to require a thirty-day notice for all marches. By the time this injunction could be contested in the courts and undoubtedly ruled illegal, it would be winter and the summer crisis would be over. The limited injunction would hold marchers in check while reassuring angry white property owners that the Mayor had the situation under control. In case the injunction was broken, there would be no mass arrest, which would dramatically increase Movement troops. It was the reaction of the Negro voter that Daley was most concerned about. His adviser on the mood of the Negro community, Alderman Ralph Metcalfe, reported that the injunction would be acceptable to most Negroes. To explain his move to the people of Chicago, Daley went before the television cameras for eleven minutes that evening.

I have appealed to the civil rights leaders to take the issue out of the streets and on to the conference table. I pointed out to them that the reduction of police protection resulting from the demonstration, strikes particularly at those areas where there are the most families and the most children. I have remarked much of the violence, most of the disturbances were being stimulated by extremists of the right and the left, not from the residents of the north, south, and west sides—but extremists who live out of the community, out of the county, and in many instances, out of the state. I said that a continuance of these kinds of demonstrations would only serve as a magnet to the hate groups which only desire to stir up racial violence and disorder. I told them and I believe that most people of the city and especially those who are most anxious to see hatred subside and discrimination because of race eliminated; do not want to see the great issue of civil rights reduced to the level of street fighting and the collapse of law and order.

The Mayor ended with a lengthy quotation from Abraham Lincoln.

King's reply was swift and sharp. He called the Mayor's talk an "act of desperation." "Mayor Daley is more of a politician than a statesman and not good at either. The people who are throwing rocks and bricks are the ones along with the realtors who need to be enjoined." King and Raby in their statement, suggested that if the police needed help, they might call upon the National Guard. "If 5,000 persons want to exercise their right of free speech and assembly, do we have to turn away 4,500?" Because the injunction was so limited and could be dealt with at the conference table, King's lawyers advised that it is "something we can live with." To the rally of civil rights marchers, King encouraged: "We aren't going to let any injunction turn us around. I am ready to go to jail in Chicago."

Privately the injunction it was felt would be difficult to break. "I'd break that injunction if I had the troops," King had confided. He knew that 80% of his marchers were middle-class, holding responsible jobs, and not eager to be detained in jail for several days and fined. Although there would be no mass arrests, enough open-ended fines could be levied against individuals to make the strategy costly and questionable. Appealing the injunction would take a couple of years and about $200,000 since it would have to go beyond the Federal District Court, controlled by Daley. Although the NAACP was

81

willing to pay some of the costs, it was uncertain where other funds would come from. Furthermore the issue over which the arrests would be made was not clear-cut. Real estate practices and open housing could not be achieved by an act of Congress.

On Sunday, August 21, more than 1,000 marchers appeared at King's south side headquarters, anxious to see how their leader would deploy them. King chose to observe the injunction. "If the injunction isn't overturned by the courts this week," King asserted that he would "defy it in the marches scheduled for next weekend." Five hundred marchers followed King to Trumbull Park, a housing project area which was the scene in the early 1950s of repeated violence by whites who had learned that Negroes were assigned there. One thousand police were on hand to maintain order. Surplus marchers were sent to two suburbs, Evergreen Park and Chicago Heights, which were outside of the jurisdiction of the injunction.

Earlier in the week, rightist David Sheehan spoke to his predominantly white Catholic audience on the southwest side. The audience lustily booed any mention of Dr. King, the civil rights movement, Mayor Daley or Archbishop Cody. The latter was accused of "prostituting his religious power." That same day, Cody was picketed outside of Chancery Office by eight Catholic members of the Chicago Freedom Movement who accused the Archbishop of showing a "lack of leadership" in the civil rights struggle by calling for a halt to the marches. That week marked the first anniversary of Cody's appointment to Chicago.

By Sunday, a curious assortment of speakers arrived in Marquette Park to address the crowds. George Lincoln Rockwell of the American Nazi Party told 2,000: "If you took the worst ghetto where Negroes live and drove them out and put white people in, the area would be cleaned up in two weeks. Negroes should go back to Africa. They are scum. They can't think. They can't talk. They won't work and they are ugly." Rockwell was warned afterwards that he would be arrested if he spoke again.

In another corner of the park, Evan Lewis of Akron, Ohio and "Imperial Ambassador" of the Ku Klux Klan attempted to speak without a permit and was promptly jailed. Elsewhere, Rev. Connie Lynch of the National States Rights Party was similarly halted.

On Monday, August 22, Mayor Daley held his first press conference since August 11th, and discussed these visitors to Chicago: "They're not Chicago citizens and they're not neighborhood people. They come from outside the neighborhood, outside the city and even outside the state. We've got commies, we've got Nazis, and everyone else you can name showing up. I wish they'd go home!" When asked whether such "outsiders" would include Dr. King, Daley hesitated and then answered: "You said that."

Over the weekend, the newspapers reported that the Movement was holding a trump card. Three thousand marchers would be called upon to march into the suburb of Cicero, a town whose name alone aroused chilling memories among blacks and whites in Chicago. It was in Cicero that two weeks of violent rioting took place in 1951 when a Negro couple tried to move into an apartment. Their furniture and apartment were wrecked and the family driven from the town. Directly adjoining the West side of Chicago, Cicero had only a slim police force that was unable to keep peace. Then Governor Adlai Stevenson had to call out National Guard troops to the white Catholic suburb. Since that time, Cicero had stood as the symbol of segregation. Now, a militant wing of the Freedom Movement considered the Cicero march a national demonstration against the closed city. With a shadow of a police force, Cicero would need hundreds of law enforcement officers to keep the anticipated thousands of marchers protected. State and county leaders immediately set about providing the needed forces. For some leaders in the Freedom Movement, the Cicero march came as news. It had not come out of the decision-making process of the full movement but only leaked out of an Action Committee meeting and was alluded to at a rally. But by Sunday, King was committed to Cicero. Meanwhile, Mayor Daley sighed a sigh of relief . . . Cicero was out of his jurisdiction.

The organizers within the Movement knew that they would be at the beginning of their real, though temporary, power, if they could compel the indigenous, poorer ghetto Negroes to join the Cicero march. Cicero was symbolic and having marched once a person was sure to march again and again. The call went out to the ghetto and new faces appeared, willing to march into Cicero.

The Thursday session of the City Council saw Alderman Thomas Keane lead the councilors in a forty-five to one vote of confidence for Mayor Daley in his taking action with the injunction: "In forty years of public life I cannot recall a greater unanimity of expression in favor of an action taken by a Mayor" to bring a problem from the streets to the Conference Table. Dissenter Leon DesPres of Woodlawn urged a substitute resolution: that segregated housing is against City policy. This was defeated.

Other aldermen had their turn to speak. Alderman John Hoellen pointed to "20,000 signatures" on a petition of support for Mayor Daley. Hoellen also urged an investigation of War on Poverty workers who were seen participating in civil rights marches. Negro Alderman William Harvey remarked: "King is a great man but he is surrounded by some people who are not right." There should be, he suggested a "sincere test of the fair housing ordinance." And, "King should turn around and look at some of the people who brought him here." For Ralph Metcalfe, Daley's injunction was "an act of statesmanship." "Some in the Movement want to see Chicago destroyed." He continued: "Negroes have come a long way" since the Days of Reconstruction and he feared "we will lose what we have gained." The militants are the "pawns of forces who do not want to see justice done." According to Negro Alderman Claude Holman, "education is needed before it (the housing problem) can be solved." Meanwhile, white Aldermen David Healy and Joseph Krska concluded, "the marches are not caused by our Negro people in the North."

By Thursday, August 25th, the Ayers subcommittee had put in sixty hours of work on the report, often working late into the evening. "At first the job was one of keeping order . . . everyone wanted to talk at once," Ayers recalls. After taking notes on the discussions, Ayers withdrew with his minutes and with the help of two secretaries one evening, put the subcommittee report together. The Movement was realizing that by putting the agreement on paper, they would inevitably lose some power. At best, any commitments would look vague and a follow-up process undramatic. The Movement had come without having done its homework on each agency and the record of their past performance in the fields of open housing. Open to question was the absence of any specific commitment of money and staff to enforce the agreement and the discouragement of timetables as a test of the agreement.

As the week wore on, Raby found himself tired and caught between the convictions of the Agenda Committee and the Action Committee. Taught by Northern experience to crusade for laws and agreements in writing, the Agenda Committee, composed mainly of Chicago civil rights leaders, was eager to put the commitments on paper. The Action Committee, led by James Bevel, was not satisfied. "I'm getting tired," cried Bevel, "of all this lawyers' talk! Tell me when can a Negro family move into a white neighborhood? When a white family wants a house, they go to a real estate office; when a Negro family wants a house, you're telling them to go to the Commission on Human Relations!" Faced by the willingness of the City to deal, Bevel returned Wednesday with a whole new set of Movement demands. Ayers flatly refused to allow this "escalation." As a sign of their good faith, city leaders were willing to make side agreements to cover those points not originally introduced by the Movement. It became clearer to all that enforcement would come only through some community-wide leadership group which would commit itself to the goals of the agreement. The Chicago Conference on Religion and Race volunteered to call this group together. As their "concession" the Chicago Freedom Movement would pledge "its resources to help carry out the program and agrees to a cessation of neighborhood demonstrations on the issue of open housing so long as the program is being carried out." There was no specific mention of Cicero, thereby leaving it as a negotiable item for the Friday conference table. Also negotiable was the Daley injunction. The *Daily News* reported on Thursday: "It was also reported that spokesmen for the city have hinted to civil rights leaders they would act to withdraw the injunction limiting the open housing marches. Such action to be taken in Court would be part of an over-all settlement of open housing issues—if such a settlement could be reached Friday." It was, the *News* reported, a point that might be thrown in, but not a large important "bargaining" concession.

With the continuing marches and backlash reaction, there was concern in Washington for the future of the vital Daley Democratic Administration in Chicago. Thus pressure was placed on the sensitive places and persons, particularly labor unions and other supporters of Dr. King. It was Bayard Rustin who had reportedly warned Dr. King: "For God's sake, Martin, this (the marches) is getting you nowhere! Settle for something!" Certainly, open housing in Chicago could not be delivered to King by Daley. Years of education within the communities led by good-willed Chicago leaders would be needed, and the Metropolitan Leadership Council might offer this. The idea of a Council to enforce the Agreement was inevitable. Chicago had a responsive business community which met regularly with the Mayor on specific issues and crises. Blue Ribbon committees were regularly formed. Members of such groups included men sensitive to social problems, committed, and action-oriented, as well as those committed to the mere enhancement of their own prestige.

On Friday, August 26th, the day of Summit II, significant breakfast meetings were being held. Daley huddled at City Hall with his advisors, Raymond Simon, Ralph Metcalfe and Thomas Keane. "Everyday I get up I'm optimistic," he told reporters. "We'll do the best we can."

Fifteen leaders of the Conference on Religion and Race ate breakfast in the Palmer House. There "fifteen different opinions" were voiced concerning what should be the Church's position when certain questions were asked: i.e. the cessation of the Cicero march and the Mayor's injunction. "We knew that the Mayor, if he got mad, would walk out," explained Gene Callahan several months later, "and we knew that the question about his injunction might do it. So we arranged for Dr. Zimmerman to respond to it when it came up."

Meanwhile, members of the Chicago Freedom Movement met at the headquarters of the American Friends Service Committee in the loop. When presented with the final Ayers Subcommittee report, many were dissatisfied and proposed that an entirely new draft, newly written, be submitted for the Movement. As in the earlier Summit session, King and Raby were the spokesmen for the Movement and any permission to speak had to be approved by them.

The Summit Conference was now moved to the third floor of the Palmer House Hotel. Television cameras were set up immediately outside and hotel security guards were posted. The second session began at ten o'clock.

Thomas Ayers read his subcommittee report. Interest was focused more on the issues of the injunction and the Cicero march. Earlier that day, Charles Swibel had approached the Movement leaders with a new deal: Mayor Daley would give up his injunction if the Movement would call off the Cicero march and give public credit to Mayor Daley for calling the Conference and delivering adequate concessions. King, on the other hand, made it clear that morning, that he was willing to call off the Cicero march as a sign of the Movement's "good faith."

As expected, the Movement was asked if they were prepared to call off the Cicero march. The Movement countered by demanding the withdrawal of the injunction. At this point, by prearrangement, Dr. Donald Zimmerman, president of the Presbyterians of Chicago, arose and urged that the Mayor's injunction ought to stand and that the Movement could challenge its legality in the courts as the final test. Dr. King argued that such a course would cost "hundreds of thousands" of dollars and would require several years. Daley made a short speech in which he defended the use of the injunction to "protect all the people of the city" and alluded to Police Superintendent Wilson's position that marches made normal crime-fighting activities difficult for his men. "Furthermore," Daley concluded, "if you don't demonstrate there won't be anything in the injunction to bother you."

"Then followed a long pause of maybe a minute or two," said one civil rights source. "Nobody came to our side from either the business or church community. For a moment, I think MLK (Dr. King) was ready to walk out," he said.

"We kept sending up notes to King to caucus, but he disregarded them for a long time," recalled one leader. Finally the Movement caucused on the fifteenth floor of the Palmer House, for twenty-five minutes. "It was a stormy session . . . everyone was losing their heads," recalls another leader. By that time, the Swibel deal was off—Daley indeed did not have to relinquish his injunction nor would the Movement make that issue the basis of a walk-out. During the caucus, Swibel turned to the Mayor and asked: "Who's going to get the credit then?" The Mayor responded: "The hell with the credit!"

The Movement reconvened and heard the end of the Ayers report. King had prevailed. The "pact" that had been reached appeared for the present—assuming it would be acted upon—too important a gain to throw away. Heineman warned the business-political community that promises to the Negroes indeed had been broken over the years. If they were broken again, "results which will be very hard to predict are bound to follow," he warned. The Mayor made a short speech pledging the "good faith" of the city in carrying out the proposals. Beatty reiterated: "Ninety per cent of the negotiations for sale and rental of homes go through real estate agents and they're in the middle . . . they get it from both sides." Next, the religious leaders were asked to respond. Bishop Montgomery stated: "The religious leaders haven't done their job and ought to do more." Archbishop Cody, who had remained silent throughout the entire conference, was asked to comment. He pulled himself up and surveyed the group: "This looks like the League of Nations," he remarked. Many in the assembly remembered what happened to the League of Nations.

When asked if there were any "nay" votes to the subcommittee report as submitted, there was silence. Officially, Heineman announced, the "pact" was unanimously adopted. "Can we expect one per cent integration by 1967?" asked Al Raby. Again there was silence. In order to insure the effective implementation of the agreement, timetables would only confuse the process, some argued.

The subcommittee had completed its work and the meeting was adjourned.

The press, radio and television recorded the sentiments. "This is a great historical day in the City of Chicago—Chicago as usual is leading the way for all other cities. I am satisfied that the people of Chicago and the suburbs and the whole metropolitan area will accept the program in the light of the people who endorsed it." (To Ben Heineman) "Ben you did a wonderful job and now we can get on to the problems of poverty and making the city a better place to live."

Heineman responded: "The City of Chicago through all the elements of society represented here have made a giant step forward through the democratic process of discussion."

King had produced his first victory after nearly a year in Chicago and this reassured him of his place and that of the nonviolent movement at the head of Civil Rights Movement in the United States. "Never before have such far-reaching commitments been made and programs adopted and pledged to achieve open housing in a community. The Chicago Freedom Movement takes great pride in providing the non-violent vehicle through which the total eradication of segregated housing can be made possible . . . the program is one of the most significant ever conceived to make open housing a reality . . . we take pride in beginning Chicago's role as a harmonious city and in healing the deep cleft of emotional and physical strife . . . this is the first step on a 1,000 mile journey but an important step."

IV. *Summary and Conclusion*

In attempting to analyze those events which unfolded in Chicago during the past year, one is struck that they represent a clash of unique forces, nearly a time of ultimate racial crisis. They are ambiguous and contradictory. When a city's sins, its fears, hatreds and tensions had reached a vivid violent peak, a victory is suddenly announced—for the people of Chicago, for the nonviolent movement, for justice. An agreement was entered into and hailed by the same persons who knew that that same agreement alone could not effect the racial composition of a city block. Two sides emerge from a conference room, both claiming victory, only to find that their problems had curiously intermingled.

In Chicago, the problems of every big city are intensified and magnified. If Chicago has laid claim to significant advances, it is likely to be true, due to the unspectacular performance of other cities. In a city one-third Negro, race is still the hidden agenda of every major decision made in Chicago. Its Mayor, like other mayors, finds himself governing two cities in one—divided sharply along racial, economic and cultural lines. And it is the coalition of these two cities that places and keeps him in power. This power is consolidated through compacts with business, industry, labor, religious and voluntary groups. It is threatened by the real or imagined loss of votes. Power is recognized and exchanged over the conference table and through the deal. Negotiation will expose that artist who as dealer knows how to assess the limits of the other's bargaining power, times his moves, and can secure agreement to his terms.

Faced with obvious bureaucratic stalling and the undramatic follow-up to the Summit Conference in Chicago, many asked, what was accomplished? Others replied that the question is rather, how much time have we left? Optimists could still answer the first question thus: for the first time in any major Northern city, all of the leadership groups publicly committed themselves to the policy of open housing and to specific actions to make it real. Others less hopeful were never under any illusion. For them, it was simply a question of power and one's ability to compel a power structure to produce on its promises.

The man of power, especially if he is the most powerful Mayor in the nation, only understands power. And it is in his shadow that other powerful men stand. Mayor Daley could see the city he built about to be destroyed. Clearly, his two cities were being further polarized because now "issue politics" had taken the place of the politics of the material reward. Yet it was not in the mind of Dr. King to destroy the boss of Chicago since such a boss was needed to grant concessions and bend. King had not succeeded in channeling the indignation of poor Negroes into a political organization. In fact, the inroads of his organization into the black ghetto were embarrassingly unsuccessful, especially because this fact was known to City Hall. The Open Housing marches were the latest in a series of tactics to test responses while providing an outlet for the slim number of middle class recruits to the Movement. The unanticipated violent response to the marches took both King and Daley by surprise. In the days that followed, there was no time for adequate reflection on the true significance, politically and socially, of the extent of the backlash. One thing was certain: it served the best interests of both groups to end the marches quickly.

To the bargaining table, then, came not strong men but frightened and uncertain men. For Daley who would face reelection within a year, the political horizon was overcast and grey. For King, his philosophy of nonviolence was under attack as was his national leadership of the civil rights movement. Both Church and labor leaders could see the division in their houses. In the leadership vacuum that developed, men from business and industry took an uncertain step and asked what its role might be. Curiously, there was now a pressure from behind. Had indeed a "coalition conscience" been formed and what was its strength? "My own view," observed Ben Heineman, "is that we have been too far committed by leadership of the entire community not to have moved."

How will this "leadership" phrase its question? How much time do we have left? Or, will we have the same time to solve our problems as it takes for us to discover them? Or, how long is a 1,000 mile journey?

APPENDIX

ARTICLES AND PERIODICALS

Sun-Times, August, 1966.

Chicago Daily News, August, 1966.

Good, Paul, "Chicago Summer—Bossism, Racism and Dr. King," *The Nation*, September 19, 1966

King, Martin Luther, "Freedom's Crisis," *Nation*, March 14, 1966.

Koko, Karen, "Chicago's Race March—A Walk on the Wild Side," *National Catholic Reporter*, August 10, 1966.

Kupfer, Marvin, "On Fighting City Hall—The King-Daley Struggle in Perspective," *Renewal*, September, 1966.

McDermott, John A. "A Chicago Catholic Asks: Where Does My Church Stand on Racial Justice?" *Look*, November 1, 1966.

Satter, David A., "West Side Story: Home is Where the Welfare Check Comes," *The New Republic*, July 2, 1966.

Schlitz, Michael E., "Catholics and the Chicago Riots," *Commonweal*, November 11, 1966.

"The Battle of Roosevelt Road," *Time*, July 22, 1966.

"The Chicago Triple," *Time*, July 24, 1966.

"Riot in Chicago," *America*, July 30, 1966.

"Open City," *The New Republic*, September 17, 1965.

"Dr. King Carries His Fight to the Ghetto," *Ebony*, April, 1966.

"Gamble in the Ghetto," *Newsweek*, January 31, 1966.

"Render Unto King," *Time*, March 25, 1966.

"Chicago—Big City Meets Its Problems," *U.S. News*, March 28, 1966.

"Dilemma for Dr. King," *Christian Century*, March 16, 1966.

"Still King," *Christian Century*, September 7, 1966.

"Chicago-King-Daley-Cody, Strong Men in Conflict," *National Catholic Reporter*, August 31, 1966.

UNPUBLISHED MATERIAL

American Friends Service Committee, Chicago Regional Office, "The Open Housing Campaign—Chicago 1966 ("A report presented to the Annual Meetings of AFSC, November 6, 1966, by Kale Williams, Executive Secretary, Chicago Regional Office)—mimeographed.

Chicago Freedom Movement—"Open City—Background Memo and Action Report,"—Monday, July 25, 1966.

Chicago Freedom Movement—"Program for the Chicago Freedom Movement," Chicago, July, 1966.

Chicago Urban League, "Commentary on Areas of Negro Residence Map: 1950-60, 64," Research Report, May 1965.

Commission on Human Relations—"A Report on the Chicago Fair Housing Ordinance," August 5, 1966.

Commission on Human Relations—Minutes of the Special Commission Meeting held on Thursday, October 13, 1966.

Riddick, Edward, "An Observation of Gage Park," and "Some Notes on Race and the Protestant Churches," (mimeographed).

PARTICIPANTS IN THE CONFERENCE ON OPEN HOUSING

Thomas G. Ayers, President, Commonwealth Edison Company, Assn. of Commerce & Industry
Warren Purcell, Cook County Council of Insured Savings Associations
Sam Dennis, Community Relations Service, Justice Department
Sydney Finley, NAACP National Office Field Director
Kale Williams, American Friends Service Committee
Rev. Arthur Brazier, President, The Woodlawn Organization
Edwin C. Berry, Director, The Urban League
Rev. Edward Egan, Archdiocesan Commission on Human Relations
Rev. Robert Spike, Professor of Christian Ministry, University of Chicago
Rev. Arthur Griffin, President, The Westside Federation
Albert Ransom, American Friends Service Committee
Dr. Martin Luther King, Jr., Southern Christian Leadership Conference
Eugene J. Callahan, Chicago Conference on Religion and Race
Albert Raby, Convener, Coordinating Council of Community Organizations
Rabbi Mordicai Simon, Chicago Conference on Religion and Race
Archbishop John Patrick Cody, Archbishop of Chicago
Ben W. Heineman, Chairman, Chicago and Northwestern Railway
Rabbi Robert Marx, Union of American Hebrew Congregations
Ely M. Aaron, Chairman, Chicago Commission on Human Relations
Mayor Richard J. Daley, Mayor of Chicago
Dr. John Gardiner, Church Federation of Greater Chicago
William G. Caples, Vice-President, Inland Steel Company
William R. Ming, Jr., Attorney, Chicago Commission on Human Relations
Roger Nathan, Illinois Commission on Human Relations
Ross Beatty, Chairman, Chicago Real Estate Board
Jack Kleeman, Chicago Real Estate Board
John Stamos, Chicago Mortgage Bankers Association
David M. Kennedy, President, Continental Illinois National Bank
A. L. Foster, Cosmopolitan Chamber of Commerce
Leonard Foster, Garfield Park Chamber of Commerce
Gordon Groepe, Real Estate Board
Arthur F. Mohl, Chicago Real Estate Board
Sgt. Samuel Nolan, Chicago Police Department, Human Relations Division
John Womer, Metropolitan Housing and Planning Council
John Baird, Baird and Warner Real Estate Company
Edward Marciniak, Director, Chicago Commission on Human Relations
Charles R. Swibel, Chairman, Chicago Housing Authority
David Schucker, Illinois Commission on Human Relations
Robert Johnson, United Auto Workers
Thomas Paul, Chicago Federation of Labor and Industrial Union Council
John Gray, Chicago Association of Commerce and Industry
William Robinson, Republican Ward Committeeman
Rev. Andrew Young, Southern Christian Leadership Conference

George Jones, President, Joe Louis Milk Company, Conference on Religion and Race
Rev. James Bevel, Southern Christian Leadership Conference
John McDermott, Director, Catholic Interracial Council
James Wright, United Auto Workers
Rev. Jesse Jackson, Southern Christian Leadership Conference
Charles Hayes, United Packinghouse Workers
Bishop James Montgomery, Co-Adjutor Bishop, Episcopal Diocese
Clark Stayman, Chicago Mortgage Bankers Association
Lewis Hill, Director, Department of Urban Renewal
John Ballew, Acting Director, Cook County Department of Public Aid
Leonard P. Spacek, The Commercial Club; Chairman, Arthur Anderson Associates
Paul Lund, Assistant to President, Illinois Bell Telephone Company
William A. Lee, Chicago Federation of Labor

NOTES

1. King, Martin Luther, "Freedom's Crisis," *Nation*, March 14, 1966, 202:288-92.
2. Chicago Urban League, "Commentary on Areas of Negro Residence Map,", May, 1965—published research paper.
3. *Ibid.*
4. *Ibid.*
5. "Dr. King Carries His Fight to the Ghetto," *Ebony*, April, 1966, p. 94-96.
6. *Ibid.*, p. 94.
7. "Riot in Chicago," *America*, July 30, 1966, p. 117.
8. *Ebony*, p. 95.
9. Good, Paul, "Chicago Summer: Bossism, Racism and Dr. King," *The Nation*, March 14, 1966, p. 240.
10. *Ibid.*, p. 240.
11. Chicago Freedom Movement, "Program for the Chicago Freedom Movement," July, 1966.
12. *America*, p. 117.
13. Koko, Karen, "Chicago's Race March—A Walk on the Wild Side," *National Catholic Reporter*, August 10, 1966, p. 1.
14. Riddick, Edward, "An Observation of Gage Park," September, 1966. Mimeographed.
15. Commission on Human Relations, *Minutes*, August 9th meeting.
16. *Ibid.*
17. *Ibid.*

Program
of the
Chicago
Freedom Movement

JULY, 1966

INTRODUCTION: THE PROBLEMS OF RACISM, GHETTOES, AND SLUMS

Racism, slums and ghettoes have been the essentials of Negro existence in Chicago. While the city permitted its earlier ethnic groups to enter the mainstream of American life, it has locked the Negro into the lower rungs of the social and economic ladder. The Negro in Chicago has been systematically excluded from the major rewards of American life; he is restricted in the jobs he may hold, the schools he may attend, and the places where he may live. In the year 1966 the Negro is as far behind the white as he was in the year 1940.

Chicago today is a divided city—segregated in all areas of social and economic activity, in employment, in education, in housing and in community organization. The Negro community is sectioned off from the larger metropolis into areas of the city that have been set aside for black ghettoes. Within these confines the Negro community is regulated from the outside like a colony—its potential economic resources underdeveloped, its more than one million inhabitants, the daily victims of personal rebuffs, insults and acts of prejudice, and its poorer citizens at the mercy of police, welfare workers, and minor government officials.

Racism in the large Northern cities has not featured lynchings, denial of the vote, or other clear injustices that could easily be removed as is the case in the South. Yet, racism in Chicago has been a stark reality, visible in many dimensions. It is reflected in the existence of the massive overcrowded ghetto that grows each year. It is reflected in the crime-infested slums where the living standards of the Negro poor often do not cover the bare necessities of urban living. It is reflected in the exploitation of Negroes by the dominant white society in higher rents and prices, lower wages and poorer schools.

Under the system of northern racism the Negro receives inferior and second-class status in every area of urban living. The Negro is concentrated in the low-paying and second-rate jobs. In housing, proportionately more Negroes live in substandard or deteriorating dwellings. In education, Negro schools have more inexperienced teachers, fewer classrooms, and less expenditures per pupil. In the maintenance of law and order Negroes are frequently the victims of police brutality and of stop and search methods of crime detection.

All Negroes in Chicago are confined to the ghetto and suffer second class treatment regardless of their social or economic status. But the worst off are the Negro poor, locked into the slum which is the most deprived part of the ghetto. The forty (40) per cent of the Negro population who make up a black urban peasantry in the slums are the hardest hit victims of discrimination and segregation. Their incomes often have to be supplemented by welfare payments dispensed under procedures that are ugly and paternalistic. They are frequently unemployed. They are forced to live in rat infested buildings or in the Chicago Housing Authority's cement reservations. Their children are all but ignored by the school system. In short they have been frozen out of American society by both race and poverty.

The subjugation of Negroes in Chicago has not been the result of long-established legal codes or customs, like those that existed in the South. Although Chicago has not for a century had any segregation laws or discrimination ordinances, the subordination of Negroes in the North has been almost as effective as if there had been such laws. Northern segregation resulted from policies, in particular the decision-making procedures, of the major economic and social institutions. The employment policies of business firms and government, and practices of realtors, and the operation of the Chicago School System have all reinforced one another to keep the Negroes separate and unequal. The system of racial separation resulting from their interaction has become so strongly imbedded in the city's life that present racial patterns are passed on from generation to generation.

In many instances, although these restrictive policies have now been formally abolished or concealed, the effects of their operations over several decades remains. Very often, Negroes are no longer excluded consciously and deliberately. In employment, personnel men need not discriminate so long as Chicago's inferior schools send their pupils into the labor market less prepared than white graduates. Realtors can justify their discrimination when white parents rightfully fear that integrated schools eventually deteriorate because the school system considers them less important than white schools. School administrators can efficiently segregate by following neighborhood school policies in allocating school facilities.

In the past, the Negro's efforts to improve his living conditions have concentrated on going through the well-defined channels of white authority. Negroes for years have been asking, begging, and pleading that white employers, board presidents, bankers, realtors, politicians, and government officials correct racial patterns and inequities. The major lesson that the Negro community has learned is that racial change through this process comes only gradually, usually too late, and only in small measures.

In this rapidly changing world where technological changes may displace the unskilled workers, where affluence makes it possible to spend millions in waging wars in far away places like Vietnam, and where the elimination of poverty and racism have become national goals, Negroes no longer have the patience to abide by the old, unsuccessful gradualism of the respectable defenders of the status quo.

The present powerlessness of Negroes hinders them from changing conditions themselves or even in developing effective coalitions with others, but the time has now come for Negroes to set up their own instruments that will direct pressure at the institutions that still adhere to racism policies. Negroes must form their own power base from which Negro aspirations and goals can be demanded, a base from which they can make a strong common fight with others that share their problems or their aspirations. Chicago will become an open city only when Negroes develop power in proportion to their numbers.

THE CHICAGO FREEDOM MOVEMENT

The Chicago Freedom Movement is a coalition of forces for the purpose of wiping out slums, ghettoes and racism. Its core is formed by the unity of the Southern Christian Leadership Conference (SCLC) and the Coordinating Council of Community Organizations (CCCO). SCLC, operating under the leadership of Dr. Martin Luther King, Jr., was invited to Chicago by CCCO because of its dynamic work in the South. CCCO is a coalition of thirty-six (36) Chicago civil-rights and Negro community organizations. Cooperating with the Chicago Freedom Movement are a number of religious organizations, social agencies, neighborhood groups and individuals of good will.

Many groups in the Chicago region share with Negroes common problems of slum housing, welfare dependency, inferior education, police brutality, and color discrimination. Puerto Rican and Mexican Chicagoans are becoming increasingly vocal about these problems, and the Freedom Movement is seeking ways to join in a united effort with its Latin American brothers. Therefore, the Freedom Movement is making many proposals that provide for the improvement and upgrading of conditions of Latin Americans, other non-whites and some white minorities.

The Freedom Movement proposals and demands are designed to set the broad guidelines for a just and open city in which all men can live with dignity. Three interrelated goals set forth the direction to such a society:

1. To bring about equality of opportunity and of results.
2. To open up the major areas of metropolitan life of housing, employment, and education.
3. To provide power for the powerless.

Many will affirm these goals and wish that they could be achieved. But very little will happen unless Negroes, Latin Americans, other oppressed minorities and their white friends join hands and organize to bring about change—for power does not yield to pleading.

The Freedom Movement will achieve its goals through the organization of a non-violent movement which provides the power to participate in the decisions which now subjugate rather than elevate, which suppress man's humanity rather than express it.

In order to generate the necessary power the movement will:

1. Organize a series of direct actions which will make the injustices so clear that the whole community will respond to the need to change.
2. Organize people in every sector of the ghettoes—in neighborhoods, in schools, in welfare unions, in public housing, in hospitals, to give the strength of numbers to the demands for change.
3. Strengthen the institutions which contribute to the goals of a just and open society and withdraw support from those institutions—banks, businesses, newspapers and professions—which drain the resources of the ghetto communities without contributing in return.
4. Demand representation of the organizations of the ghetto community (Chicago Freedom Movement) on decision-making bodies at every level of government, industry, labor, and church, affecting the lives of people in the ghetto.
5. Promote political education and participation so that the needs and aspirations of Negroes and other oppressed minorities are fully represented.

The Chicago Freedom Movement and its constituent organizations use many means to bring about change. Community organization, education, research, job development, legal redress and political education are all weapons in the arsenal of the Movement. But, its most distinctive and creative tool is that of non-violent direct action.

Non-violence is based on the truth that each human being has infinite dignity and worth. This truth, which is at the heart of our religious and democratic heritage, is denied by systems of discrimination and exploitation. The beginning of change in such systems of discrimination is for men to assert with simple dignity and humanity that they are men and human and that they will no longer be oppressed or oppressors. A just society is born when men cease to be accomplices in a system of degradation.

Then specific injustices and discriminations must be exposed by direct actions which reveal, without excuse or rationalization, the extent and nature of the problem. They bring into the open, as conflicts, social antagonisms that in the past had been hidden as subjugation or exploitation. The methodology of non-violence keeps attention focused on the real issues of injustice and discrimination rather than on false issues which arise when conflict becomes violent.

The non-violent movement seeks to create a community in which justice and equality provide the framework for all human relationships and are embodied in its institutions. The practice of justice is the evidence of a community based on respect for every person and of a society in which human values prevail over cash values. A genuine human community does not exist until all citizens are given an opportunity to participate to the fullest limits of their capacity. In this way each person contributes to the community's solution to its problems and fulfills himself as a member of the community.

The Chicago Freedom Movement commits itself to the struggle for freedom and justice in this metropolis and pledges our non-violent movement to the building of the beloved community where men will live as brothers and no group or class or nation will raise its hand against brother.

AN OPEN AND JUST CITY

To wipe out slums, ghettoes, and racism we must create an *open* city with equal opportunities and equal results. To this end we have drawn up program proposals for employment and income, housing and metropolitan planning, education, financial services, police and legal protection. We only sketch the major ideas of the full program here as that document shall be released shortly.

Two different approaches are necessary to do the job. The first approach involves gigantic development programs for the slum ghettoes similar to those for underdeveloped nations. The second involves proposals for the various institutions of the whole metropolitan area.

We propose three major redevelopment program areas for three slum areas. The redevelopment projects will constitute a concrete application of the domestic Marshall Plan idea. A redevelopment authority, with majority control by persons and institutions in the area, will shape a unified plan for housing, employment, educational, social, and cultural development. Massive expenditures would create a climate for further public and private spending. The objective would be to make what are now the slum ghettoes as good places to live as any in Chicago.

In education our program is based on proposals that all schools should have at least the same expenditures as the best suburban public schools. Racial separation should be broken down by such new ideas as educational parks and city-suburban educational cooperation.

In employment our program proposals call for fair employment by the elimination of all forms of job bias and of all measures which screen out minority groups. The proposals call for full employment at decent wages by the creation of tens of thousands of new jobs in rebuilding our city and in new sub-professional positions in health, education, and welfare. We call for effective job training and retraining with the provision of a job at the successful completion of the program.

In housing our program calls for an open city in which no man is discriminated against. We call for adequate financing and programs for the redevelopment of slum and deteriorating housing and for the elimination of exploitation by slum lords. We call for humanization of the present public housing projects. We propose the development of a vastly increased supply of decent low and middle cost housing throughout the Chicago area.

In planning we call for the development of a metropolitan-wide land and transportation plan, including the city of Chicago, that will promote and facilitate access to jobs and housing for all men throughout the entire region; the plan would include the development of new areas, the eradication of slums and the redevelopment of these blighted areas both in Chicago and the older suburbs.

In welfare we call for the elimination of welfare dependency by a guaranteed adequate annual income as a matter of right with provision for payment in the most dignified manner possible. In the immediate future, pending the change in the manner of income distribution, we propose measures to humanize the welfare system and to strengthen the autonomy and rights of recipients.

In politics and government we call for increased representation of Negroes, Latin Americans, and other exploited minorities.

We call for measures to equalize protection from police and the courts, including a citizen review board to monitor complaints of police brutality and arbitrary arrest.

The task of wiping out racism, slums, and ghettoes in order to make Chicago an "open city" is large, but necessary. We recognize that many of the proposals in our full program are long-range ones—and Chicago is receiving its total benefits. However, a good number of our proposals can be implemented this summer by the action of government and private executives; therefore, it is these proposals that constitute the demands for the summer campaign of the Chicago Freedom Movement.

Since people and organizations resist change, the Freedom Movement shall have to demonstrate by the tools of non-violent direct action that our summer demands can be implemented. We shall prove that the Chicago metropolitan area can be an open city. For this purpose we have chosen a small number of specific target demands, around which we shall organize non-violent direct action campaigns. With the creative help and pressure of the Freedom Movement, government and private organizations will find that the target demands can be met. Then they will be able to meet the other immediate summer demands.

SELECTED IMMEDIATE ACTION DEMANDS—SUMMER 1966

For our primary target we have chosen housing. As of July 10 we shall cease to be accomplices to a housing system of discrimination, segregation, and degradation. We shall begin to act as if Chicago were an open city. We shall act on the basis that every man is entitled to full access to buying or renting housing that is sound, attractive, and reasonably priced.

DEMANDS FOR OPEN HOUSING

From the Real Estate Boards and Brokers:

1. All listings immediately available on a non-discriminatory basis. This means that no realtor or real estate broker will handle a property that is not available to anyone, without regard to race, color, creed, or national origin.
2. Endorsement of, and support for, open occupancy.

From the Banks and Savings Institutions:

1. Public statements of a non-discriminatory mortgage policy so that loans will be available to any qualified borrower without regard to the racial composition of the area, or the age of the area, a policy

that takes into account years of discrimination against Negro borrowers.

2. Creation of special loan funds for the conversion of contract housing purchases to standard mortgages.

From the Chicago Housing Authority:

1. Program to rehabilitate present public housing, including such items as locked lobbies, restrooms in recreation areas, increased police protection and child care centers on every third floor.

2. No more public housing construction in the ghetto until a substantial number of units are started outside the ghetto.

From the Chicago Housing Authority and the Chicago Dwelling Association:

A program to increase vastly the supply of low-cost housing on a scattered basis. The program should provide for both low and middle income families.

From the Governor of Illinois:

Enforcement of his Fair Practices Code, especially by revoking the licenses of real estate brokers who discriminate.

From the Illinois Public Aid Department and the Cook County Department of Public Aid:

Direct the housing placement of welfare recipients so as to use the entire housing market.

From the Federal Government:

1. An executive order for Federal supervision of the non-discriminatory granting of loans by banks and saving institutions that are members of the Federal Deposit Insurance Corporation or by the Federal Savings and Loan Association.

2. Passage of the 1966 Civil Rights Act with a provision to make it illegal to discriminate in the sale or renting of property on the basis of race, color, creed, or national origin.

From the Mayor and City Council:

1. Ordinance giving ready access to the names of owners and investors for all slum properties.
2. A saturation program of increased garbage collection, street cleaning and building inspection services in the slum areas.

From Advertising Media:

No advertising media will list either housing or jobs not available for every man.

DEMANDS FOR OPEN EMPLOYMENT

From the Mayor and City Council:

1. Publication of headcounts of whites, Negroes, and Latin Americans for all city departments and for all firms from which city purchases are made.
2. A compliance program that checks on all contractors on a routine basis.
3. Revocation of contracts with firms that do not have a full-scale fair employment practice.

From Business:

1. Racial headcounts, including white, Negro, and Latin American, by job classification and income level, made public.
2. Radical steps to upgrade and to integrate all departments, at all levels of employment.

From Unions:

1. Headcounts in unions for apprentices, journeymen and union staff and officials by job classification.
2. A crash program to remedy any inequities discovered by the headcount.
3. Support for the organization of the unorganized minority workers since Negro and other minority workers are concentrated in the low paying, unorganized industries.
4. Indenture of at least 400 Negro and Latin American apprentices in the craft unions.

From the Governor of Illinois:

1. Prepare legislative proposals for a $2.00 State minimum wage law and for credit reform, including the abolition of garnishment and wage assignment.
2. Publication of headcounts of whites, Negroes, and Latin Americans for all State departments and for all firms from which state purchases are made.

WELFARE DEMANDS

From the Illinois Public Aid Department and the Cook County Department of Public Aid:

1. Recognition of welfare unions and community organizations as bargaining agents for welfare recipients.
2. Regular meetings between representatives of the recipients and top department administrators.
3. Institution of a declaration of income system to replace the degrading investigation and means test for welfare eligibility.
4. Change in the rules and procedures to speed up the issuance of emergency checks and to eliminate withholding of checks pending investigation.

EDUCATION DEMANDS

From the Chicago Board of Education:

1. Announce plan for desegregation of teachers in Chicago schools during the 1966-67 school year.
2. Immediate publication of the achievement scores of all schools by grades.

From the Federal Government:

Executive enforcement of Title VI of the 1964 Civil Rights Act regarding the complaint against the Chicago Board of Education.

OTHER DEMANDS

From the Mayor and City Council:

Creation of a citizens review board for grievances against police brutality and false arrests or stops and seizure.

From the Political Parties:

The replacement of absentee precinct captains, with the requirement that precinct captains be residents of their precincts.

From the Federal Government:

Direct funding of Chicago community organizations by the Office of Economic Opportunity.

DEMANDS OF OURSELVES

From the People:

1. Financial support of the Freedom Movement.
2. Selective buying from firms that do not practice racial discrimination in hiring and upgrading of employees.

3. Deposit money in banks and savings institutions with clean records on hiring and lending policies.
4. Selective buying campaigns against businesses that boycott the products of Negro-owned companies.
5. Participation in the Freedom Movement target campaigns for this summer, including volunteer services and membership in one of the Freedom Movement organizations.

The Summit Negotiations: Chicago, August 17, 1966– August 26, 1966

JOHN McKNIGHT

This is a report of the meeting in Chicago on Wednesday, August 17, 1966, between the power people of the city of Chicago and the Chicago Freedom Movement. [Editor's Note: See pages 93-94 for a complete listing of the individuals attending, along with their affiliations.] The meeting was called by the Chicago Conference on Religion and Race. Chairman of that Conference is the Suffragan Bishop of the city of Chicago, Bishop James Montgomery. The meeting was chaired by Ben Heineman, Chairman of the Board of the Northwestern Railroad. Also in attendance were myself and

John McKnight was invited to attend these negotiations by the Chicago Freedom Movement in his capacity as Midwest Director of the United States Commission on Civil Rights. He took careful notes of what was said in the meetings and then dictated them into a tape recorder immediately after each session. This document is a transcription of his dictation. While quotation marks have been used to indicate that a particular person is speaking, the words within the marks are the essence of their point rather than the precise spoken words.

Sam Dennis, a representative of the Community Relations Service of the Justice Department.

The press was not permitted in the meeting. The meeting was held in a large meeting room in the parish house, the Cathedral House of the Episcopal Diocese. It was held there because the group calling the meeting, the Conference on Religion and Race, is chaired by the Episcopal Bishop who provided the space for the meeting. It is perhaps of some significance to note who was not in attendance. Particularly notable as non-attendants were the Chicago Negro Aldermen and Congressman William Dawson. Here at a moment of great meaning for the Negro community, their elected political representatives were not even present, and they were not present because they are irrelevant: the Mayor could make any decisions that were necessary without them.

The immediate cause of the meeting was the demonstrations of the Chicago Freedom Movement in all-white neighborhoods. The political machine was being challenged. The political machine had always straddled the ghetto and had lived in and outside the ghetto and now this situation challenged the machine. The basic fact revealed by the meeting was that the marches had been so damaging politically to the machine that Mayor Daley was ready to overcome all of his pride and engage in some significant negotiations.

The meeting had been announced as a two hour meeting beginning at 10:00 a.m. to be over at 12:00. It turned out to be a meeting that lasted much longer. That was the result of the Mayor's determination that everything possible should be done on this day to end the marches.

With that background I will report what was said at the meeting. And in most cases rather than to say that person said it I will say who said it and say it in the first person. I will try to say from my notes what he said the way he said it to the degree that is possible.

The meeting was opened by Bishop Montgomery, Suffragan Bishop of the Episcopal Diocese. He was chairing a meeting where people were sitting around three large long tables laid out in "U" fashion. At the base of the "U" was seated Ben Heineman and the religious leaders of Chicago. The left hand column of the "U" held Mayor Daley and the political and economic leaders of Chicago. On the right hand arm of the "U" were seated the Freedom Movement. In the middle of the "U" were seated some trade union representatives, at a little table that was positioned there.

Bishop Montgomery opened the meeting by explaining that the church needed to be relevant to the concerns of our time and his group felt that the church should provide the meeting ground for all the people to be present and to begin to discuss this great issue of an open city. Then he introduced Ben Heineman whom he said would be chairman, and he said that Ben Heineman, who was not a member of the Conference on Religion and Race, which had called the meeting, was to be the chairman because the conference members wanted to be free to speak. They did not feel that they were neutral; they agreed with the demands of the Chicago Freedom Movement.

Then Ben Heineman, after making brief remarks, asked the Mayor to speak. Now this was in violation of the agreements that had been made with the Freedom Movement the night before, when it was agreed that Dr King would speak first, then Daley would speak, and then King would present the demands. The meeting actually developed so that Daley spoke first, then King, and Daley's people, the Commission on Human Relations, placed their proposals, and the Movement's proposals were placed last. The meeting could have foundered on that point if it had not been for the fact that the Mayor seemed willing to negotiate. Heineman turned to the Mayor and asked him if he would like to say something and he said (and incidentally, everything that I am reporting as being said, was said, but I only noted the most important and significant things that were said), "proceed to restore peace and tranquility. I want to congratulate all of you for your participation. We have to do something to resolve the problems of the past few weeks." He was noncommittal about anything else.

Heineman then turned to Dr. King. Dr. King stood up and said, "I want to thank the Conference on Religion and Race. This is the kind of constructive dialogue that is necessary." Then he went on to describe the ghetto in terms of dualism, and I think that's very significant. "We have a dual school system, a dual economy, a dual housing market, and we seek to transform this duality into a oneness. We can not solve this alone: we need the help of the people with the real power. I have recently been in Jamaica where I was very impressed with the motto of that country which should enlighten us today, 'Out of many people, one people'."

Then Al Raby, the Co-chairman of the Chicago Freedom Movement, spoke, and he said, "I am very pessimistic about the negotiations today because my experience with negotiating has indicated that our success has always been very limited. We need everybody here, including myself, to know that we have just not done the job that is needed. Fifteen years ago in Cicero a Negro family moved in and there was a riot and they burned their house down. Fifteen years later when Negroes again say they may go into Cicero everyone is agreed that it will take the National Guard to protect any Negroes who go in that city. So there has not been any significant change through the natural process. The Movement has exposed by its marches how we all have failed. We must admit that this dialogue that's beginning today would not have occurred without the marches. But there will be no resolution of this situation until we have a factual change in the circumstances of Negroes. We will not end our marches with a verbal commitment."

At that point Al Raby ended his presentation and Heinemen turned to Ely Aaron of the Commission on Human Relations who had a series of proposals to present. As mentioned earlier it was at this point that it had been agreed the Chicago Freedom Movement was to present its proposals.

After Aaron read the proposals of the Commission, A. L. Foster, the Negro executive of the Cosmopolitan Chamber of Commerce, stood up and said that one of the Commission's proposals—that the Chicago Real Estate Board support open occupancy—was key. He said, "Since the Chicago Real Estate Board was the agency that designed the nationwide system of exclusion that was developed through the restrictive covenants, it is particularly appropriate that they now be asked to take the leadership to revise the situation. You may not remember" said Foster, who was an older man, "that the Chicago Real Estate Board brought its proposals for establishing a network of restrictive covenants to the National Real Estate Board in Atlantic City and sold restrictive covenants, a device for racial exclusion, to the nation. So it is particularly appropriate that we demand of them that they now completely change their position and sell the national real estate industry on the proposition that it has got to support open housing rather than closed housing." Then the president of the Chicago Real Estate Board was asked if he had any comments and he stood up (and before saying what he said it should be noted that he said nothing that indicated any change from positions that the Chicago Real Estate Board has taken for the last ten years including their presentations before the United States Commission on Civil Rights in 1960. It is as though they did not realize that times had changed.) The president, Ross Beatty said, "This meeting is a good thing and the most important thing for us to understand is what the situation really is as it exists; not what we would like it to be or want it to be but what it really is. Also we must approach things on the basis that the past is past. My associates are decent honest gentlemen. They are leaders in their community. And now I want to tell you how they feel. This is our statement. We are not here to negotiate because the problem can't be solved between us and the civil rights people. We have Negro members and we are proud of our record. Not all brokers, you must remember, are realtors and therefore we can't speak for the real estate industry totally. Many apartments are operated by businessmen, not by realtors. You must understand that realtors accept property as an agent. The realtor doesn't own or control the property. And it is this agency relationship—we are the agent that binds the realtor under the laws to the person for whom he is an agent. Now we have concluded after considerable experience that we cannot persuade property owners to change their attitudes about whom they want to sell their property to. And therefore we will reflect their attitudes. Now we know that there are problems and we are the ones that are easy to blame since someone is needed to blame. But the problem is not ours. The realtor is an agent; we must represent our clients. And therefore, because our clients are opposed to the open occupancy law, we must oppose the law if we are to honestly represent our clients. We would propose that a market research corporation be hired to assess community attitudes to see whether or not the community is properly reflected by our position. We are asking also that there be conferences with community leaders to see if they will take the leadership in changing attitudes. The realtors cannot take the lead in this for various reasons. We would also like a clearer definition of the Chicago city open occupancy ordinance and we will urge our people to obey the law. And we will ask our Board to restate their position."

Then Al Raby said that the Chicago Freedom Movement had its demands and he read those demands. Then Leonard Foster of the Garfield Park Community Organization or Garfield Park Chamber of Commerce, a Negro man, the son of A.L. Foster, said, "I've heard Beatty's position and he says we are not responsible, yet he has in the Real Estate Board the key people for setting trends. The Board has excluded Negroes until recently and he says the Board people are only agents but the client's capacity, the agent-client capacity, is not one in which the agent must do and does do anything the client wants. There are many directions that realtors take or that clients take from their agents. Basically, they now assume that the client is discriminatory and they take his listing as discriminatory unless the client indicates the reverse." And, finally, he said he thought that several of the Freedom Movement demands could be acted upon today.

Clarke Stayman of the Chicago Mortgage Bankers, with whom we have been working, then stood up and said that the demands that mortgage availability be made in all neighborhoods without regard to race or religion could be absolutely accepted by the Mortgage Bankers Association; this was a good first break-through.

Then Mayor Daley asked if the demonstrations would stop if the demands were met. And then Dr. King said, "Yes, the demonstrations in the neighborhoods might stop but," he said, "we have demands also in the areas of education and employment and you are hearing here only our demands in the area of housing." And then Daley said, "If we do all we can as a city, then why can't the marches stop. I thought this was supposed to be a kickoff for a conference table."

Heineman tried to clarify the various positions of King and Daley. And then King asked Daley if he agreed specifically to the demands placed upon him, which were the demands listed A through F. And so the Mayor picked up the sheet of paper and read each demand and agreed that he would do each of those things. Then Al Raby questioned the Mayor about some of the statements he had made and the Mayor responded affirmatively. Then Raby said that he wanted to make it clear, (and I couldn't tell why he was saying this at the time, it didn't seem to be appropriate) that the Freedom Movement would always try to negotiate first before engaging in demonstrations. (I think Raby felt that there had been implications that these things were new demands and he wanted to say that he felt there had been negotiations previously on these things).

Then Heineman asked for a clarification about what King meant when he said that neighborhood marches would end. And then it became clear that what King was saying was that if these demands were met, the neighborhood marches for the purpose of securing open occupancy by marching to real estate offices would end. But he made clear that marches to neighborhoods for purposes relating to employment or education would not be excluded as a possibility. John Baird, the president of Baird and Warner, one of our biggest real estate management firms, and the president of the Metropolitan Housing and Planning council, then said, "The Mayor can't really do all the things that he has said here immediately, with all due respect," although the Mayor had said he was going to do them immediately. "Will the marches stop before the Mayor has been able to accomplish the specifics." And rather than answer that Al Raby said that the Mayor has only answered what he was willing to do and he said we must hear from everyone.

Then Chuck Swibel, the president of the Chicago Housing Authority, said, "I can't say immediately that we will cease building high-rises in ghetto neighborhoods, because I think the elderly should have high-rises and also we should ask the county and the suburbs if they would provide us land to build low-rises on. But we will agree that we will build non-ghetto low-rise as much as is feasible."

Then Bill Berry of the Urban League said, "On the high-rise we are talking about apartments for families and we are not talking about the elderly." He said, "There is the question of the present twelve sites that you are going to build all in the ghetto and most of them high-rise. We are talking about no more now. That you would not build high-rises in the ghetto on the present sites or those present twelve buildings." And then the Mayor said, "Basically it is the Federal regulations that cause the high-rise because of the costs, because of the dollar value that's allowed for an apartment you have to build high-rise once you pay for the land costs in the city." Then Bill Berry said, "Let's discuss site selection. The Chicago Housing Authority always blames the City Council" and that they are really responsible for the ghetto sites and all the sites are in the ghetto. He said, "Can you get sites out of the ghetto?" Now the Mayor gave an answer and this whole issue was not joined as clearly and directly as it should be. (And the Mayor, when the Mayor talks, he always tends in this area to blur things either intentionally or because of the way he speaks). The Mayor said, "Well, let's get the slums out of our cities and replace them." He said, "I know about public housing; we've got Negro neighborhoods where they don't want public housing, just like white neighborhoods. Now I don't want to concentrate all the poor people in one place, but we've got to put public housing someplace in some neighborhoods." And then he went off on something he said twice and which is apparently a big personal thing in his mind, "I can't see how we can keep lecturing to children that they live in ghettos because it gives them a ghetto mentality. We should say to them what we can do to make public housing a good place to live in even if it has been a mistake in the past. We're building up great frustrations in our public housing projects." Then Bill Berry again asked Chuck Swibel about the high-rises built without specific community approval. Swibel went on to say that they are now leasing apartments throughout the city and he said that if there must be high-rises built because of Federal regulations, that they wouldn't be multi-purpose bedroom apartments. And then he mentioned the suit filed by the American Civil Liberties Union against the Chicago Housing

Authority for building on ghetto sites and he asked the Movement to ask that suit be withdrawn. Then Ed Marciniak of the Chicago Commission on Human Relations said. "Regarding the problems of the Housing Authority you're talking about a metropolitan problem." And he said to the Movement people, "Have you asked the Cook County Public Housing Authority about whether or not they will help give us vacant land sites and what is their response?"

Then Arthur Mohl, representative of the Chicago Real Estate Board, who has been a power in that organization for years, an ex-president, spoke. (And he and the other realtors, as they spoke, increasingly revealed themselves as people in a dream world. In a situation of great crisis, which focussed on their industry, they seemed to be almost completely confident that they would be able to continue pursuing their past practices. They were cocky. They talked as though the people there were going to have to understand how things really were and they just didn't quite seem to realize that this was the real confrontation, that the game was over. And although the meeting went on and on and on, one couldn't tell whether or not they really understood by the end of the meeting what their real position was). Arthur Mohl then said, "Let me make clear that the Chicago Real Estate Board will obey the Chicago city open occupancy ordinance. (He means they will obey it while it is being tested in court; it is now being tested in the Illinois Supreme Court). In our view each member can interpret his action with his lawyer because we are a trade association and what his legal position is will be defined between himself and his lawyer." He said, "Most of what we are doing here is nit-picking." (He was trying to take the focus off the Real Estate Board.) "Twenty-five percent of the rental housing in this city," he said, "is actually controlled by realtors and the rest is controlled by individuals who are not realtors who own buildings. Now, if we are going to be realists, we must ask how can we deal with the bigoted attitudes in the neighborhoods. You can accuse us as though we created that bigotry until the end of the world but we are not the creators, we are the mirror. (It is interesting that in this setting he agreed that they were a mirror of bigotry). We need a cooperative venture here, not bullying, but a program to sell people in the neighborhoods on the idea that the world won't end if a Negro moves in." (Of course, it was the Chicago Real Estate Board which sold the neighborhoods on the opposite proposition but now its position is that they can't reverse that educational effort of theirs). And then he closed by saying that the Chicago Real Estate Board is not in the business of resolving social problems.

Dr. King then said, "I disagree. But I want to hear reactions to our specific demands. All over the South I heard the same thing we've just heard from Mr. Mohl from restaurant owners and hotel owners. They said that they were just the agents, that they were just responding to the people's unwillingness to eat with Negroes in the same restaurant or stay with Negroes in the same hotel. But we got a comprehensive civil rights bill and the so-called agents then provided service to everybody and nothing happened and the same thing can happen here."

Then Heineman said that, because several people had said that they wanted to be sure that such and such point was raised he said, "I want to make clear that I don't intend to recess today until we have resolved these issues." And this was a surprise because it had been understood that this was a two hour meeting. And, undoubtedly, the Mayor had indicated, as he said later, to Heineman that Heineman should get this issue settled today. And so, (and this is another part of the initial agreement that was broken), rather than it being a two hour meeting, Heineman said, "We're going to stay here, I have no plans to recess except for lunch; I'm going to stay here all day."

Then Thomas Ayers, president of the Chicago Association of Commerce and Industry, and the president of the local electric company, stood up and said that basically he agreed with King about the importance of the law and he reviewed the fact that the FEPC law had a very effective positive effect on bringing about compliance on the part of employers, and that the Association had supported that law. And then he said (and this was the first key statement of reaction from one of the power elite) he said, "I think we support all the points in the proposals of the Chicago Freedom Movement."

So, the head of the Association of Commerce and Industry and the Mayor had both indicated that they were behind everything that had been asked of them. The president of the Chicago Federation of Labor, Bill Lee, was not there so a spokesman said, "We endorse the reforms here, and I will call our executive board immediately to discuss our role in carrying them out."

Then Jim Bevel spoke and he said, "The key problem, the core problem is that realtors refuse to serve Negroes in their offices. And that must change. That is insulting and it is humiliating. And the burden is to change service to Negroes. If the city were opened, then everyone would stop discriminating against Negroes." And then he said, "We have a big problem in Chicago; it's safer now in Birmingham than it is here in Chicago and George Lincoln

Rockwell is leading this city and the Chicago Real Estate Board should begin to lead it." Then the man from the Real Estate Board said that there were three members of the Board there and that the Board would be meeting this afternoon and that he wanted a smaller meeting to discuss this. He didn't like this large forum. And he said, "All of the real estate industry must get together too, not just ourselves, we're only a portion of it." And he said the people who were there were not empowered to answer the specifics that were placed upon them.

Heineman then clarified the positions that various groups had taken. He said to the Real Estate Board, "Were you saying that there should be a sub-committee of the Conference on Religion and Race, the Freedom Movement and the Chicago Real Estate Board to talk about this further?" Then Beatty said, "We can't sit across the table and bargain with the civil righters for something that we don't have the power to give." And then Gordon Groebe, another representative of the Real Estate Board, said, "If King would come out against the fair housing ordinance then he would lose his supporters and he would lose his position and he would not be a leader. And you've got to realize that you're asking us to do the same thing. When we ask our realtors to abrogate their position as agents then you're asking us to do what you'd be asking Dr. King to do if you told him he had to come out against the fair housing ordinance."

Then Dr. King spoke, "I must appeal to the decency of the people on the Chicago Real Estate Board. You're not negotiating this question with us. You are men confronted with a moral issue. I decide on the basis of conscience. A genuine leader doesn't reflect consensus, he molds consensus. Look at myself. There are lots of Negroes these days who are for violence but I know that I am dealing with a moral issue, and I am going to oppose violence if I am the last Negro in this country speaking for non-violence.

Now the real estate people must act on principle in that same manner, or they're not leaders. The real estate industry has not only reflected discriminatory attitudes, it has played a significant part in creating them. In fact, in California, the real estate people spent five million dollars to kill the open occupancy law there. Now don't tell me that you're neutral." He also said that the day before he'd been talking with Attorney General Katzenbach about another problem and that Katzenbach had told him that if the money that the real estate industry was using to fight the Federal open occupancy law were available to the government that they could eliminate all the slums in one major city. He said, "I appeal to the rightness of our position and to your decency. I see nothing in this world more dangerous than Negro cities ringed with white suburbs. Look at it in terms of grappling with righteousness. People will adjust to changes but the leadership has got to say that the time for change has come. The problem is not the people in Gage Park, the problem is that their leaders and institutions have taught them to be what they are."

Then the man from the Real Estate Board said that, "Well we will recommend to our Board that we sit down with you and discuss this further. But we have got to be clear on what the Chicago open occupancy ordinance really requires." Now he said this several times and it's an amazing thing because that ordinance has been on the books since 1963. And then he said, "We must find a way of reaching the people."

Then the chairman of the Church Federation, a Presbyterian, head of the Presbytery, named Zimmerman, said, "I want to call us back to the three points in the Freedom Movement demands and these demands are basically for the Real Estate Board to change its present actions in regard to legislation and laws and I think the Chicago Real Estate Board can act on these." (This was a very astute comment. He was saying we don't have to depend on the neighborhoods to get the Chicago Real Estate Board to stop its litigation against the city's open occupancy ordinance. We don't have to rely on the neighborhoods to get the Chicago Real Estate Board out of the courts trying to enjoin the open occupancy bill).

Then Rabbi Marx, representing the Union of American Hebrew Congregations, said, "We have heard this same thing from the Real Estate Board over and over. They must understand that we must have a change now." Then Bob Johnston, the regional director of the United Auto Workers, said, "I agree we must have change. This is an urgent situation. The Real Estate Board must realize that there must be a change now. All the realtors are not going to go out of business if they change their practices. The Mayor has made a good statement. We must continue to meet. No one can stand in the road of progress. You can't go back now and do your business as usual. We should establish a permanent committee of this type and at the community level we should hold meetings to try to change attitudes."

Bishop Montgomery then said he agreed with the Chicago Freedom Movement's demands of churches and he wanted to specifically accept the blame for the failures of the religious community and to admit that the religious community had not translated its ethics.

Then Al Raby suggested that the meeting be adjourned. Mayor Daley then said, "No, let's not adjourn the meeting. The Chicago Real Estate Board should get on the phone to their members and do something about these demands now," which really surprised everybody and placed a terrific burden on the Chicago Real Estate Board. But, the Real Estate Board representative, even in the face of the combined power structure telling them, "Gentlemen, now is the time to move," said, "We cannot possibly deal on the phone; we cannot possibly work out a resolution to these things today."

Then Ben Henineman said, "Let me summarize. Gentlemen, the big stumbling block here is the Chicago Real Estate Board and what it's going to do about the demands on it. And the representatives of the Real Estate Board must realize that they are the key to this thing. The monkey, gentlemen, is right on your back, and whether you deem it as fair or not, everyone sees that the monkey is there. And the question is how are you going to deal with the demands placed on you." And then Chuck Swibel, the chief cheerleader for Mayor Daley, and president of the Housing Authority, stood up with a final little statement which ended with, "We need a victory for Mayor Daley, a victory for the City of Chicago." And when he said a victory for Mayor Daley there was a groan from the Freedom side.

It was then agreed that the meeting would be reconvened at four o'clock to hear what the Chicago Real Estate Board had been able to accomplish at its meeting in the afternoon, which had been previously scheduled. And it was agreed that nobody would say anything to the press. Generally, statements were not given to the press, except that apparently the *Chicago Daily News* did have a contact because at the close of the meeting they seemed to have the story and the other papers did not. The meeting adjourned between 12:30 and 4:00, for the main purpose of waiting with bated breath to see whether or not the Chicago Real Estate Board was going to meet the basic demands placed upon it.

These demands were that they would immediately withdraw their support of the suit they had initiated contesting the legality of the Chicago fair housing ordinance; that they would withdraw their opposition to the Governor's fair housing executive order; and to the fair housing provision of the 1966 Federal Civil Rights Bill; and that they would persuade other realtor groups to cease their warfare against the order and the proposed Federal legislation. And that they would pledge to support an effective state fair housing law to apply to property owners as well as brokers in the coming session of the state legislature.

The Movement people had lunch and caucused and discussed whether or not and under what conditions they would agree to a moratorium on the marches. It was rather clear that they were unwilling to agree to a moratorium without results and that they wanted to focus on the reality of an open city rather than a law.

When the meeting was reconvened at four o'clock (and everybody was there promptly at four o'clock) the newspapers were allowed in for a few minutes to take pictures and sent out. Heineman opened the meeting and asked Mr. Beatty of the Real Estate Board to report. And then Mr. Beatty read a statement. It was a very confusing statement and was read rather quickly. Basically, the statement said as follows, and copies of it were distributed shortly thereafter, as soon as they were prepared: first, that they would support the principle of freedom of choice in housing as a right of every citizen (it never was determined what that meant); second, that they believed that race relations progress was produced only by a favorable climate and that the techniques of street demonstrations hardens bigotry and slows down progress, and that if demonstrations, and I'm reading this incredible sentence specifically, "if demonstrations do not terminate promptly we may lose control of our membership and be unable to fulfill the commitments we have here undertaken;" third, they said that as a Chicago organization (and this was their major agreement, really), they would withdraw all opposition to the philosophy of open occupancy legislation at the state level provided it is applicable to owners as well as to brokers; that they would reserve the right to criticize detail as distinguished from philosophy; and that they would also request the state association of real estate boards to do likewise; and, fourth, they agreed they would remind their members that it is their duty to obey the Chicago fair housing ordinance. But they said, "as their lawyers interpret its meaning," meaning, as the realtors' lawyers interpret its meaning. But they said, "We do not accept the Governor's order as proper and will not ask compliance so long as it is under injunction." Finally they said, "We object to the proposal by the Freedom Movement that the city or citizens engage in testing real estate offices, this is an unwarranted harassment." (The Movement had asked the City to engage in affirmative compliance testing). And they couldn't sacrifice the principles they had espoused in their objection to the Constitutionality of the Chicago ordinance. So, basically, they were meeting none of the specific demands and agreeing only that they would not oppose in the future a state open occupancy law as they had opposed one in the past.

123

Al Raby then said, "I want to see that in writing, but we have nine demands here and we haven't gone over all of them, there are others to go over, so let's go over them." Then King said he would like Beatty to clarify what he had said and so Beatty, from the Real Estate Board re-read his statement, and it was a little more understandable the second time around. It was still not exactly clear what the situation was as a result of the Real Estate Board's statement. So Raby asked Beatty, "We've heard your statement. We're not sure what you're saying. What is your position on our demands A,B, C?" Basically the response Beatty gave was, "On your demand A, which is to withdraw our support from the suit testing the legality of the Chicago Fair Housing ordinance, no. B, to withdraw our opposition to the governor's fair housing executive order, no." C, they did not agree to support an effective state fair housing law but they did agree to withdraw their opposition to a law.

Then Jim Bevel stood up and said what he said almost all the time during the meeting, "Gentlemen, I don't think the important thing is what your position is about A, B, and C. The question is whether Negroes are going to be served at your office tomorrow morning." Then Bob Ming, who is a professor of law at the University of Chicago, key member of the NAACP Legal Defense Committee, and a member of the Chicago Commission on Human Relations, in which capacity he was at this meeting, said, "The ordinance is clear. Ever since September, 1963 every broker has been obliged to abide by practices which are in compliance with what it is that Mr. Bevel wants. The Negro is protected by this ordinance. He must be served under this ordinance by realtors." Then Bill Robinson said, "It is obvious that there are wholesale violations of this ordinance." Bob Ming said, "The City has opposed the Chicago Real Estate Board suit and we fought it in the courts. Brokers got on the stand and made it clear, and the evidence showed that they really decide on the tenants in buildings that they control. Although they are pleading that they don't control things, they do make the decision on the race of tenants, in contrast with sale buildings." John Womer, of the Metropolitan Housing and Planning Council, then said that he thought the proposals of Chicago Freedom Movement were very restrained, but he thought it was inconsistent with a free society for them to try to stop people from seeking legislation or litigation that they wanted.

Then Jim Bevel stood up again and said, "Gentlemen, in Memphis, in 1960, we had a series of marches to try to open up the restaurants, and, finally, we had a meeting like this and what was agreed was not that they were going to pass a law or anything like that. The power structure said that they were going to see to it that we could eat in Memphis and one week later we went out and we ate and we have been eating in Memphis ever since. Now that's what we want here today. I want to re-emphasize that we need Negroes to be served in real estate offices. And you people here can see that will happen. That's a conservative, simple, humane request, and let's not confuse the issue with all these A's, B's and C's."

Then Andy Young, Dr. King's chief aide, stood and said, "Now, gentlemen, I want to reaffirm what has been just said here. In Savannah, for instance, in 1960, in Savannah, in the deep south, we got change in a movement activity there in the schools. Legislation, and a court decision in the schools followed that but we got the change before the legislation and the courts. Now, we need leadership to bring a result. Where they have had ordinances and laws, they don't work to produce the result we want. We need a plan to do right and not a law to stop wrong." And Beatty said, "I couldn't agree with you more; (always trying to get off the hook) we should take the monkey off our back and put it on the back of all the people."

And then Art Brazier, of TWO, said, "The question is whether a member of the Chicago Real Estate Board will obey the law." Then the president of the Church of Federation of Greater Chicago said, "Does the ordinance provide that realtors should do what Mr. Bevel says, that is, serve Negroes?" And Ming said, "Yes." Then Zimmerman said, "When you tell your people to obey the ordinance, will you tell them that they should serve Negroes?" And Beatty said, "We're still not clear on some points of the ordinance. We can ask them to obey the law." Zimmerman, of the Church Federation, said, "Can you exercise your leadership by explaining to them about serving everyone?" This was a little bit coy and not stated so directly that the Real Estate Board couldn't wriggle out.

Then Al Raby said, "Now, I want to know when the Mayor will see that an ordinance is enacted to require that all real estate dealers post in their windows the open occupancy law and a statement of policy on nondiscrimination." The Mayor said, and here he was a little flustered, "I said already this morning that I would do that, and I keep my word and that will be done and actually I've got my corporation counsel checking on it right now to see whether we can do it without an ordinance, whether we can just require it under the existing law." Then Bill Robinson said, "What about state law?" And Daley said, "The Democrats have always supported a state open occupancy law and the Republicans have fought it. We need a state law that covers the metropolitan area." Then Arthur Mohl of the Real Estate Board said, "We are hesitant to give our people advice because we've been told as brokers we can't do that, but we'd be glad to submit the interpretation of the Human Relations Commission as to what the law means to our brokers."

Then Rabbi Marx, in a very astute comment, asked the president of the Chicago Real Estate Board to look at his statement that he had presented at the beginning of the afternoon and he called attention to the fact that this sentence was in the statement of the real estate brokers, and he said, "If demonstrations do not terminate promptly, we may lose control of our membership and be unable to fulfill the commitments we have undertaken." Rabbi Marx, after reading that statement said, "You have been here all morning saying to us that you don't have control over your people and that therefore we are asking the wrong people to change. Now, do you have control or don't you have control?" Then Jesse Jackson, of Dr. King's staff, said, "Let's go back to the basic issue," and then he talked about the theological issues involved and then he said, "I'm not concerned about your law. Dr. King has told you what the needs are and your law must come to a higher level than it has come. It must come to the theological level."

Then Al Raby said, "I think we must ask, can a Negro walk into a real estate office and be served? If we find that in fact is true, then whatever it is that the Real Estate Board is trying to say in its statement will not be of any concern to us because that's what we want. And if we find that's true in fact, then your statement is all right. If not, it is not." Bill Berry said, "It seems to me that outside the first paragraph, your statement is totally unacceptable, and I want to ask Mayor Daley, if the Chicago Real Estate Board can't do something about our demands, can you?" And then Daley, having previously put the finger on the Real Estate Board, came to its defense. He said, "I think they've done a lot. It shows a real change that they've come in here indicating that they will no longer oppose open occupancy. We will act as an agency through the Human Relations Commission. We shouldn't ask the Real Estate Board to withdraw its suit. We have agreed to virtually all the points here and everyone says that they are going to move ahead. Now let's not quibble over words; the intent is the important thing. We're here in good faith and the City is asking for your help." And then Ben Heineman said to Bill Berry, whom he knew very well, "Bill, now you said the statement is worthless, but isn't point three, the willingness of the Board to stop opposing the state open occupancy law, a significant change?" And Bill was caught a little off guard by that, and he said, "I've had long experience with them; they'll say that they will withdraw it but they're still fighting the principle in court." And then Heineman still tried to make a virtue of the statement. And Bill said, "Well, on fourth reading I would have to concede that the third statement is something." And Heineman said, "It is a concession."

Then King said, "I hope that people here don't feel that we are just being recalcitrant, but we do have a little history of disappointment and broken promises, and I certainly wouldn't want to argue with Mr. Ming. Mr. Ming was my lawyer who saved me in court in Alabama from ten years in prison and he's my great counselor, but I would remind him that ten years ago we got a court decision and a law three years ago now that says that segregation is illegal and we now have 8.8% of the children integrated in the South. And Bob Ming is telling me now that the ordinance will do the job. We see a gulf between the promise and the fulfillment. We don't want to fool people any longer; they feel they have been fooled; so we are asking today that Negroes can buy anywhere. When will that be? Tell us, so that we won't fool the people. We need a timetable, something very concrete. We want to know what your implementation is." Then Ben Heineman said, "We don't see you as recalcitrant. Anyone here can understand why you want to nail down the terms of this agreement."

Then Heineman said, "I want to try to attempt a summary here. The Mayor has accepted your demands on him. The Real Estate Board has stated that it will withdraw its opposition to a state open occupancy law. And this is a great victory, a major victory, and probably insures passage of that legislation. The other demands have been mainly accepted. The only one that hasn't been involves the Federal Deposit Insurance Corporation and they aren't here and I can pass your claim along to them." And here he left the neutral chairman's position and he said, "The Chair feels that we are well on the way to realization and that the demonstrations could now cease until we see if these agreements are working out."

And then Jim Bevel said, "Most all the laws have not been effective in providing men housing. We're asking the Board of Realtors and the city of Chicago to go beyond that law. We don't want a commission investigation. If you discriminate against a man trying to find a place for his family, that's a crime. Let's deal with our principles. I can't suggest anything to the Negro people of this town until I can say to them, to a man, to a Negro man, 'You can buy land from the people who sell land.' Nothing less. Now white men don't go to commissions to get a house, and I'm a man like white men and I go to a real estate office and anything that you come up with, any scheme or game, that's short of that is inadequate."

Then A.L. Foster, or rather the son of A.L. Foster said, "The Chicago Real Estate Board, now, we've got too many myths here. The Chicago Real Estate Board has moved a little and it doesn't have absolute control over the market, but it is not just an agent, and we've got to realize that they just can't play this game anymore. Homes are not sacred things. Today statistics show that most people are moving once every three to five years. They are buying autos every three to five years, so homes are being sold just like autos and, if tomorrow, all the automobile dealers were to die, we'd have to have more automobile dealers and, you don't have to worry, people will be buying and selling houses and needing brokers to do it. And therefore, a change in your policy isn't going to hurt anything."

Then Bob Spike, who had been the director of the Conference on Religion and Race in New York for the National Council of Churches and is now on the faculty of the Chicago Theological Seminary, University of Chicago, said, and I think that everybody was rather surprised by his position, "I consider the change by the Chicago Real Estate Board as profound and I don't think, on the other hand, that we should take Bevel's frustration lightly. But we've got to make clear here that the Chicago Freedom Movement didn't say, in its three demands to the Real Estate Board, what Bevel is saying, and that is that Negroes would be served in all the offices. I think we need some terms here for a moratorium." And he was the first person outside the establishment who had said anything for a moratorium.

Raby said, "Now, I want to say that I don't think we're nearly so clear on all of these things as Mr. Heineman thinks. I'm not very clear on where we are on points four, five or six for instance." So then they began to go over those points. One of these points had to do with the Department of Public Aid placing welfare recipients only in ghetto neighborhoods, Negro welfare recipients. And so the chief of the Housing Department of the Department of Public Aid stood up and said, "We let people pick their own housing, and we have fifty housing men who are in thirteen district offices and they go around and look up and try to find housing for people and certify housing. We try to find housing for everybody and we're controlled by price ceilings." Then Bill Robinson stood up, and in very strong language, said, "Negro families are encouraged by your people to find housing inside the ghetto."

And then the Mayor said, "Now, the real fact is that the recipients pay the rent, not the Department, so they control things." And Robinson refuted the Mayor and said, "No, there are all kinds of recipients who are paid directly from Springfield." And the man from the Public Aid Department said, "No, there are a limited number of these people." Then Kale Williams of the American Friends Service Committee, who is a relatively silent person, stood and said a very profound and certain thing, and that was that he felt the common thing about point three, four and five, which Al Raby had raised, which had to do with the Public Housing Authority, and the Public Aid Commission and the Urban Renewal Commission, the important things were that the public policy and practice of these agencies had not had any effect on opening up the city and that if their tenant placement and site selection policies were affirmatively administered they could be used to begin to provide an open city. A very important point to be made.

Then Andy Young said, "The question is, 'Who is going to bear responsibility for desegregating the city?' The society must change the patterns so that the individual can and will be moved out, rather than producing laws that put the individual in the position of having to move himself. We must take the responsibility here for implementing a plan for an open city. We need a plan to aggressively desegregate this city." He said, "And as to your fears of violence, let me say that it is more dangerous in Lawndale with those jammed-up, neurotic, psychotic Negroes than it is in Gage Park. To white people who don't face the violence which is created by the degradation of the ghetto, this violence that you see in Gage Park may seem like a terrible thing. But I live in Lawndale and it is safer for me in Gage Park than it is in Lawndale. For the Negro in the ghetto, violence is the rule. So, when you say, cease these demonstrations, you're saying to us, go back to a place where there is more violence than where you see violence taking place outside the ghetto."

Mayor Daley then, apparently intentionally or out of emotion or ignorance, responded to this superb statement by saying, "Did I hear you say that we are going to have more violence in this city?" And then Andy Young, who is always very cautious and kindly in his answers, said, "No, I'm saying that Negroes who are jammed into ghettos are people who are forced into violent ways of life, I'm saying that the Blackstone Rangers are the product of what happens to people when you live in a ghetto. I'm saying that the ghetto has to be dispersed, that this city must be opened up, and this high concentration ended, or we will have violence whether there is a movement or not." Then Mayor Daley said, "The city didn't create this frustration or this situation. We want to try to do what you say." And then Young said, "Well, we need a program. We need to know how much is going to be accomplished in thirty days, and how much in sixty days. We will find families to move into twenty communities in the next thirty days. The United Auto Workers could find twenty or twenty-five families to move near their plants rather than being so far away from their plants. We've got to have a plan for an open city to take to the people."

And then, having really begun to talk about some real realities for affirmative planning for an open city, the Movement was caught up a little in the anomaly of having defined its goals in terms of specific actions rather than results. And, since the demands were actually more conservative than the results which Andy Young and James Bevel had been defining, Ben Heineman, the chairman, said, "Now, I think we've got to understand what we're talking about here. We understood that your proposals were on these two pages, and it sounds now like you're changing things." And then Andy Young backtracked a little, and said, "No, what I'm talking about is a plan to implement what is on those two pages. For instance, we say that the Public Aid Commission will end its enforced ghettoization of Negro recipients. So, the woman who works in a hospital on the North side who is an aid recipient who lives in the apartment below our apartment, the Public Aid Commission would go out and look for a house for her on the North side, near the hospital where she is working so she wouldn't be spending an hour an a half every day getting to work and an hour and a half going back. And the Public Housing Authority would go out and find a site in Jefferson Park where we could build the next low-rise public housing units."

Then Chuck Swibel, of the Chicago Housing Authority, stood up and said, "I will pledge to you that we will move people out. Take our word. I want to see these marches ended today. If we are dealing on top of the table, then call off the marches for twelve months. (There was a groan from the Freedom Movement people when he said twelve months). We can't get an okay on Jefferson Park public housing sites in less time than that because the Federal government will require so much red tape." Then, a couple of not very significant statements were made, and Al Raby said, "I think the Movement would like fifteen minutes to adjourn to talk among themselves."

And before the adjournment, Charlie Hayes of the Packinghouse Workers, a Movement person, said, "I think that you need to be a Negro to really understand what the situation is here. I represent Negro people, laboring people. I am a Negro first; I was born that way; I'll die that way. I am a trade unionist since I was nineteen. And I want you to know that there are a whole lot of people in this town who believe in Jim Bevel. And no one here is holding anyone responsible, but what we're asking, what I'm saying here, is, we've got to see that we're in changing times and we can't go out after these negotiations and tell the guy on the street that what we got was an agreement from the Chicago Real Estate Board that they philosophically agree with open occupancy. The people want to hear what we're going to do for them now. If I as a union negotiator ever came back to my men and said to them, I got the company to agree that philosophically they were in support of seniority, I'd be laughed out of court." And, somehow, that statement was very real, I think, to people who were there and they recognized that what was being said was the case.

The meeting was then adjourned while the Freedom Movement people got together to review their position. At the meeting which they had, there was no one who felt that the agreements were such that the marches should cease. Coming back into the meeting, everyone turned expectantly to Al Raby as he stood to announce the results of the discussions that had just transpired. He said, "We view this meeting as very important and significant. For the first time there are verbalizations at least that show that we have some opportunities for change. But I would remind you that the important thing, that we stressed at the beginning of the meeting was the actuality, the implementation; that's the key. We can see the need for further discussions. In your mind the question may be a moratorium, but we would have to say that we would have a moratorium on demonstrations if we had a moratorium on housing segregation. We would like to see a meeting one week from now to see what you're doing in terms of implementation. In the meantime we would meet in a sub-committee on specifics. I can remember everything this city did to see that a bond issue was passed and we need that same kind of campaign on open housing. During this week we will have to continue our present plans." Then Heineman asked him to clarify whether that meant that there would be demonstrations in the next week. And the answer was, "Demonstrations will continue for the next week." And then the Mayor stood up abruptly and said, "I thought we were meeting to see if we couldn't, if there couldn't be a halt to what is happening in our neighborhoods because the use of all the police and the crime rate rising throughout our city. I repeat, as far as the city is concerned, we are prepared to do what is asked for. I appeal to you as citizens to try to understand that we are trying. I ask why you picked Chicago? I make no apologies for our city. In the name of all our citizens I ask for a moratorium and that we set up a committee. We're men of good faith and we can work out an agreement. The police can't give our people adequate protection now. What's the difference between today and a week from today with men of good faith? We're defending your rights, and also there's no question about the law. Can't you do today what you would do in a week?"

Then the president of the Association of Commerce and Industry said, "We started on this document, this two-page document, I don't think we should leave it now. We've gotten substantial agreement; we ought to make sure at least that we know what the outstanding areas are." Raby said, "Well, let me give you an example. Is the Mayor going to ask for the legislation to require brokers to post the ordinance in their window; will he ask for that legislation next Tuesday and will he get it? Will that actually be implemented? The Mayor said, "We've got to show the City Council that you'll do something. We'll pass what we said we'd pass if we get a moratorium." This was the first time that there was any indication that this was a trade.

And then Raby was infuriated and said, "If I come before the Mayor of Chicago some day, I hope I can come before the Mayor of Chicago with what is just and that he will implement it because it is right rather than trading it politically for a moratorium." Then Ben Heineman tried to cool things down and to censure Raby a little, and he said, "In a cooler moment, I think you'll realize that the Mayor cannot help but want fewer demonstrations, he's concerned about the safety of the people. And the Mayor is accustomed to having his word taken."

Well, Raby was just not satisfied with that statement by Heineman and he said, "I won't reply to what you've said for the sake of harmony." But he went on then, in a very angry and tense voice, to go down the list and to make clear just exactly how vague the agreements were and how specific he wanted the agreements to be. And I think that this was a very effective moment because it did make clear to everybody just exactly what the Movement was expecting to be done and how far the agreements that had been made were from the specifics, that Raby was talking about. "So," he said, "the Real Estate Board hasn't done anything meaningful here. I'm not clear on what the Chicago Housing Authority is really going to do about high-rises. The Cook County Department of Public Aid has got to change;

it can't tell us that it has all Negro recipients in one area and all white recipients in another area and that's an accident. That's an insult to our intelligence. The Urban Renewal program is going to have to do something about its relocation policies. I want to hear the details about what the Savings and Loan people are going to do. The open city program must be like the bond issue program. I want to see companies and unions who have been asked to do something here to kick out their members, to kick out their employees who are acting like Fascists in the neighborhoods. If they steal something, if an employee stole something and was arrested, they would be fired immediately, but when they're stoning Negro cars and innocent Negro people nothing happens at all. I am not going to go back to our people with a philosophic program. We want a real program; a moratorium on discrimination will bring a moratorium on marches." This was a very hot statement.

And then Dr. King stood up and with the grand and quiet and careful and calming eloquence which he has, changed the mood completely. "This has been a constructive and a creative beginning. This represents progress and a sign of change. I've gone through this whole problem in my mind a thousand times about demonstrations, and let me say that if you are tired of demonstrations, I am tired of demonstrating. I am tired of the threat of death. I want to live. I don't want to be a martyr. And there are moments when I doubt if I am going to make it through. I am tired of getting hit, tired of being beaten, tired of going to jail. But the important thing is not how tired I am; the important thing is to get rid of the conditions that lead us to march. I hope we are here to discuss how to make Chicago a great open city and not how to end marches. We've got to have massive changes. Now, gentlemen, you know we don't have much. (He meant the Movement.) We don't have much money. We don't really have much education, and we don't have political power. We have only our bodies and you are asking us to give up the one thing that we have when you say, 'Don't march.' We want to be visible. We are not trying to overthrow you; we're trying to get in. We're trying to make justice a reality. Now the basic thing is justice. We want peace, but peace is the presence of justice. We haven't seen enough for the massive changes that are going to be needed. To the Chicago Real Estate Board, I want to say particularly that your second point about the demonstrations being the wrong approach bothers me. Because the problem is not created by the marches. A doctor doesn't cause cancer when he finds it. In fact, we thank him for finding it, and we are doing the same thing. Our humble marches have revealed a cancer. We have not used rocks. We have not used bottles. And no one today, no one who has spoken has condemned those that have used violence. Maybe there should be a moratorium in Gage Park. Maybe we should begin condemning the robber and not the robbed. We haven't even practiced civil disobedience as a Movement. We are being asked to stop one of our most precious rights, the right to assemble, the right to petition. We asked Chicago to bring justice in housing, and we are starting on that road today. We are trying to keep the issue so alive that it will be acted on. Our marching feet have brought us a long way, and if we hadn't marched I don't think we'd be here today. No one here has talked about the beauty of our marches, the love of our marches, the hatred we're absorbing. Let's hear more about the people who perpetuate the violence. We appreciate the meeting. We don't want to end the dialogue. We don't see enough to stop the marches, but we are going with love and non-violence. This is a great city and it can be a greater city."

A commissioner from the Illinois Commission on Human Relations then asked if it wouldn't be possible to have symbolic marches in one place to take the heat off the police. Then Bevel said, "You're still saying that the problem is the demonstrations, and that's not the problem." Then Andy Young said, "We need a working committee. The Real Estate Board did a good job, they moved along in the hour and a half they had, and tomorrow by noon we could start working out a program. As soon as concrete proposals are worked out we can get back together." Then Bob Johnston of the UAW made a long plea that the negotiations be continued. He said, "The UAW has struggled a lifetime for freedom. I know about negotiation, we've talked with Bill Lee of the Chicago Federation of Labor and his reaction was a hundred per cent in favor of the Movement's demands. Let's meet tomorrow. We should get together tomorrow. We're talking about the future of America and we can't work it out in one day. We should meet tomorrow. I believe we shouldn't break off negotiations. Let's find out by tomorrow night how much further we can get than where we are today."

Then there was a consultation and I'm not exactly sure what happened, because it seemed to me as though the Movement people might have accepted this promise, but instead, and rather surprisingly, Heineman made a new proposal. He said, "The Chair will appoint a committee, under the chairmanship of Bishop Montgomery, that will be composed of no more than five representatives of the Freedom Movement, two representatives of the Real Estate Board, the president of the Association of Commerce and Industry, an officer of the Commercial Club of Chicago, a representative of labor, and the Mayor of Chicago or his representative. And they will meet at the call of Bishop Montgomery. We'll re-convene this group to have a report from them. I propose that we re-convene this group a week from this Friday." Which made ten days and was more time than anybody thus far had talked about, and it was obvious that there wasn't going to be a moratorium until this group came back.

Somebody asked Heineman what the purpose was, and he said, "The purpose of the sub-committee is to come back with proposals designed to provide an open city." And so Bishop Montgomery called for the first meeting of the sub-committee on Friday, giving a day in between, Thursday, for the groups to consolidate, to work on their various positions, I presume. The remainder of the meeting was a lengthy discussion about what should be said to the press. And Heineman proposed that he would say, in company with Bishop Montgomery, "We had a full discussion; it was profitable but not conclusive; a sub-committee has been appointed to work out details, if possible;" and that he had recommended that the group be called together again a week from Friday. "As to the demonstrations, there was no commitment to terminate them in the interim, but the Chairman hopes that whatever is done will be done with the view to the overall interests of the city, and that the Movement would proceed with great restraint."

The Movement people were very unhappy with that conclusion, and most of the debate which followed was to persuade him that he shouldn't say anything about the demonstrations that would make people in the city feel as though there were going to be a change. And Dr. King said, "Can't you say that if there are demonstrations, you want to call on the violent people to be restrained?" And Mayor Daley wanted it made very clear to the press that there weren't any agreements reached at the meeting today. The CHA president made one final plea that the marches be called off. And Raby said, "That question has already been answered."

There was considerable debate about whether or not Heineman should say that the Movement will proceed with restraint. And Dr. King said, "I think we've been restrained." Bevel suggested that he say that he hoped that in the interim rather than that the Movement would be restrained, that Negroes wouldn't be discriminated against. Bob Ming suggested that some showing be made that progress was underway and that they not just say that a committee had been appointed. He suggested that it be said that everybody

135

agreed that they can't solve the problems of this city and maintain the present residential segregation and that the problems can't be solved by violence. Al Raby said, in a disgusted voice, "I can stand anything you say about me, I really don't care. The important thing is what is the substance of what we're willing to do to open up this city." It was then obvious that there couldn't be an agreement reached as to what ought to be said, so Mayor Daley stood up and said, "I think everybody should be allowed to say anything they want to and that it be made clear that this is a continuing meeting, and that this has been a beginning." And the meeting just sort of dissolved in a babble. And then King made his statement; Daley made a statement; the Chairman made a statement. All of the statements were rather neutral and there were not any significant charges by one party or another.

On Friday, August 26, at 10:00 a.m. in the Monroe Room of the Palmer House Hotel in Chicago, the full negotiating committee was re-convened. For ten days the sub-committee of the negotiating committee had been meeting, actually doing the negotiating, and this was a meeting to report back on the agreements that had been reached. The tables in the room were in a "U", the religious leaders at the base of the "U", the Chicago establishment on the left hand leg of the "U" and the Freedom Movement on the right hand leg of the "U." I sat with the Movement people, next to Rev. Arthur Brazier of The Woodlawn Organization, and Sam Dennis of the Community Relations Service, the other Federal agency that was represented. Shortly before the meeting was opened, the press was allowed in for a few minutes to take pictures. Then the meeting was opened a few minutes after the press was dismissed by Bishop Montgomery, the chairman of the Chicago Conference on Religion and Race and Suffragan Bishop of the Episcopal Church. It was opened with a prayer. He then turned the meeting over to Mr. Ben Heineman, the president of the Northwestern Railroad.

Heineman said, "This is a closed meeting. I want to ask the sub-committee chaired by Thomas Ayers, president of the Chicago Association of Commerce and Industry to report on their work. They have been working for sixty hours." Then Thomas Ayers distributed the written recommendations of the sub-committee and he read the report to everyone. [Editor's note: see pages 147-154 for the full text.] Ayers is a rather mild mannered, youngish man who is president of Commonwealth Edison and the Association of Commerce and Industry. After reading the report (which struck me as being much more general than I had expected the report to be coming from this committee), Heineman thanked the sub-committee. Ayers said that the report had been unanimously accepted by the negotiating people, although the representatives from the Chicago Freedom Movement had said they would have to review the document with their constituency and thereafter Ayers moved the acceptance of the report. Mayor Daley was then asked if he had any comments and he stood and thanked the sub-committee and said, "When men of good faith sit down and talk they can solve problems. We said at the last meeting we would do everything possible as a city to meet the demands. I asked therefore for the assembling of a permanent organization to solve at the negotiating table these problems before there would be any further demonstrations. We want to recognize the right of people to demonstrate, but there isn't any reason why men of good faith can't bargain before there are any demonstrations." He then moved a vote. Before a vote could be called Al Raby of the Chicago Freedom Movement, said "Well just a minute here, we are all concerned in the Freedom Movement about the personal commitments of the individuals who are here. For instance, we want to know whether or not the churches will take responsibility for a specific number of Negro families in each all white community. Will we be able to have one per cent Negro occupancy in every community in the city of Chicago by 1970? Will there be a concrete date when the city and the Chicago Real Estate Board can guarantee us that the communities are opened to all. And the ultimate question is still the question raised by Jim Bevel, 'When do we foresee the time when a Negro can go into a real estate office in Chicago and be served?'" And as Raby said "In Chicago", Mayor Daley interrupted him and said "And the suburbs" which indicated Mayor Daley's great concern that there be a movement to evacuate Negroes from the city to the suburbs. (An idea, to my personal knowledge, that he had had for the last few years. It is an idea that I suspect is purely political, because he understands that his political base is being eroded by the increase in the Negro population and the decrease in white population).

Bishop Montgomery stood up at that point and said that he thought that he could speak for all the faiths and say that they do endorse the agreement, they recognize their responsibilities and their failures. And he said that, for the Episcopal Diocese, he could pledge that everything in the diocese's power would be preached in every parish and every pulpit. Since Raby had raised the question about what the actual commitments of the member bodies were, it seemed that everybody then felt, after Bishop Montgomery spoke, a move to make their own statement of commitment and although I will report these they were to me not significant commitments because they did not have any specific content. They were statements of good will and good faith but nobody was really throwing anything into the pot, saying, "and to demonstrate our commitment we will do this or we will do that."

Next stood Archbishop Cody of the Roman Catholic Archdiocese, saying "I endorse the agreement and pledge our support: In fact you will note in this morning's paper that the Rogers Park Community Council has already spoken up and indicated its willingness to accept Negro families. This is the first community that has done this and we have encouraged this effort. I believe that with the relief in the tensions that we are working out today we can now sit down and discuss and find some solutions. We have already had priests in many parishes working with select groups of laymen. We have 454 parishes and all ethnic groups. We are like a little United Nations and we will commit our moral, financial and religious resources to the fulfillment of this agreement." Then Rabbi Marx of the Union of American Hebrew Congregations stood up and said, "A week ago, one of our congregations in Rogers Park called me and asked 'What should we do? Our real estate offices are being tested' and I think the answer we gave is indicated by the statement in this morning's paper which shows the first results; all faiths participated in Rogers Park in the statement that was just released indicating that community's willingness to accept Negro families. We have here today the new president of the Board of Rabbis, who has personally acted to bring Negro families into his community of Glencoe. We are ready to make a total commitment." Rev. Zimmerman, President of the Church Federation said, "The Church Federation is composed of twenty-seven denominations and I can assure you that when our Board next meets, that the Board will accept these agreements. Any document," he added, "needs a means for amendment, and the genius of this document is paragraph ten which provides for a continuing committee which will audit and be able to revise the agreements here and move them forward and this is vital." Rabbi Siskind, the new chairman of the Chicago Board of Rabbis, then stood and said that the rabbis supported the agreement.

He was followed by Bill Lee, the president of the Chicago Federation of Labor, who made a rather lengthy statement. (Lee speaks in the vein of Mayor Daley—many words, but they have so little content, they're so general, that you are not sure that anything has been said when the individual who spoke is done). Bill Lee spoke in this manner and he said in terms of content only that labor had wanted such a conference as this and that labor intended to carry out its commitments in this document to the letter.

Then Mr. Beatty, the president of the Chicago Real Estate Board stood and said, "We had a meeting yesterday of the Chicago Metropolitan area realtors; these included non-members of the realtor group as well as the suburban Boards and it was a long and frantic meeting and everyone there felt that this was a area-wide problem and not just a Chicago problem. It was a very, very difficult meeting but it seemed to be a first move. (And one had the feeling that even Mr. Beatty of the Real Estate Board sitting with this group assembled and seeing the great concern and commitment of so many, felt that he had an obligation to try to do something, to try to move things along.) He said, "We accept this document but we have to say that the fact remains that there is a tremendous job ahead of us. Ninety per cent of the transactions in real estate are handled by real estate men and while we believe in what is being done here, we want to say as strongly as possible that we need everyone's help, because the realtor is usually a small businessman in a small office and we are placing a tremendous burden upon him."

Dr. King then interrupted and said "Now I think that it would be very bad to have any wrong statements made by anybody that would hurt the acceptance of this agreement by our people." He said, "I am wondering about a statement that you made yesterday on the radio, Mr. Beatty. It went to the effect that if realtors are forced to sell and rent to Negroes, the real estate industry will go out of business." Beatty then responded in a very confusing way saying that he had been widely quoted and misquoted and not agreeing or disagreeing that he had made such a statement. He said, "But this is a complicated thing; it is extremely difficult, and we will do all we can." Then he began to equivocate and express the fact that I am sure is prevalent among real estate men. (They are completely out of touch with their time when, with their backs to the wall, when even wanting to do something, they are so far out of touch that they don't even know what to do. They don't understand. They are the last people to be dragged into our century.) He expressed this in a way that one could see looking at Mayor Daley that even upset Mayor Daley. He went on to say in response to King's request "We'll do all we can, but I don't know how to do it. Frankly, I am confused. The last two weeks have been the most confusing of all my life. I think that there are a lot of specifics that we just aren't going to be able to work out here. But I hope that everyone will understand that we are all not bums. Real Estate dealers are people and we need commitment from all people in this community, but on the other hand we are not hedging on anything." Well, his statement made everybody very nervous, even Mayor Daley. I could see that Daley was afraid that Beatty was going to blow the deal, because it sounded after his statement like nothing was firm.

Bishop Montgomery then jumped into the picture and said, "Well I want to say that we all recognize this is a joint problem and Section 8, Part 3, of the agreement speaks to Mr. Beatty's need. I know it is hard for Mr. Beatty to represent those that he does not have authority over. But we need to give, and we are committing ourselves to give massive support to the Chicago Real Estate Board in its efforts."

Then Bob Johnston spoke, Regional Director of the United Auto Workers, the only union person who has attempted to keep a close relationship with the Movement but still a person with a close relationship with the Democratic party and Mayor Daley. (At one point it was clear that he was acting as an agent for the status quo and the administration but counter pressures were applied and he moved close to the Movement. None-the-less, the Movement was unhappy about his role). He said, "This is a historical document that we can accept with pride. No city has had a similar breakthrough and no one ought to leave without a definite and a full commitment. The executive committee of the AFL-CIO met last week and reaffirmed its commitment to non-discrimination and I called Walter Reuther this morning and he said 'We will do everything we can do to cooperate in the implementation of this agreement.' And I have gotten specific commitments of support for this agreement from many unions. Specifically the following unions have made agreements: Amalgamated Clothing Workers, Furniture Workers, the State, City, County and Municipal Employees Union, Oil and Chemical Workers, United Auto Workers, ILGWU, Shoe Workers, Metallurgical Workers, United Transport Workers, Packinghouse Workers, Textile Workers, and the International Association of Machinists. Also I want to say that I have a staff of forty-three members and all of them are going to be committed and totally committed to the implementation of this agreement." Then he went rambling on in a speech making points that one could not discern. He closed by saying that Milton Olive, Jr. would represent the UAW in further meetings of this nature and that he felt that this agreement could be a design for every major city.

Al Raby then said "Before we vote, I think we should understand that this vote is indicative of an intent to facilitate the agreement. We can't accept a vote that is binding. It should only be an indication of sentiment."

Ben Heineman, together with Mayor Daley, was pushing for a vote that made clear the fact that all were in complete agreement with the document that had been established. Heineman said, "Let me say that the Chair concedes that there has been a lot of hard work in getting this document together. And normally I don't believe in votes; I don't believe in overly structured efforts of this nature, but I would think that the Chicago Freedom Movement would want a unanimous and a binding vote and on the other hand I am sure that those who are committing themselves to the Movement's demands, want also to see the Movement's commitment." Then Al Raby said, "Well, before we take such a vote I think we may need to caucus on the details. We want to be sure of some things. It is unfair for any of us to make commitments unless we are perfectly clear, so I ask for a fifteen minute recess." It was clear that Heineman and Daley were not enthusiastic about this idea, and that they wanted a vote and acceptance, and to close the affair. But the meeting was adjourned for a fifteen minute recess.

During the recess the Freedom Movement people walked out, and it was my understanding that in the debate the people who were not in favor ultimately of accepting the agreement were Jim Bevel and Jesse Jackson, who were the two essential Negro Southern Christian Leadership Conference leaders of the marches. (I think this has great significance, that the two people who had been leading the marchers, who were most in touch with them and who would have to sell the marchers on discontinuing the marches, were the people who were most opposed to the agreement as it stood. And I suppose I should record here that in my mind after ten years of working with and in government that the document as it read in my mind was so vague as to be an unreliable instrument for securing significant progress.)

When the meeting was reconvened, Dr. King spoke first. "We have decided that we are prepared to vote on the issue before us and we want to agree that this is a most significant document. However, we have one or two questions that still remain. First, while we recognize that this was not a matter involved in these negotiations, we are much concerned about the injunction we face." (Here he was speaking about the injunction that Mayor Daley had secured after the initial negotiating meetings; the injunction that limited the Movement to one march a day, in the daytime, twenty-four hours

141

notice, no more that 500 people, in one neighborhood only). "We feel that injunction is unjust and unconstitutional. Thousands of people were deeply hurt as a result of the injunction. Now if we want to have a great meeting at Soldiers Field and to march to City Hall with thousands of people as we did then, we can't do that. This denies freedom of assembly. If we want to have a great march, only 500 people can march and thousands of people will be denied their freedom of assembly. We are acting in good faith and since we are, we will agree to limit the demonstrations. And, therefore, we want to know if the City will withdraw the injunction; we make the request of the city 'What will you do?' Second, we are very concerned still about implementation. Maybe we are over-sensitive but there have been so many promises that haven't materialized, that this is a great thing in our minds. We want to know if the continuing body that will be established to hammer out the specifics will be an action body or whether it will be just a forum. We want to know how soon it will be underway. Because ultimately we want to know how soon a Negro can go to a real estate office and feel reasonably sure that he will get fair treatment: that he will be served. And we also want to know how we can deal with the Negro that is not served."

Bishop Montgomery then said, "On Monday, we hope to have the organizing body set up and an action group and ready to roll."

Rev. Zimmerman of the Presbytery of Chicago and Chairman of the Church Federation of Greater Chicago stood up and made a speech which stunned everyone. I think he said, "This matter of an injunction has troubled me and I remember at our last meeting we heard one individual" (he was referring to James Bevel) "who said that he did not like the legal recourse as an approach to resolving these problems and that he felt that he wanted to go to a real estate office and be served and not to a commission. However, recourse to the courts is the basis of our society, and indeed it is a right and an obligation to use the courts and I would like to see this injunction tested in the Supreme Court of the United States, so that we can know, finally, what rights people have to assembly and petition." Dr. King interrupted and said, "I'm sure you're aware that this will take at least three years and $200,000 of the Movement's resources to get an answer to." "Well," said Zimmerman, "perhaps it could be at least a continuing item to be discussed on the agenda." Al Raby was so affronted by Zimmerman's proposal that he stood up and said, "I am forced to respond here. I don't see that the judicial process has really helped the Negro. I think it is very gratuitous of anyone to suggest that we suffer this injunction for three years just to get a legal opinion, because legal opinions haven't done us much good. The same process, the process of legal opinion, got us twelve years ago a decision of the United States Supreme Court that would have integrated schools, that segregation would be done away with. And the result of that legal opinion twelve years later is largely insignificant. We want from the city an answer and not a debate. I felt it was bad faith for the City on Wednesday to say that they would negotiate with us and then go out on Friday and seek an injunction against us."

Mayor Daley then stood and was not flustered when he said, "People can make all the statements that they care to about bad faith." Then he went on to make this statement (which was the most coherent and relatively reasonable statements I have ever heard Mayor Daley make), "Last Friday I acted on the recommendation of the Superintendent of Police of Chicago. I want you to know that I was raised in a workingman's community in a workingman's home. My father was a union organizer and we did not like injunctions. I know the injustice of injunctions. But I also faced the decision of what to do with three and a half million people. Because the Superintendent of Police had said that the crime rate was soaring as his police resources, crime fighting resources were being thrown into protecting the Freedom Movement. He also told me that the Freedom Movement wouldn't cooperate on giving him the routes or giving him advance notice or in any way helping him in an effort to provide protection. So the decision had to be made. There were many people who were demanding that we stop the marches entirely, but we said that they had a right for the marches. The course I took was the only one that I could take. I took an oath to preserve law and order and the Constitution. Now as far as this agreement and injunctions are concerned if this agreement is made and everybody keeps to it you will have no worry about the injunction because you won't need to march. And if we agree to the document, then the injunction means nothing to you. We don't want long litigation either and long legal fees and this matter can be heard as an emergency matter, I think. It was with heavy heart, yet firmness, that I sought that injunction. There was no other course for me."

Martin Luther King then said (and I felt here that he felt that Al Raby had gone too far, and he was trying to back away from Raby's position), "I appreciate what Mayor Daley has said, and I know he made the decision with heavy heart. I don't want to stress bad faith. I hope we are operating here by the law of life which is that reconciliation is always possible. But I think

143

I've got to say, that if that injunction stands, somewhere along the way we are going to have to break it. We are going to have to break it tomorrow, or in a week, or a month, or sometime as the Movement proceeds."

Then Ben Heineman interrupted Dr. King and said, "Now I haven't seen the injunction and I'm not interpreting it legally, but as I see it, this agreement has to do with the cessation of neighborhood demonstrations, and I think Dr. King, that you are saying that this injunction isn't limited to neighborhood, enjoining neighborhood marches, but to assemblies as well. Now, Mr. Mayor, would you be willing to sit down with the legal representatives of the Chicago Freedom Movement to negotiate a modification that will allow them broader demonstration rights outside of neighborhood demonstrations?" Mayor Daley said, "The city will sit down and talk over anything with anybody. Speaking specifically, we can amend our injunction, I know, as a lawyer, and we would be glad to sit down and discuss . . ." (Interruption on the tape) ". . . asks whether or not the Mayor will withdraw his injunction and I think we deserve an answer to our question." Before the Mayor could answer, Ben Heineman said, "I think that the Mayor is saying, he will not at this time withdraw the injunction but he will discuss its amendment." The Mayor nodded and then said, "I call for a vote." Al Raby said, "No, let's wait. We want to discuss this more." Then there was a hurried conference around Dr. King with many people saying many things and finally Dr. King said, "I don't think that we can accept a conference to modify the injunction because we are opposed to the injunction totally, but we would accept a separate negotiation through the continuing body on this issue." (Incidentally this position, it seemed to me, was a very, very reasonable one).

At that point the question was called, again by Ben Heineman pushing always for this resolution, and the vote was unanimous.

Ben Heineman then said, "Given the tensions and the problems we faced, I think everyone has conducted themselves in exemplary fashion, and I want to thank everyone who is present here. I am familiar with the trail of broken promises, but I think we are all committed here to seeing that cynicism will not grow as a result of the work of this group. I want to thank everyone."

Mayor Daley then stood and said he wanted to thank Ben Heineman and Tom Ayers for the fine work that they had done. And then Dr. King stood and in his beautiful and magisterial terms, said these closing words. "I do want to express my appreciation for everybody's work and the appreciation of the Chicago Freedom Movement. I want to thank the subcommittee. We read in the scripture, 'Come, let us sit down and reason together,' and everyone here has met the scriptural mandate. There comes a time when we move from protest to reconciliation and we have been misinterpreted by the press and by the political leaders of this town as to our motives and our goals, but let me say once again that it is our purpose, our single purpose to create the beloved community. We seek only to make possible a city where men can live as brothers. I know this has been said many times today, but I want to reiterate again, that we must make this agreement work. Our people's hopes have been shattered too many times, and an additional disillusionment will only spell catastrophe. Our summers of riots have been caused by our winters of delay. I want to stress the need for implementation and I want to recognize that we have a big job. Because I marched through Gage Park, I saw hatred in the faces of so many, a hatred born of fear, and that fear came because people didn't know each other, and they don't know each other because they are separate from one another. So, we must attack that separation and those myths. There is a tremendous educational job ahead of us. Now, we don't want to threaten any additional marches, but if this agreement does not work marches would be a reality. We must now measure our words by our deeds, and it will be hard. I speak to everyone on my side of the table now, and I say that this just be interpreted, this agreement, as a victory for justice and not a victory over the Chicago Real Estate Board of the City of Chicago. I am as grateful to Mayor Daley as to anyone else here for his work. I think now we can go on to make Chicago a beautiful city, a city of brotherhood." And following his speech, there was the only applause of the meeting.

Then Ben Heineman suggested that all the major principals join together in a joint press conference. But Mayor Daley, said, "No, Ben Heineman, why don't you speak for all of us and we will all sit and listen to you." So the press was admitted and while everybody sat, Ben Heineman spoke and as he spoke he said, "This is a great day for Chicago. We are all gathered here and through the great democratic process, we have worked out an agreement."

When Ben Heineman said, "We have worked out through the great democratic process, Al Pitcher turned and started to walk away and said to me, "Democratic process, shit, it was forced out of them!"

The 'Summit Agreement'

AUGUST 26, 1966

Report of the Subcommittee to the
Conference on Fair Housing Convened
by the Chicago Conference on Religion and Race

For the last week, this subcommittee has been discussing a problem that exists in every metropolitan area in America. It has been earnestly seeking immediate, practical, and effective steps which can be taken to create a fair housing market in metropolitan Chicago.

In the City of Chicago itself, the policy of fair housing has been established by the clear statement of purpose in the Chicago Fair Housing Ordinance enacted in 1963. It provides:

1. It is hereby declared the policy of the City of Chicago to assure full and equal opportunity to all residents of the City to obtain fair and adequate housing for themselves and their families in the City of Chicago without discrimination against them because of their race, color, religion, national origin or ancestry.

2. It is further declared to be the policy of the City of Chicago that no owner, lessee, sublessee, assignee, managing agent, or other person, firm or corporation having the right to sell, rent or lease any housing accommodation, within the City of Chicago, or any agent of any of these, should refuse to sell, rent, lease, or otherwise deny or withhold from any person or group of persons such housing accommodations because of the race, color, religion, national origin or ancestry of such person or persons or discriminate against any person because of his race, color, religion, national origin or ancestry in the terms, conditions, or privileges of the sale, rental or lease of any housing accommodation or in the furnishing of facilities or services in connection therewith.

The subcommittee has addressed itself to methods of making the Chicago Ordinance work better, the action which can be taken by various governmental groups, the role of the Chicago Real Estate Board, and how to make further progress towards fair housing in the months ahead. It would be too much to expect complete agreement on either the steps to be taken or their timing. Nevertheless, the representatives at the meetings have undertaken specific and affirmative measures to attack the problem of discrimination in housing. Carrying out these commitments will require substantial investments of time and money by both private and public bodies and the wholehearted effort of many Chicagoans of good will, supported by the cooperation of thousands of others.

In the light of the commitments made and program here adopted and pledged to achieve open housing in the Chicago metropolitan community, the Chicago Freedom Movement pledges its resources to help carry out the program and agrees to a cessation of neighborhood demonstrations on the issue of open housing so long as the program is being carried out.

The subcommittee believes that the program can be a major step forward. It has confidence that this program, and the more extensive measures bound to flow from it, will achieve the objective of affording every resident "full and equal opportunity to obtain fair and adequate housing without discrimination because of race, color, religion, national origin or ancestry."

The participants in this conference have committed themselves to the following action:

1. The Chicago Commission on Human Relations is already acting to require every real estate broker to post a summary of the City's policy on open housing and the requirements of the Fair Housing Ordinance in a prominent position in his place of business. To obtain full compliance with the Fair Housing Ordinance, the Commission will give special emphasis to multiple complaints and will follow up on pledges of non-discrimination resulting from prior conciliation proceedings. The Commission will increase its enforcement staff and has already requested budgetary increases to support a significantly higher level of effective enforcement activity. This will include year-around inquiry to determine the extent of compliance in all areas of the City, but without placing undue burdens on any broker's business. The Commission will initiate proceedings on its own motion where the facts warrant. It will act on all complaints promptly, ordinarily initiating an investigation within 48 hours, as is now the case. In order to facilitate

proceedings on complaints, it has changed its rules to provide for the substitution of attorneys for Commissioners to preside in conciliation and enforcement hearings. Where a formal hearing justifies such action under the ordinance, the licensing of an offending broker will be suspended or revoked.

The City will continue its consistent support of fair housing legislation at the State level and will urge the adoption of such legislation at the 1967 session of the State Legislature.

2. In a significant departure from its traditional position, the Chicago Real Estate Board announced at the August 17 meeting that its Board of Directors had authorized a statement reading in part as follows:

As a leadership organization in Chicago, we state the fundamental principle that freedom of choice in housing is the right of every citizen. We believe all citizens should accept and honor that principle.

****

We have reflected carefully and have decided we will—as a Chicago organization—withdraw all opposition to the philosophy of open occupancy legislation at the state level—provided it is applicable to owners as well as to brokers—and we reserve the right to criticize detail as distinguished from philosophy—and we will request the state association of Real Estate Boards to do likewise but we cannot dictate to them.

While not willing to dismiss its appeal from the decision of the Circuit Court of Cook County upholding the validity of the City's Fair Housing Ordinance, the Board has committed itself effectively to remind its members of their duty to obey the ordinance and to circulate to them the interpretation of the ordinance to be furnished by the Chicago Commission on Human Relations. The individual representatives of the Board also committed themselves to join other realtors to participate in a continuing organization, should one by formed, to promote effective action implementing the principle of freedom of choice in housing.

3. The Chicago Housing Authority will take every action within its power to promote the objectives of fair housing. It recognizes that heavy

concentrations of public housing should not again be built in the City of Chicago. Accordingly, the Chicago Housing Authority has begun activities to improve the character of public housing, including the scattering of housing for the elderly across the city, and initiation of a leasing program which places families in the best available housing without regard to the racial character of the neighborhood in which the leased facilities are provided. In the future, it will seek scattered sites for public housing and will limit the height of new public housing structures in high density areas to eight stories, with housing for families with children limited to the first two stories. Wherever possible, smaller units will be built.

In addition, in order to maximize the usefulness of present facilities and to promote the welfare of the families living in them, a concerted effort will be made to improve the opportunities for satisfactory community life in public housing projects. In order to achieve this improvement the participation of all elements in the surrounding communities will be actively enlisted and utilized.

4. The President of the Cook County Board of Commissioners has advised the chairman of the subcommittee by letter that the Cook County Department of Public Aid will make a renewed and persistent effort to search out the best housing for recipients available within the ceilings authorized by the legislature, regardless of location. Each employee of the Department will be reminded that no recipient is to be prohibited or discouraged from moving into any part of Cook County because of his race, color, or national origin. The Department will not be satisfied if recipients live in less satisfactory accommodations than would be available to them were they of a different race, color or national origin.

Department employees will be instructed to report any discriminatory refusal by real estate brokers to show rental listings to any recipient to the Chicago Commission on Human Relations or the State Department of Registration and Education through the Chief of the Bureau of Housing of the Public Aid Department. Department employees will also encourage recipients who encounter discrimination in dealing with brokers to report such experiences to the same agencies. The Chief of the Bureau of Housing will maintain a close follow-up on all matters that have been thus reported.

5. The Urban Renewal Program has had some success in achieving stable residential integration in facilities built in renewal developments, with the

cooperation of property owners, property managers, community organizations and neighbors. To that end, the Urban Renewal Program will devote itself to producing the same results in its relocation activities and will earnestly solicit the support of all elements of the community in the City, County and metropolitan area in these efforts.

In relocating families, the Department of Urban Renewal will search out the best housing available regardless of location. Each employee of the Department will be reminded that no family is to be prohibited or discouraged from moving into any part of the Chicago metropolitan area because of his race, color, or national origin. Department employees will be instructed to report any discriminatory refusal by a real estate broker to show listings, to the Chicago Commission on Human Relations or the State Department of Registration and Education through the Director of Relocation. They will also encourage families who encounter discrimination in dealing with a broker to report such experiences to the same agencies. The Director of Relocation will maintain a close follow-up on all matters that have thus been reported.

6. The Cook County Council of Insured Savings Associations, by letter, and the Chicago Mortgage Bankers Association, at the Committee meeting on August 17, 1966, have affirmed that their policy is to provide equal service to and to lend mortgage money to all qualified families, without regard to race, for the purchase of housing anywhere in the metropolitan area.

7. Assistant Attorney General Roger Wilkins, head of the Community Relations Service of the United States Department of Justice, has advised the chairman of the subcommittee that the Service will inquire into the questions raised, under existing law, with respect to service by the Federal Deposit Insurance Corporation and the Federal Savings and Loan Insurance Corporation to financial institutions found guilty of practicing racial discrimination in the provision of financial service to the public. While the matter is a complex one, it will be diligently pursued.

8. The leaders of the organized religious communities in the metropolitan area have already expressed their commitment to the principle of open housing.

The Chicago Conference on Religion and Race, which is co-sponsored by the Catholic Archdiocese of Chicago, the Church Federation of Greater Chicago, the Chicago Board of Rabbis and the Union of American Hebrew Congregations, pledges its support to the program outlined and will enlist the full strength of its constituent bodies and their churches and synagogues in effecting equal access to housing in the metropolitan area for all people. They pledge to:

(1)   Educate their membership on the moral necessity of an open and just community.

(2)   Urge owners to sell or rent housing without racial restriction.

(3)   Support local real estate offices and lending institutions in their cooperation with this program.

(4)   Cooperate with and aid in the establishment of responsible community organizations and support them in the implementation of these programs.

(5)   Undertake to secure peaceful acceptance and welcome of Negro families prior to and at the time of their entrance into any community.

(6)   Use their resources to help make housing available without racial discrimination.

(7)   Establish, within 30 days, one or more housing centers, with the assistance of the real estate and housing industry and financial institutions, to provide information and help in finding suitable housing for minority families and to urge them to take advantage of new housing opportunities.

9. The representatives of the Chicago Association of Commerce and Industry, the Commercial Club, the Cosmopolitan Chamber of Commerce, Chicago Mortgage Bankers Association, Metropolitan Housing and Planning Council, Chicago Federation of Labor and Industrial Union Council, and other secular groups represented in these discussions recognize that their organizations have a major stake in working out the problems of fair housing. Each such representative welcomes and pledges support to the program outlined in this report. Further, each undertakes to secure the support of his organization and its members, whether individuals, corporations, locals or groups, for the program and their participation in it, including education of their members on the importance to them of fair housing throughout the Chicago metropolitan area.

10. The Chicago Conference on Religion and Race will initiate forthwith the formation of a separate, continuing body, sponsored by major leadership organizations in the Chicago metropolitan area and built on a nucleus of the representatives of the organizations participating here. This body should accept responsibility for the education and action programs necessary to achieve fair housing. It should be headed by a board consisting of recognized leaders from government, commerce, industry, finance, religion, real estate, labor, the civil rights movement, and the communications media. Its membership should reflect the diverse racial and ethnic composition of the entire Chicago metropolitan community.

The proposed board should have sufficient stature to formulate a strong and effective program and to provide adequate financing and staff to carry out that program. To the extent of available resources, it should carry forward programs such as, but not limited to, the convening of conferences on fair housing in suburban communities to the end that the policy of the City of Chicago on fair housing will be adopted in the whole Chicago metropolitan area. There must be a major effort in the pulpits, in the school systems, and in all other available forums to educate citizens of the metropolitan area in the fundamental principle that freedom of choice in housing is the right of every citizen and in their obligations to abide by the law and recognize the rights of others regardless of race, religion, or nationality. The group should assist in the drafting of fair housing laws and ordinances. It should make clear the stake that commerce, industry, banking, real estate, and labor, indeed all residing in the metropolitan area, have in the peaceful achievement of fair housing. The group should emphasize that the metropolitan housing market is a single market. The vigor and growth of that market is dependent upon an adequate supply of standard housing available without discrimination. The group should promote such practical measures as the development of fair housing centers after the model now being established by the Chicago Conference on Religion and Race. The group should in the immediate future set up specific goals for achievement of fair housing in the Chicago metropolitan area. Finally, the board should regularly review the performance of the program undertaken by governmental and non-governmental groups, take appropriate action thereon, and provide for public reports.

Although all of the metropolitan areas of the country are confronted with the problem of segregated housing, only in Chicago have the top leaders of the religious faiths, commerce and industry, labor and government sat down together with leaders in the civil rights movement to seek practical solutions. With the start that has been made, the subcommittee is confident that the characteristic drive of Chicagoans to achieve their goals, manifest in the Chicago motto of "I Will," will enable the Chicago metropolitan area to lead the rest of the nation in the solution of the problems of fair housing.

Respectfully submitted,

THOMAS G. AYERS,
Chairman

The Chicago Freedom Movement: What is It?

ALVIN PITCHER

Is there a Chicago Freedom Movement? To answer that question formally is very difficult because the formal existence of the Chicago Freedom Movement is very tenuous. It may well be that the formal organization as such will not exist very long.

Informally it is a loose arrangement of cooperative action in which the Coordinating Council of Community Organizations, the Southern Christian Leadership Conference, the Industrial Union Department of AFL-CIO, and a few other groups work together.

The real focus, so far as there is any formal organization of the Chicago Freedom Movement, is the Agenda Committee. After struggling for many months to develop a formal organization, it was decided to operate somewhat informally with an Assembly of the Chicago Freedom Movement and an Agenda Committee. The Agenda Committee was approved by the Assembly, but in a sense it was not legitimated in any way; CCCO delegates never really voted to accept it as the organization of the Chicago Freedom

This paper was written in November, 1966. It is published here for the first time.

Movement. It was hoped that if the Movement operated informally for a time, its legitimacy would evolve from action. This unfortunately has not occurred. The Agenda Committee was appointed by Albert Raby, Convener of CCCO and Martin Luther King, President of SCLC. The members of the committee included representation from most of the main Civil Rights groups in the city. These are the Urban League, American Friends Service Committee, Catholic Interracial Council, The Woodlawn Organization, West Side Federation, United Auto Workers, Packinghouse Workers, and City Missionary Society. West Side Organization, a so-called grassroots organization, and Operation Breadbasket are also represented. Representing full-time staff for the Movement are Andrew Young, James Bevel, Jesse Jackson, and Alvin Pitcher. IUD, JOIN, and KOCO were scheduled to become a part of the Agenda Committee but because of disruptions in CCCO, this has never taken place. It was the thinking that this base would be broadened as soon as an organization obtained a certain measure of power (particularly community organizations would be added to the Agenda Committee); then the base would be shifted from the old-line organizations to the community-mass organizations. The Agenda Committee, then, is still the operative base of the Chicago Freedom Movement. How long it can retain its power is difficult to predict.

There are a whole series of activities that are very loosely connected to the Agenda Committee; this is why the whole organization is so loose. Movement activities take place usually not on the initiative of the Agenda Committee but by the initiative of the Movement staff. Once an action is underway the Agenda Committee usually baptizes it. The lay leadership of the Freedom Movement is involved in big human relations organizations and their energies and creative possibilities are almost totally absorbed by those responsibilities; therefore, since their time is limited for overall Freedom Movement activities, it is only logical that the initiative comes from the full-time staff.

There are several staffs involved, but primarily the Movement projects are carried out by three—the CCCO staff which involves about four people, the SCLC staff which has twelve to fourteen people, and the IUD staff which employs labor as well as Movement people. Other organizations also have staff for the various activities which feed into the Freedom Movement and are considered part of the whole Chicago operation.

To illustrate the involvement of organizations in a Movement activity, one could study the Englewood Action Program. The Englewood Action centers around the problem of urban renewal in that community. For five years the Green Street Association has been fighting the hard battle to save their homes from becoming parking lots. The Englewood Civic Organization, a more militant organization has also joined the battle against urban renewal and the business community. This program was presented to some of the CCCO-SCLC staff as a situation that could be escalated into a fight against the whole program of urban renewal as well as a fight for improving the total community. This program seemed to be an ideal situation for the Freedom Movement. The community has the second largest business center in the city, the third in the Metropolitan area; therefore it was a very visible target. If the community, mostly Negro, could withdraw its purchasing power from the businesses, there would be a real leverage for helping the whole community. The business community happens to be very influential in the power structure of the city. The president of the Chicago City Bank in Englewood and the president of Sears, which has a large store in the community, are both very close to the Mayor and the machine. Furthermore in the process of evolving Operation Breadbasket, which is a force to secure jobs for Negroes, Jesse Jackson has developed a group of Negro and white ministers that are very loyal to the Movement and to King. They have the potential to be the vehicle for mobilization in that community. Therefore there seemed to be an ideal mobilizing device and a good target to try to influence. This discussion and calculation took place in the staff coordinating committee. Thus a decision was made almost apart from the sanction of the Agenda Committee. In theory the responsibility for such a decision for the Movement was recognized but things moved ahead, in fact, without the approval of the Agenda Committee. Eventually they baptized the project.

The Englewood Action Committee is made up of the Green Street Association, the Englewood Civic Organization, SCLC, CCCO, Operation Breadbasket, and the Student Union. This illustrates the way in which forces that represent a lot of different facets of the Movement come together in an action.

The major coordinating device other than the Agenda Committee is the Staff Coordinating Committee. This is a very loose control of staff. It is an attempt to bring representatives of the different projects that claim to be part of the Freedom Movement together in order to discuss the various activities—their progress, their problems, and possible solutions. It is an informal device because nobody truly runs the committee. James Bevel, Stoney Cooks, Jesse Jackson, Bernard Lafayette and Al Pitcher attempt to get the various people to the weekly meeting. Jesse Jackson represents Operation Breadbasket, Sol Ice represents CHA and CCCO, Bill Moyer represents the Open Housing Follow-up committee, Chickulas and Ted Black represent IUD and the Labor Center. Representing the tenant Unions are Bill Briggs for East Garfield Park, Sam Smith for Lawndale and Bernard Lafayette for the Federation of Tenants Union. Al Sampson represents the Co-op and Jim Wilson represents the Student Union. The Englewood Action Committee is not formally represented at Staff Coordinating committee nor is the Education committee which is really a CCCO activity, not a Movement activity. There are other operations which are also part of the loosely defined Freedom Movement. The Student Union and the Co-op are both SCLC activities. The Labor Center is a combination, SCLC provides and pays the salaries of eight people, IUD provides and pays the salaries of ten, and CCCO pays the salary of one of the staff of the center. This description, although somewhat confusing, may give some feel for what the Movement is and is not. It may also show how loose it is but how real it is in terms of the kinds of things that are going on.

In order to determine just what is going on in the city, it is necessary to look at a few of the operations linked to the Freedom Movement.

Operation Breadbasket is a movement instituted by SCLC that endeavors to get jobs for Negroes. The Chicago operation, like the Philadelphia operation and like the Atlanta operation, asks companies to reconsider their hiring policies. If they refuse, pressure is applied in terms of picketing and the withdrawal of purchasing power. If this is effective, then the atmosphere is right for negotiating for jobs and for the upgrading of Negro employees. There are plans to expand this program—to relate to major economic institutions where the Negroes can gain some power. There is hope of taking insurance companies, construction companies, and developing Negro economic power by relating the self-interest of these various phases of the Negro community with the Freedom Movement so that the Freedom Movement will profit in many ways. We already have profited by the kind of support it gets when there is a real economic benefit, for example from some Negro manufacturers who can now put their products in major chain stores, at least in the ghetto. There are problems, of course, in terms of their using the Movement for their own purposes, but Operation Breadbasket is expanding quite rapidly and successfully.

The open housing follow-up committee is attempting to police and to renegotiate the open housing summit agreement. It is striving to figure out what could be the solutions in achieving open housing for the total city.

The urban renewal committee is a new committee that has just been formed as a result of the Englewood action, when it became evident that there should be an attempt to tackle the whole problem of urban renewal in the city. Various people attend the meeting—professors of architecture, city planners, former city planners, the community people as well as people just interested in the whole problem of urban renewal. We hope it will develop a program, as was done in open housing, first to see what justifiably could be asked for, and then to work out some strategy in order to get enough power to bring about real change. The Englewood Action, in a sense, is a part of this urban renewal action but it is also a separate action too. It is not responsible to this committee and the only relationship is that some of the people from the Englewood action program participate in the city-wide committee. The Agenda Committee can do little about the committee except perhaps to remove some of the staff. This points out again that things are done independently. Even though there are affirmations that things have to be cleared through a central committee, the control is very indirect.

The Labor Center, again, is a very independent action. Its chief power is the IUD which came in with the thesis that they had to develop a community program as over against a mere labor organizing program in order to develop their own interests. The labor center is chiefly active in organizing hospital and retail workers. (These activities have been stymied by various problems. The Hospital Organization has been dropped.) It also provides staff for the tenant unions. The Federation of Tenant Unions is also seen as a loose part of the Movement. In a sense East Garfield Park and Lawndale are more closely allied to the Movement than are the others in the Federation such as JOIN, South Shore, KOCO, and TAC. This informal relationship is due partly to the fact that they relate to SCLC and that they receive financial support or staff from SCLC. IUD was allegedly going to provide some money for Lawndale but backed out when the Federation voted thirteen to two to make it mandatory that representation on the Federation Board was to be tenants only. Charlie Chickulas, chairman of IUD, had previously chaired the tenant union group. Although this was good participatory democracy, the result was that IUD withdrew its financial offer from Lawndale. Although somewhat sketchy, this is the essence of the program of the Chicago Freedom Movement. There are various operations that are under loose sponsorship of the informal Freedom Movement.

DISCUSSION OF THE FREEDOM MOVEMENT

Question: Are you saying that IUD is basically in favor of the support of the staff of the Tenant Unions but that it does not favor the committee being made up of tenants rather than staff?

Answer: IUD withdrew support on the basis of the Lawndale Union's support of the tenants as the real power over against the staff.

Question: You mean that if IUD did not have a real power voice in the organization they were not going to support it?

Answer: The implication is, really, that they were going to bargain for a more significant role other than just an advisory role. This is a real problem in their functioning, they are better organized and they favor a tight organization. IUD is, also, supporting an office in the Spanish community which is more or less very informally tied to the Movement. They are providing the money for the Spanish American people to picket and boycott and do other things in the interest of minority groups.

STATUS OF SCLC STAFF

Question: Is the reduction of SCLC staff significant of anything at all?

Answer: It's a shortage of money and a deterioration of morale, purpose, and meaning. People are leaving—going to school, going to other places. I'd say that there is a deterioration in the morale.

Question: The staff has dropped from about forty-five to twelve, hasn't it?

Answer: I'd say it is about thirty, but I never know what the staff is. There are so many people who volunteer on the staff that you can't quite tell who is on the staff.

Question: Why the deterioration?

Answer: The deterioration was due to a lack of administration and to the disillusionment with our achievements. Some of these people who did not know what to do before are now attached to something. The theory now is to attach each staff person to someone in one of the actions and then they will begin to function. Many have been floating around without the direct supervision that seems to be necessary in order to get accomplishments. One of the SCLC theories, as I understand it, is that each is given a kind of personal freedom. However there is a limit to the kind of freedom that many people can use constructively. The staff wants, just like children, both freedom and a lot of guidance and direction. They want a project which calls them there at 9 o'clock in the morning and demands a certain amount of discipline. The Student Union is an example. It was to be a city-wide organizing attempt. Our thesis was that there was no point in organizing a union in the city unless there is an outlet for it in some action. Therefore we have tried to relate everything to tie in with something, where there is not only some kind of control but where there is some action instead of a kind of diffuseness of the programming that seems to characterize some of the SCLC. I must say that many Chicago operations are equally diffuse.

THE AGENDA COMMITTEE

Question: Does the nature of the Agenda Committee represent a kind of compromise between formal organization and informal leadership? It is not really a source of power, is it?

Answer: It is a source of power. Formally it is the authority in the Freedom Movement. What I was trying to say about it emphasized the loose way in which it exercises its authority. This can be illustrated by the summer Open Housing program. The summer action that created an atmosphere for negotiations with the powers of the city was produced by the action committee composed chiefly of staff. But the summit agreement was negotiated by the Agenda Committee. The staff represented on the Agenda Committee (Bevel, Jackson, Pitcher) were not really considered on the same level with the other members. To emphasize this, in the first negotiation of the summit conference, only Bevel and Burt Ransom were included from the action committee. In the first appointment neither Jackson nor I was included. Bevel objected and so Jackson was included; it was not until later that I was included. However the leadership was taken by the Agenda Committee; therefore the Agenda Committee conceived of itself as a real authority. This became clear in the continual fight between Raby and the action committee for control. There was not much effort to exercise informal authority but a real effort to establish the fact of authority even to the point of having documents written that clearly stated the relationship between the action people, or the staff people, and the formal authority in the Agenda Committee represented by Raby.

Question: It would be fair to say that the Agenda Committee is a representative kind of structure that can decide who is really going to speak, such as in some negotiations?

Answer: The Agenda Committee discusses that and appoints the people. There are no rules of procedure for operation in the Agenda Committee.

Question: Does a majority carry it?

Answer: I don't recall any occasion when it was necessary to be that formal—once or twice.

Question: What about when another group is brought in?

Answer: Nobody has really been brought in since the formation. There was a proposal about other groups, and that would have been announced by King and Raby at the Freedom Movement Assembly. Raby would have probably pushed it through on his authority. Now this is what they are resenting and reacting against.

Question: Wasn't Chester Robinson brought in?

Answer: No, he was in from the beginning. All of the members of the Agenda Committee were formally announced when it was initiated.

Question: How were the members of the Agenda Committee selected?

Answer: On the basis of their power. There were two things functioning—economic contribution and potential troops.

Question: Was Lucas barred?

Answer: No.

Question: Is there any provision for a review or a replacement of the Chicago Freedom Movement.

Answer: There is no formal constitution or by-laws. John McDermott of CIC prepared a new constitution in detail but nothing ever came of it. There is a real lack of executive leadership in the Freedom Movement. It takes real pressure to carry something like that out and this just doesn't happen. We took another way because of the problems of getting anything accepted. Part of it is time. The Agenda Committee members are busy. Part of it is Al Raby's leadership. Part of it is the lack of strong SCLC leadership. Young, who represents King's authority is in and out of the city. Hence, coordination of CCCO-SCLC leadership is difficult.

Question: Is it also a lack of power on Raby's part?

Answer: No, I don't think so. I think at any point at which the kind of leadership of the Freedom Movement represented by the Agenda Committee had decided it wanted to get something done and would pay the political price to organize the people, it could have gotten something accomplished. It had to pay some political price in terms of time and education, but I think they could have won the day just with votes. But it takes a lot of energy.

Question: I would like your reaction. I think that Raby is constitutionally grooved, and that he is very uncomfortable.

Answer: SCLC operates, I'd say, without much formal organization. They will assert this in principle, and Andrew Young will represent this to the highest degree. Bevel may believe in organization but he does not execute it. From the very beginning it was clear that a strong person as executive director of the Chicago Freedom Movement was needed. The person who could be appointed had to be strong enough to work with Bevel; there are only three or four people in the country that could possibly qualify. It is not only a question of control, it is also a matter of informal relations, respect and trust. We were not able to find the person. At first it was thought that Young had to be here all of the time, but that wasn't possible. It was thought that possibly Walter Fauntroy from Washington, D.C. could take the position, but that did not work out. Therefore everything that is on that chart in one sense is an annotation to the lack of anybody to direct. It has all been instituted in a way in order to try to get informal control. Bevel doesn't really function as staff coordinator. He frequently chairs the meeting but all the work is done by other people. In coordination, Stoney Cooks works with the SCLC staff without any formal authority or power, status or anything else. I also try to work with the coordination. Still one does not have the formal authority, and in a sense Bevel or Jackson can upset anything one does do because no one really has control over them.

Question: Would a decision to fight CHA in East Garfield Park be brought to the Agenda Committee?

Answer: No, that decision would probably be discussed in the urban renewal committee and the Staff Coordination committee because the real fight involves the staff. It involved King, Bevel, Jackson, or Lafayette. I have great confidence in the strategy ideas of Bevel, Jackson, and Lafayette; without them, it would seem to me, that we would fall back into the same CCCO pattern of a kind of thrust here and a thrust there without any overall view of how to develop a strategy with a purpose for direct action.

Question: Is the Staff Coordinating Committee more of a strategy committee than the Agenda Committee?

Answer: That has been called the great debate. The action committees were first called strategy committees; then there was a debate because the Agenda Committee felt that it ought to make strategy, so we called them action committees. There is still a debate as to the difference between strategy and tactics and there always will be. I was quite content not to define it but tried to see what we could do to get as many decisions as possible taken to the Agenda Committee for their approval either before or after action began.

Question: What kind of things are brought up in the Agenda Committee, summit negotiations, representation issues?

Answer: Not only the representation but also the content of the summit agreement. They all went to meetings and spent a lot of time dealing with the content. The whole committee met several times to deal with the proposals, and a subcommittee met innumerable times to deal with the preliminary proposals.

Question: Does the Agenda Committee OK agencies that spring up or new organizations?

Answer: For the most part they do not institute them. They don't do that kind of planning. The finance committee is an example. Since the Movement is in bad shape financially, I suggested to Bill Stein, SCLC fund raiser, that we ought to get a finance committee formed in order to raise some money. I suggested persons for the committee to Raby, he suggested some changes, and then we took the committee proposal to the Agenda Committee. We also discussed primarily a kind of budget; they approved of doing something about the financial situation. Occasionally we get the committee to be a planning group that thinks things through. It really needs to meet three times longer than it does to fulfill its functions. Our agenda usually includes eight major items and we usually cover two.

Question: Do you think that the Agenda Committee is a viable instrument?

Answer: I think that it is a necessary instrument, but it could function more creatively and constructively. It could legitimate a lot of the things that now have to happen informally; this would avoid a lot of the frictions that have occurred. If it had been strong, we would have had a legitimate Freedom Movement a long time ago. The kind of frictions that are now occurring on the basis of a failure in process and a failure to legitimate, would not have occurred. The kind of oppositions that would have occurred would have occurred in a different climate. They would have had to deal with the content and not the process, and that would have taken a lot of the sting out of the opposition although there still would be opposition.

Question: I think that up to now there has been an inverse relation between the Agenda Committee and CCCO, that the Agenda Committee has acted to get rid of the constituency.

Answer: What needed to happen was more meetings of the Chicago Freedom Assembly in which the members of the CCCO were really the major ingredient. In this way they would have all participated in these decisions, by hearing reports, by being informed about what was going on, and then by making commitments to programs adopted. This did not happen because of a lack of leadership and lethargy.

CCCO—WHAT IS IT?

It is now important to engage in a formal discussion of what CCCO is. The major group, in size, in the Chicago Freedom Movement is CCCO. It is divided into types of organizations. The civil rights citywide and national organizations are Urban League, NAACP, CORE, SNCC, NALC and the National Lawyers Guild. The church groups that are represented are CIC, ESCRU, liberal churches, the United Church of Christ, Methodist, AFSC and the Lutherans. United Auto Workers and Packing House Workers represent labor. The particular Chicago civil rights groups are Committee to End Discrimination, the Chicago Medical Institutions, Freedom of Residence, Cook County Physicians, Citizens Housing, Lincoln Dental Association, Social Workers for Human Rights and Teachers for Integrated Schools. There are the Community Organizations which number twelve including JOIN. WSO is the only community group that has been active in the Movement and is not a part of CCCO. CCCO was ready to accept organizational dues, but it never got any statement of WSO's desire to join. It could be negotiated. They gave $1,000 to CCCO. City Missionary Service gave them $2,000 with the understanding that CCCO would get $1,000.

Austin Community Organization and the Urban Training Center faculty have applied to CCCO but have not been accepted yet. Special church groups include the Ecumenical Institute, the University of Chicago Divinity School, etc. Other special groups are Tenants Action Council, Association of Social Workers, IUPAE, etc.

We then have the SCLC spawned groups—East Garfield Park Tenant Union, Lawndale Tenant Union, the Co-op, Student Union, and Operation Breadbasket.

IUD sponsors hospital workers, retail workers, etc. They work with the Federation of Tenants Union. It is not something that they spawned but they provide services for it. They also support TAC, Lawndale Tenants Union, LADO, and East Garfield Park Tenant Unions.

The SCLC staff should be considered to be a unity. SCLC really functions as a staff, a kind of entity in and of itself. This, then, is a general picture of organizations that make up the Freedom Movement.

DISCUSSION OF THE ORGANIZATIONS

Question: Within CCCO, what are the strengths or contributions? Can you differentiate the title of Coordinating Council of Community Organizations from the category called community organizations and how are these loosely based community organizations participating?

Answer: TWO is participating very little. Rev. Brazier occasionally comes to the Agenda Committee and stays only a short time. JOIN is increasingly active and cooperative. Rennie Davis, for example, is very active in the Urban Renewal Committee. CCCO is relevant in the Movement; it is not simply a SCLC operated thing. The Urban Renewal committee has a large number of our own organizations. South Shore is new and not very strong. West Side Federation is a paper organization so far. West Chatham Improvement Organization is a middle-class organization that could be powerful and has quite a constituency which could be related. Roseland Heights is not too strong. Morgan Park Planning Association is weak. Mile Square does not relate very much; they do come to meetings and they do produce troops on almost any major occasion. KOCO is having her own problems, but it has been related. For example, in Gage Park KOCO people lost five cars indicating they were part of the summer activity. Englewood Civic Organization is weak and the Englewood Community Organization is the opposition in a real sense. Chatham-Avalon has really pulled out. Altgeld Murray is very weak in terms of its cooperation. When these organizations are surveyed, it points out the lack of strength in the Freedom Movement.

In the beginning strategy, the Open Housing action was conceived of as using the Community organizations in order to build platoons which would feed into the activity. One day one organization would go into and test a community. The next day another organization would do the same thing. The effort to escalate that action fast, because King wanted it escalated in the light of many things, may have destroyed that possibility because there was not enough staff or time to develop these community organizations. It became a city-wide Movement based on mass meetings and press relations. However in its intent it was to combine the two factors, as Bernard Lafayette said, two days a week to work for the Movement and five days to work in their own communities. We failed to accomplish this task. In the Englewood Operation we have the Englewood Civic Organization which we hope to develop during the course of events. In the Urban Renewal program as a whole, there will probably be five or six community organizations. KOCO, Lawndale, Englewood are part of the urban renewal operation now. The whole Urban Renewal push if developed in the right direction should feed in, develop and strengthen the whole organization. This would happen because we would be servicing our community organizations. This would be ideal for the Freedom Movement—to strengthen its community organizations, to service them by giving them planning help as well as other things. Stan Hallett of the Church federation has agreed to take the planning aspect in terms of the whole community and to provide a group of planners to be of service. Nobody can do that on his own, but as a part of the whole picture, this service could be provided. This is the kind of scheme that could be worked on so that the organizations would be tied into the whole. They would feel a need for the total organization and the whole would feel a need for each part.

Question: It has been said that the Movement goes on somewhat apart from CCCO. I have a feeling that it goes on somewhat apart from the neighborhood community organizations.

Answer: CHA depends upon CCCO staff; Operation Breadbasket, Open Housing, Urban Renewal, the Labor Center, Englewood Action, the Co-op or the Student Union do not rely directly upon CCCO for support. Very few activities are dependent upon anything CCCO supplies. One of the reasons is that CCCO does not have much to supply. Not counting myself, because I work in most of these areas, CCCO has only three people. Gene Tournour is working with the hospital workers, Sol Ice works generally, and Loretta Hall works with CHA. As far as direct resources are concerned,

CCCO does not have any money so if we do not provide staff, we do not do much. Al Raby and I relate to many of the actions in many different ways. There are, in addition, some people who on many occasions can come through in various ways—with resources. CCCO has meetings at the Packing House, or at the Labor Center—these will provide resources, occasionally money, and occasionally a kind of power and representation.

Question: Is it still a question of who is CCCO? The neighborhood community organizations are not doing a great deal.

Answer: The NAACP is out, CORE does not amount to much, SNCC is not active in CCCO, NALC is very weak although they are being revised and may gain some strength. CIC is very strong, active and very loyal. ESCRU does quite a bit, PIC has not done much, the Methodists have a small amount of leadership, and, the United Church of Christ is weak. The American Friends have provided Lafayette, Moyer, and Ransom—three full time persons for the Freedom Movement. Lafayette is active on the West side in various projects. Moyer is head of the Open Housing Follow-up committee which requires full time attention. He was head of the action center on the south side during the summer marches. It was the Friends and the SCLC staff with some assistance from me and my assistant that ran the summer activities. A very concrete kind of participation and help that is invaluable came from the Friends. I use this illustration in order to show the concrete way in which organizations could supply staff and resources.

Question: One way of looking at the problem of CCCO or any of these groups is to say "What is the quality and number of staff that can really back the action?" This is decisive.

Answer: That is why I started to work on finances because we do not even have the finances to keep this staff after the first of November. The only real permanent source of income to CCCO comes from a group of Negro businessmen who contribute regularly.

THE FUTURE OF THE MOVEMENT

One other aspect that needs to be treated formally is the question—where is the Freedom Movement headed? I do not have concrete answers, but I think that it is headed toward Urban Renewal. I do not know who will make the decision. It is headed toward the organization of the unorganized among the Negro population. It is headed toward development of Negro economic institutions and jobs for Negroes. It is headed toward the development of tenant unions. I think that these are the major programs. That does not mean that there is no work being done in the field of education. As you have seen in the papers, members of CCCO are to work on educational task forces. As far as the Movement is concerned, pressure on the Board of Education will be held in abeyance probably for three or four months until Dr. Redmond is tested and tried for PR purposes if for no other.

SCLC is kind of withdrawing. I do not know if it will continue in that direction. Somebody said King was to write a book beginning in December.

The other thing that we don't have is politics because formally we don't have any group that is dealing with it. In spite of the fact that somebody made a motion at a meeting, we have not formed the committee.

Question: In the area of urban renewal, in what direction are you headed? Does this mean communal area renewal, housing, etc. in the ghetto, or does it mean something rather specific?

Answer: What it really means is the redevelopment of communities using the instrument of urban renewal, but it could be another instrument such as demonstration cities or something completely different.

Question: Tenant unions?

Answer: Yes, in many ways, but so far it hasn't been linked to a program, it has to do chiefly with tenant-landlord relations. We have a committee working on legislation in tenant-landlord relationships.

Question: Tenant unions are not oriented politically at this point, are they?

Answer: They are barely organized. The problem is that a number of victories have been won in terms of agreements, but we have not developed the unions. Developing a union is a long slow job, just like any organizing job. It takes a lot of personnel, it takes a lot of time and training. The temptation is to work for agreements but not to develop the organization.

Question: Does the Movement have in any of these major areas key persons who are trying to tie into the local organizations where there are issues, and where they have organizations they can call up? For example, on the Near West Side, we are dealing with the urban renewal problem there. Is it the idea to work with ABC, then, which has already formed an urban renewal committee?

Answer: Florence Scala comes to our city-wide urban renewal committee meetings. She is a prime mover in the Near West Side urban renewal area. In Lawndale, Bernard Lafayette is saying that we really ought to tie the whole urban renewal program in with the aldermanic elections in February. If we developed our program, began to agitate and to educate immediately in the communities, it would become clear who was responsible for what happened to the community—the relationship would be shown between the problems and the machine.

Question: I would think that really putting resources into an urban renewal campaign that would naturally lead to politics would be better than just having a committee on politics.

Answer: I agree, but we still ought to have a committee on politics in order to hammer out the approach. That would be the formal way. The informal way would be to do the job politically as one moved along and that is probably what will happen.

Question: The problems are clearly illustrated in the Near West Side struggle. Apparently Florence Scala has urban renewal as her interest and is separating from WSO. There also seems to be Owners vs. Tenants.

Answer: Yes, but she would say that "without WSO nothing would happen."

Comment: In a meeting on the west side, it was the homeowners who were being catered to by the renewal people. They are not really going to lose. A WSO guy said, "It's irrelevant what is going to happen to the people who have been sweating out their lives as tenants." And then the meeting just broke up.

Answer: You have to find a coincidence of interest, somewhere. If you take the Lawndale area, the CHA comes in with a higher standard than the city code. Condemnation then proceeds on the basis of CHA. Urban renewal uses the CHA code as a basis of condemnation, they tear down almost any building that they want.

Question: When one looks at the objectives as you mention them, it looks as though the Freedom Movement is focusing on what Harold Baron calls institutionalized racism. The Movement is not focusing on the level of a collective power, but really using various ways to express institutionalized racism as discriminatory patterns.

Answer: The problem of getting power is a problem that is usually avoided.

Question: You are hitting on economic power, of course, which is one aspect of this.

Answer: It is a minor aspect when we think of what we'll be able to do over against what the job is. You have to be able to make a contract of ten or fifteen million dollars out of which you make two or three in order to get real economic power. If there is no institution which is capable of handling that kind of contract, it is impossible to make some of the major money in the city. I do not know where that kind of collective economic strength will come from. We're trying to do something about it by bringing economic forces together, but there is so little to begin with in terms of economic power.

STRESS AND STRAIN IN THE MOVEMENT

There are the grassroots organizations versus the old line organizations. No one knows exactly what grassroots are. I think that what is meant by grassroots, generally, is a Negro organization with a below middle-class constituency. Most of the organizations in CCCO are middle-class. Those that are not certainly have middle-class staff that provides the initiative and a great deal of leadership. KOCO has the potentiality of being something else, also Miles Square. JOIN now has a big staff, many middle-class, but they are really closer to the grassroots organization than others. They are white so that eliminates them in many ways although they have been accepted due to their success.

Question: Is JOIN grassroots directed or is it SDS directed?

Answer: I think that it is grassroots oriented. Rennie Davis came with the thesis that everybody on the Tenant Federation Board should be a tenant. If one took this thesis then it would be the militants versus the conservatives. If this were carried to its logical conclusion the role of CIC, Urban League, NAACP, AFSC, UAW and Packing House Workers would be rejected. Then one would have to find out what grassroots were. This is the strain and stress on ideology.

There are those who are concerned with the action versus the process. Some are concerned more with the way things are done than with actually getting things accomplished. There would be a great debate as to whether or not things had to be taken through a debate in the assembly of CCCO or the Freedom Movement, before anything was done.

Then there is participatory democracy versus leadership. This may be the same thing as the process but it is another way to state the problem.

There are the anti-Daley forces which may or may not be the same as the anti-machine forces. There is a whole group which is always anti-Daley versus the anti-total system where Daley is an instrument of the system. It would not matter who was there, even King. Therefore the problem is not Daley and in a sense it is not the machine. It is the way in which the machine is run and the problem is to get the power to force the machine or Daley to move in the "right" direction.

There are certain personality needs that are causing stresses and strains. People have been rejected who apply for jobs. Ego needs often get in the way of important decisions. Leadership abilities are often questioned. All of these factors tend to "hang up" the Movement at crucial times.

Then you have white vs. black. The Hyde Park liberal white is in the worst position vs. the black. The Agenda Committee, depending on whether Archie Hargraves or Don Benedict represents the City Missionary Society, has either three or four whites. This is a decrease of whites in the CCCO decision making group. There is a movement away from white leadership and dependence on whites. However the influence of the white leadership was felt at the summit conference. The sensitivity to the color problem is increasing in the Negro community so I do not discount the statements of those who say this is so knowing that they represent a lot of people, although I know that they do not represent as many as they claim to.

The summit agreement is a real point of stress and strain within the Movement. I have already indicated the question about process. It is a contribution to the debate about how you decide things; we made a major error, in not taking the agreement back to the assembly. Why that was not done is unknown. It could be attributed to the great pressure during that time. The debate was really on the content of the agreement.

The maintenance needs of members' organizations versus the needs of CCCO often cause problems. The membership organizations expect CCCO to produce everything on any issue that is voted upon in the delegates meeting. For example, they will vote to oppose the school bond issue and then expect CCCO to implement the decision. CCCO does not have much to help with, neither money nor personnel. Organizations will also need servicing of all sorts and kinds and will expect CCCO to be at their call. Most of their needs are legitimate; and if we had the time and staff this kind of service would be given to member organizations. When one thinks that TWO has thirty-six full time staff people and we have only four to service the whole Freedom Movement, it does not balance out.

The CCCO and SCLC relationship often causes major stress. SCLC through some of its leadership treated CCCO as if it did not exist both in terms of behavior and in terms of verbal statements—thus undermining CCCO as an organization. The nonviolent philosophy would support the idea of strengthening all people in all institutions as over against trying to destroy them, to help them become what they are meant to be. Bevel does not admit any contradiction in the relationship to CCCO although this is the line he took with CCCO. To him it did not exist, it was nothing, it would become nothing and therefore it was not worth making into something. This idea pushed Raby into the background; this became evident during the action particularly PR wise. This caused a real problem with our constituents because the spokesmen for the action became staff of SCLC as opposed to the CCCO convener. The staff of SCLC were also the leaders because of their conception of leadership. That would be my interpretation of the problem—of the difference of the way they operate. They do have a leadership principle; they do not believe, really, in letting the people run the action. They believe in letting a lot of people into the action, but the leadership is in the hands of a few and these few also get the PR. It could have been handled in a different way.

Question: Who brought Bevel here?

Answer: Bevel came here on his own at the invitation of the West Side Christian Parish to become its program director. He had decided that Chicago was the place to start a Northern movement.

Question: Who gave Bevel his authority?

Answer: His authority in the Movement is established by the fact that he's necessary for the Movement. He is a master strategist in action. He called almost all the shots all summer. He is a clever, intelligent, perceptive guy. I wouldn't go into a direct action movement without Bevel or somebody like him.

Question: How does one control Bevel?

Answer: One does not control easily a man like Bevel who spawns ideas, sees what ought to be done, sees what forces need to be brought together and goes ahead and pushes it. But he does not follow through; he does not communicate with the other forces in the city who have a self-interest and who will be miffed if they are left out. Someone needs to work with him and be a person to whom Bevel could relate and communicate. Jackson and Bevel can do that. I am not completely rejected by him. Jackson and Lafayette are better organizers. At one point the idea of Bevel becoming executive director with Jackson and myself acting as administrative assistants was discussed. However nothing was done about it. It is so hard to communicate with King about these problems; therefore decisions frequently take a long time or are never made.

Question: Is SCLC really trying to build a Chicago movement?

Answer: That is part of the maintenance needs of SCLC that creates some strains and stress. They have need for a public image and for a national victory. They are very scattered and unless they have action going and unless they have a public image, it is very difficult to raise the money needed to keep the organization going. They give lip service to the proposition that mobilization ought to serve organization, but they don't know what to do about it. Now, insofar as they are now really trying to work on the organization of tenant unions, they will have contributed. One of the problems there is that those tenant unions may give way to urban renewal unless a more thorough program is discussed.

Question: Is there any anxiety about SCLC's commitment to Chicago?

Answer: That would be another source of strain. King pledged to stay in Chicago through next summer, but he often talks of longer commitments. Their own maintenance needs and frustrations may drive them into something else. I think whether they remain or leave will depend in part on two things:

1. Whether or not the implementation of this housing agreement will produce anything, or

2. If we could develop another issue so that over the winter we would have won another victory. We will be on our way, perhaps, by then to the development of an issue.

The other strain between CCCO and SCLC is the philosophy of nonviolence and integration as these are set over against black power. The fact that is particularly important here is the nonviolent philosophy and whether or not CCCO really has to be pushed in that direction. SCLC with its image of integration and nonviolence has some real need for achievement. This creates a real strain with the organization, a pressure upon it and creates a real situation in the relationship in Chicago because it is necessary to push for this demonstrative action over the long haul which would involve the organization in a much slower process. King came to us and said that August was coming and that it was the months of riots. We had to have an alternative to them. His suggestion for stepped up action also was probably based on other maintenance needs as well as the fear that they would be associated with riots. So the action committee changed its pattern of development for the open housing action. That was the reason for the proposed all-night vigil in Gage Park, the beginning of the summer tension—a direct result of King's personal interference. SCLC made the decision for the most part to escalate. In the action committee Bevel presented it as if it were an idea that needed to be followed through, not as King's request. As a result, we escalated as over against what we had planned to do.

Another frustration of the Freedom Movement is the lack of power, the lack of ability to get anything done. There seems to be no real projection of a way to amass real power in the face of the machine. There is the example of the injunction, and putting Frank Ditto in jail for six months. Now Raby is waiting to hear about his sentence. He is subject to one year in jail and X amount of money. Appeal is expensive. But the Movement is fighting a machine that has several methods to stifle opposition. This certainly adds to the frustration of getting things done.

Question: You say that the lack of power is due to the existence of such exorbitant power in the machine?

Answer: If the Movement doesn't produce some TWO's or power somewhere it will be hard to sustain anything.

Question: Isn't futility experienced in the Movement because of the unlimited goals that it entertains? In fact, it is hard to see that goals are even entertained.

Answer: In the summit agreement, it seemed that open housing was not the kind of issue that had a clear target or victory in view. Bayard Rustin said: "Get out. You have the semblance of a victory. Defend it as a victory and get on with some of the other areas. You are not going to get a lot of people to move immediately anyway, so how do you win? What is the victory? Even if you got the real estate agencies to change their practices, people would not move."

Question: In relation to the point about specific goals or visualizing your goals, isn't the other side of this the power in people? It seems to me that the way you talk and the way you picture this thing is that staff is the key thing. No matter about the power of the machine, if the Movement could build community organizations or groups that had strength, they may be able to make some change. And in that way, I'm thinking that staff is the key thing—how to recruit them, support them and sustain them. Staff has been a problem for the Movement. In CCCO there never really was a staff until after the Freedom Festival and then partly because we received some money from the Unitarians. That was the first time that we even had anybody that resembled an executive director of CCCO. Even if we had the finances now, it would be hard to find a good staff. Ever since I have been in the Movement I have been looking for staff.

Question: What is the purpose of having a lot more staff and organizers on a supra-parochial level? I think that if you had twenty-five people it would be better to put four each in x number of forces rather than put all twenty-five people in a large task force.

Answer: I would not give them to TWO. I would pay their salaries, put them in an area and be in control of them (that is what Brazier said and I'd take his advice). If we had twenty-five people, we could place them in KOCO, Englewood and other areas. They would be out in these communities relating to action and the temporary power through direct action would feed into permanent organizations. Some of the time they would have to function in the direct action, but a good deal of the time, they would be mobilizing the troops, organizing them and building them into a permanent organization. Tournour is organizing hospital workers. We pay his salary. That is the way to use the staff. There should have been a person in the action center this summer whose whole concept was to make the action center relate to the community organization. But highly trained, skilled people are needed and I do not know where they are. One of the most important things is the training of leadership. SCLC has a group of people, some of whom could be trained if we had done it right. Three or four people could have been made into organizers. But they had to be related to somebody who would use them in that capacity; train them and develop them in that way. This has not really become the thinking of the movement as yet.

Perspectives on

Operation Breadbasket

GARY MASSONI

This paper was originally written as a Master's thesis in 1971 for the Chicago Theological Seminary. It is published here for the first time. Minor editorial and stylistic changes have been made, but otherwise it is published as it was written.

Contents

Preface 1989

We are ordinary people doing extraordinary things.
Jesse Louis Jackson
(1969 and 1988)

Looking back at old love letters carries an odd blend of nostalgia and anxiety. You are reminded of the warmth of the relationship, but you also worry that you might have misread the situation, that there might have been more—or perhaps less—than you remember in the letters and in the relationship. There is the feeling that you are looking at what someone else has done, that you are not reading what was written by the person you are now. Your choices and experiences and thinking in the intervening years have made you different and the reminder of who you were earlier can be a little discomforting.

Rereading in 1989 the Masters thesis I wrote in 1971 was a little like reading old love letters, reviving some of the old intensity of concern, and reminding me that much has changed in the subsequent two decades. I had written the thesis in the "heat of battle." It was a time of high idealism for those of us involved in the Movement, despite the assassination of Martin Luther King, Jr., and the continuing war in Vietnam. We on the staff of Operation Breadbasket felt that we were involved in revolutionary changes to make America better. The program and Jesse Jackson were gaining national attention because of what we were able to accomplish. Yet, there were problems; I felt the program was capable of being even more effective. With great intensity, then, I set about writing the thesis in order to understand better my experience in Operation Breadbasket, to analyze some particular organizational problems, and to suggest some long-term improvements. It was not a dispassionate, objective analysis in a normative, academic sense, but an analysis "from within", with a definite point of view and purpose.

An obvious question, looking back from 1989, is: "What would I change in the thesis?" The section that stands out for revision now is Chapter Six: "Disintegration of the Threads." In retrospect, the word "disintegration" is too strong. At the time, it was used to sound a warning that there was a danger of disintegration. The interests and directions of the program had expanded beyond the resources available to sustain them; the consequence could be a collapse of structure, and of staff. From a political point of view, the expansion was appropriate. The organization was responding to issues and opportunities in the world around it. From an organizational point of view, however, it had stretched beyond reasonable capabilities. The organization did, in fact, "regroup" and consolidate somewhat. The credit for the survival of the organization goes to the dedicated staff who, as they consistently did, rose to the challenge of new demands with high motivation and deep commitment.

Today I can also recognize my limited vantage point. I addressed a narrow range of organizational issues and operational considerations. It was not easy—perhaps not even possible—to appreciate the many forces acting on and within Jesse Jackson in the shaping of Breadbasket directions. I now have a greater appreciation for how Jesse was able to sense opportunities, to see where things could go, to balance the pressures and resources, and to guide events appropriately.

What other organizational changes have occurred since the days of Operation Breadbasket? In December of 1971, SCLC's Operation Breadbasket in Chicago ceased to exist, and a new organization was born on Christmas day: People United to Serve Humanity—Operation P.U.S.H. This new entity continued the issues and direction of Operation Breadbasket, it carried over nearly all the staff, and retained most of the financial contributors. And, predictably, it carried over organizational problems and questions. The story of Operation P.U.S.H., however, will be left for someone else to write.

Operation P.U.S.H. was the major entity for Jesse Jackson's work until his decision to run for the presidency of the United States of America in 1983. Following the 1984 election campaign, which brought new life to the political process, Jackson decided that a new entity was needed to consolidate the wider interest and support generated in the campaign. The result was the formation of the "Rainbow Coalition," which became the entity to carry Jackson's progressive political agenda until the 1988 presidential campaign. While his 1988 candidacy was viewed at the beginning by some analysts as a "symbolic" or "protest" campaign, the Jackson for President 1988 campaign was neither symbolic nor marginal. In most areas, Jackson quadrupled his voter support; he won more states than most observers had dreamed possible, placing first or second in forty-six of fifty-four contests (primaries or caucuses in the fifty states, the District of Columbia, Puerto Rico, the Virgin Islands, and American Samoa). While the resources of the campaign were limited, especially during the first months, the results were impressive. Again, the credit must be shared between Jackson's unique abilities and the capabilities and dedication of his staff.

Does this document have any particular relevance for today? I am aware that in the current political climate, some analysts will look to Jackson's leadership in Operation Breadbasket for clues to support their views about his suitability for national public office. My hope is that this analysis will not be misused. Charismatic authority remains a two-edged sword in organizations. It is not, however, a question of "good" or "bad," nor should it be allowed to be modified or excluded. Rather, the question continues to be how to build on the strengths of charisma and how to minimize the unstable elements. My recent experience as National Director of Scheduling for the 1988 Jackson for President Campaign again confirms my great respect for Jesse. His national leadership arises from his abilities to motivate and mobilize people, and to communicate a powerful, unifying vision for the nation and the world. Jesse Jackson is changing politics in the United States. He is bringing new people into the political process, both in terms of voter registration and in terms of active participation. He is helping people of all colors and backgrounds see their "common ground," the ways their interests are mutual and overlapping. Barriers will continue to come down as people join him to work toward his vision of a nation and a world at peace, where justice is the norm, and all persons are respected.

One note should be added here about what is included in this version of my thesis. The text of the document is presented with no substantive modification, just a few editorial clarifications. There remains the language uncertainty of that time about "Negro," "Black," and "Afro-American," not to mention the 1989 preference for "African American." Even the embarrassingly sexist language of those days has not been made inclusive. Most of the original seventy pages of appendices are not included. Only three items that seemed of special interest are reproduced here:

(1) a guide for Operation Breadbasket Consumer Clubs (1967)
(2) Guidelines for the Organization of Breadbasket Outposts (September 1968)
(3) Jesse L. Jackson's position paper on Human Subsidy (May 1969)

As always, thanks and appreciation are due to many people for many reasons. Thanks are in order for Frank Watkins, May Louie, Betty Magness, and other friends from the Southern Christian Leadership Conference, Operation Breadbasket, Operation P.U.S.H., the Rainbow Coalition, and the Jackson for President 1988 Campaign. Thanks to David Garrow and Ralph Carlson for including my thesis in this publishing project. There are not adequate words to express my thanks to Jesse L. Jackson for being who he is—an inspiring leader and friend. My family also deserves a good deal of appreciation for putting up with my anxiety and "stewing" over this project—the original thesis and this new presentation: thanks, Betty, Dara, and Gina.

Preface 1971

This study of SCLC's Operation Breadbasket in Chicago grows out of my involvement as a member of the staff for the past five years. I have attempted to write the history of Breadbasket, since no one else has prepared an extensive review of the development of the operation. In addition to making the story available, I have attempted to analyze the internal problems of the organization. My effort to clarify the current situation and to suggest some directions for the future is based on my hope that Breadbasket can learn from an evaluation of itself and thus maximize its potential for creative social change.

In presenting the historical analysis of Operation Breadbasket, I am fully aware of the difficulty of writing anything approaching a perfectly "objective" history. It is simply not possible to record all the facts, and there is always some limited perspective guiding the selection of materials to present. I have been aware that my own involvement and profound respect for Breadbasket and for Jesse Jackson have affected my outlook. My extensive participation in Breadbasket, however, should be seen not simply as a limitation on my perspective, but as an additional source of information and interpretation.

Despite my own closeness to Breadbasket, I am painfully aware of the limitations of the sources I have used. Although I have been able to draw on a great variety of materials, I have found that nowhere is there a complete written account or record of events, especially covering Breadbasket's early development. I have pieced together the story from many sources, including: position papers, press releases, news stories, interviews, staff reports, inter-office memoranda, notes from staff meetings and many other meetings, calendars and date-books, my own memory and numerous discussions with other staff members and volunteers. Since several sources were used to review many events, I have not cited sources for most of the material presented, except where I have quoted at length from a specific source.

I owe a great debt of gratitude to many people for their assistance in preparing this study of Operation Breadbasket. I want to express particular appreciation to Dr. Alvin Pitcher and David Wallace for generously opening their files of Breadbasket materials for my use. I also want to thank Rev.

Richard Lawrence, Richard Thomas, and my wife, Betty, for many extended discussions about Breadbasket's past and present situation. Most especially I want to acknowledge my indebtedness to Rev. Jesse L. Jackson for inspiring me to serve with him on the staff of SCLC's Operation Breadbasket and for sharing with me his many insights into meaningful living.

With what shall I come before the Lord,
  and bow myself before God on high?
Shall I come before him with burnt offerings,
  with calves a year old?
Will the Lord be pleased with thousands of rams,
  with ten thousands of rivers of oil?
Shall I give my first-born for my transgression,
  the fruit of my body for the sin of my soul?

He has showed you, O man, what is good;
  and what does the Lord require of you
but to do justice, and to love kindness,
  and to walk humbly with your God?

Micah 6:6-8 (RSV)

Part I

Historical

Perspective

ONE

Setting the Stage

Integration is no longer in vogue; freedom is no longer the focus. The issue now is power. The orientation of the civil rights movement has decidedly shifted.

The cries of "black power" that so disturbed and frightened this predominantly white nation during the summer of 1966 are often seen as marking the turning point in the struggle for equal rights for minorities. This change, however, can be understood as a response to an earlier shift in the attitude of white Americans, according to Dr. Martin Luther King, Jr. In his view, the dramatic events surrounding the efforts of Negroes to register to vote in Selma, Alabama, and the subsequent march from Selma to the state capitol in Montgomery, created a national consciousness that no citizen should be brutalized and denied basic Constitutional rights. The signing of the Voting Rights Act of 1965 marked the conclusion—in the minds of many people—of this "struggle to treat the Negro with a degree of decency."[1] Dr. King pointed out, however, that the national consciousness missed the main point of civil rights efforts, namely the realization of full equality. During the first phase of the "Movement," there was a degree of unity among blacks and concerned whites in seeking to eliminate the more extreme forms of barbaric conduct against Negroes. This unity began to erode, however, when the attention of the Movement turned to the primary goal of fulfilling the promise of equality. Whites were reluctant, by and large, to pursue the question of equality to its conclusion for black citizens. Dr. King noted that white allies who had been incensed by overt brutality and coarse degradation of blacks failed to show the same concern for eliminating poverty, exploitation and more subtle forms of discrimination. Dr. King pinpoints the reorientation among blacks about how the Movement should proceed with the divergence of expectations between blacks and whites.

For the Southern Christian Leadership Conference, this reassessment of direction meant, among other things, an assault on the problems faced by blacks in the ghettos of the North. At the SCLC Board meeting in April of 1965, Dr. King, the president of SCLC, vowed to launch civil rights campaigns in the North. A tour of several northern cities was organized in the summer of 1965. In July, Dr. King joined with other civil rights leaders in Chicago for a series of rallies on the issue of quality education in the public schools. An outgrowth of this tour in Chicago was the development of plans for an urban Movement by SCLC in conjunction with the Coordinating Council of Community Organizations (CCCO). On January 7, 1966, Dr. King for SCLC and Al Raby for CCCO announced a general plan to attack "the total pattern of economic exploitation under which Negroes suffer in Chicago and other northern cities."[2] This plan was modified to become a multifaceted "strategy to end slums," much of which eventually came to be known as the "Program of the Chicago Freedom Movement" for the summer of 1966.

Part of this plan in Chicago was an effort to involve the religious leadership in the nonviolent Movement. Dr. King announced that:

Negro ministers will be introduced to SCLC's Operation Breadbasket concept, which, in Atlanta, Georgia, alone, has added fifteen million dollars to the Negro community's purchasing power by obtaining jobs. The Breadbasket concept is a simple one, in which a Negro minister puts pressure on employers to hire and upgrade more Negroes, especially members of their own congregations.[3]

The Breadbasket concept was indeed simple, yet it combined various themes of community power, equality expressed in terms of the black community's own aspirations and definitions of needs, and concern for economic issues. As an extension of the Movement into the North, this program offered great potential for a successful pattern of action.

Actually, Operation Breadbasket was not a new idea on the northern urban scene. The program followed the pattern of the "Selective Patronage Program" organized in May of 1960, in Philadelphia, Pennsylvania, by Rev. Leon Sullivan, Rev. Alfred Dunston and Rev. Joshua Licorish. Even the Philadelphia program, however, was only reviving and reapplying a strategy whose theoretical significance had already been developed and which had been successfully applied in practice earlier in the century. The militant Negro newspaper *The Chicago Whip* launched a "spend-your-money-where-you-can-work" campaign in 1929, which resulted in about 2,000 jobs for black workers in white-owned stores as well as some additional business for black merchants.[4] Several other cities saw "don't-shop-where-you-can't-work" boycotts in the early 1930s. In 1934, William Edward Burghardt DuBois wrote an editorial for the *Crisis* magazine in which he supported the judicious use of such boycotts for economic gains for Negroes. Although he believed that more fundamental changes were needed to correct "the evils of the American profit system," he nevertheless asserted that "wherever a careful survey of local conditions seems to justify it, colored people should organize and campaign to secure jobs in some proportion to their spending power."[5] DuBois later expanded his thinking on the essential importance of economic development for Negroes, and in 1940 proposed an extensive program that included organizing the consumer power of black people and increasing the role of blacks in capitalist enterprise as part of an attempt to democratize industry in America.[6]

Although Dr. King invited Rev. Sullivan of Philadelphia to explain the "Selective Patronage Program" to the SCLC staff in Atlanta, the concept of organized consumer power and boycotts were not new even to SCLC. The Southern Christian Leadership Conference was founded as an extension of the successful 381-day bus boycott in Montgomery, Alabama, which projected Dr. King and the plight of black people into national prominence. However, SCLC had no continuing program of disciplined consumer power until Operation Breadbasket was officially established as a department of SCLC in September, 1962.

After some initial successes in securing more jobs for black workers in Atlanta, Georgia, SCLC decided to spread the program to several of its affiliate chapters in other southern cities, with Rev. Ralph David Abernathy as a leading spokesman. By the beginning of 1966, with Rev. Fred C. Bennett as Director, there were SCLC affiliates with Breadbasket programs in eight Southern cities, with similar groups unrelated to SCLC starting in several other cities. The results of these efforts in the South were encouraging. In Atlanta, for instance, the operation won at least 5,000 new jobs for Negroes between 1962 and 1967. As a program of the SCLC affiliate chapter in Jacksonville, Florida, Breadbasket joined forces with a local labor union in organizing the employees of a laundry firm and significantly improved their wages and benefits. Breadbasket programs were also instrumental in breaking down employment barriers against Negroes in some governmental agencies in Florida, Georgia and Kentucky.[7]

Although the introduction of Operation Breadbasket in Chicago was consistent with SCLC's new thrust into the urban North, it was not at first part of the general plan of the Chicago Freedom Movement, as the coalition of SCLC and CCCO was called. The program might not have been started in Chicago at all if it had not been for the position of a particular group of ministers who had been discussing means for increasing their participation in a Movement. Jesse L. Jackson, who was a second-year student at the Chicago Theological Seminary and, as of October of 1965, working for the Urban Training Center for Christian Mission under a Ford Fellowship, related the story in a report to the Urban Training Center in the Spring of 1966:

> Last summer with an anticipation of a movement developing in Chicago and a deep respect for the potential power of the church, I started working with one minister as the first step of bringing the clergy of Chicago into full understanding and participation in the freeing of people in the slum. Rev. Clay Evans, pastor of Fellowship Baptist Church and president of the Baptist Ministers Conference of Chicago and Vicinity, was the focus of my attention. In the growth of our relationship and the deepening of commitment to each other we explored the Biblical understanding of man and his relationship to God along with the causes and conditions of the slums.
>
> Our relationship led to the expansion to include other pastors. By early fall we formed a ministers' cadre meeting weekly. Six to ten ministers met with Dr. Littell of Chicago Theological Seminary, Dr. Alvin Pitcher of the Divinity School, and myself to share discussion of the ministry and understanding of the conditions under which we labor. Rev. Evans invited Dr. Martin Luther King to address a meeting of three Baptist ministers conferences in November to build support among the Negro clergy for a movement in Chicago.
>
> In the meantime, discussions were carried on with Rev. Evans and other clergymen about ways of bringing ministers into full participation in a Chicago movement. It was clear that the ministers preferred a separate, but related program to the movement. Operation Breadbasket, which had worked well in the south, was raised as a possible program of ministers. The cadre became the backbone of ministers invited to meet with Dr. King in January to lay the ground work for Operation Breadbasket.[8]

The introduction of Breadbasket into Chicago, then, was at first something of a concession to several ministers who agreed with the overall goals of the Movement, but who wanted to pursue a program under their own supervision rather than merge into the mass actions being projected. In any case, the foundation for support of the Movement in Chicago among ministers was started in the relationship between Jesse Jackson and Rev. Clay Evans, which grew into the weekly ministers' cadre with Dr. Franklin Littell and Dr. Alvin Pitcher and less than a dozen other ministers. Their interests were broadly spread in the "Joint Meeting of Chicago Baptist Ministers Conferences" on November 19, 1965, which included representatives from the Baptist Ministers Conference of Chicago and Vicinity, the Baptist

Ministers Alliance of Chicago and Vicinity, the Westside Ministers Conference, the Baptist Pastors Alliance, and the Baptist Ministers Union. From these preliminary gatherings, more specific support for the Breadbasket program emerged, so that Dr. King included Operation Breadbasket among the projected activities of the "Chicago Plan" announced on January 7, 1966. More meetings were held with Dr. King, Jesse Jackson and several ministers, including one on January 28, another on February 4, and a larger meeting on February 11, 1966. Although there was general unanimity of support in the earlier, smaller meetings where the purposes and techniques of Operation Breadbasket were explained, the February 11 meeting was considerably larger and included some ministers who were reluctant to participate. Nevertheless, this meeting issued a statement about the problem of Negro unemployment and called for more Negroes to be hired by "bakeries, dairies, coffee plants, soft-drink bottlers, chewing-gum plants, radio and television stations, newspapers, magazines, utility firms, and oil companies."[9] The nearly two hundred ministers at this meeting at Jubilee Temple (CME) were called upon to form committees to investigate employment opportunities for blacks in various companies. Their response to this appeal by Dr. King is considered the birth of SCLC's Operation Breadbasket in Chicago.

TWO

Negotiations Program

SCLC's Operation Breadbasket in Chicago followed the pattern worked out in Philadelphia and Atlanta: ministers from the black community demand more and better jobs for Negroes as a way for white companies to relate to black people in terms of economic justice. The demand for jobs was backed up by the threat of a "selective buying campaign" or a "consumer withdrawal." The process of negotiating the employment demands was modeled after the strategy of nonviolent direct action developed in other civil rights activities in the southern Movement. The first step was always a matter of "information," of gathering the facts so that the injustices being challenged could be documented in concrete terms. Nonviolent action must be based on truth, not rumor or opinion. The basic information required by Breadbasket was the employment data from specific companies, giving the total number of workers in each job category compared with the number of black workers in these same jobs. The next step was "education," or interpreting the relevant information to both the general community and to the particular adversary involved so that there could be both understanding and support for the negotiating program. The third step was a matter of "negotiation" over specific demands to correct injustices, such as hiring a specified number of black workers to fill jobs previously closed to blacks. The intention was to win over the opponent, not to conquer or victimize him. If this step failed to produce the necessary changes, however, the next step was "demonstration," or direct action as a nonviolent witness against the protested injustices. In the case of Breadbasket actions, this usually meant leafleting to inform people of the particular problems and picketing to pinpoint the cause of the injustices. Such action was intended to move the negotiation toward a final step of "reconciliation." The purpose of the nonviolent action was to heal wounds and seek ways of living together in mutual respect and justice. The conclusion of direct action was to establish new relationships of cooperation.

Although Operation Breadbasket followed this basic outline for nonviolent direct action, there was one notable omission in the northern urban setting.

Following the step of "negotiation" and before the "demonstration," there was another step called "purification," which was a period of spiritual preparation for action, a time to sort out ill-conceived motives and act as much as possible in the spirit of nonviolent, reconciling love. This stage of purification was missing in descriptions of the negotiating process in Chicago.[10]

In addition to modifying the pattern of nonviolent action, Breadbasket in Chicago also altered the basic structure of the operation. An SCLC brochure described the format in Atlanta and Philadelphia:

> A Breadbasket program is intentionally organized just as loosely as a particular situation will permit. In Philadelphia and Atlanta, "call men" are selected who call the associate ministers together to deal with specific employers. The "call men" positions are rotated frequently, and there are no other officers. No more formal organization is necessary.[11]

The ministers who responded to Dr. King's appeal at the meetings on February 11, 1966, were grouped into "target committees." On February 18, there were forty-one ministers assigned to one of four committees: (1) bread companies, (2) milk companies, (3) soft-drink companies, and (4) soup companies. These committees were to pursue information about the employment of various companies within the respective industries, but they could not make decisions about actual negotiations. This power was reserved for the larger "Steering Committee" composed of all interested ministers. With these committees, Breadbasket in Chicago soon took on additional dimensions of formal structure. The concept of rotating the positions of the "call men" who had the authority to call the Steering Committee together was affirmed, but somewhat modified. In actual practice, Rev. Jesse L. Jackson, now an associate minister at Fellowship Baptist Church, presided over nearly all negotiations and meetings of the Steering Committee. Late in April, 1966, Rev. Fred Bennett, the National Director of Operation Breadbasket, stressed again the "call men" format, emphasizing that no single person should be in charge of the program so that it would be more protected from legal sanctions. Nevertheless, Rev. Jackson was considered the "director" of the program in Chicago and was formally acknowledged as "spokesman" for the Steering Committee, and continued to chair most meetings.

Between February 11 and March 25, 1966, Operation Breadbasket in Chicago spent most of its time getting organized, expanding the number of ministers involved, discussing various issues and conditions in the community, and working out an operating procedure. Rev. Joseph Boon from the Breadbasket Program in Atlanta came to Chicago for the February 28 Steering Committee meeting to assist the ministers with some of the details of requesting information from companies about their employment patterns and of evaluating the data. The four target committees requested the necessary employment information from various companies in the four target industries. For most of the month of March, the ministers were met with delays by the companies. Most of the executives contacted had no sensitivity to the problems of minority employment in their operation, and had developed no methods of compiling comparative data for each job classification. Almost every company asked for additional time to prepare the requested information. Several companies finally provided some figures, but not the specific data requested so that even more time was taken to get useful information. One company claimed that as a matter of company policy they could not release information without approval from their headquarters in New York, which would mean additional delay. One company was openly hostile to the ministers and refused to cooperate in any way with the information-seeking committee. At a meeting on March 16, 1966, an official of Country's Delight Dairy, a subsidiary of Certified Grocers of Illinois, flatly refused to give the Breadbasket ministers any information, saying that he did not let union officials tell him how to run his company and he was certainly not about to let Negro preachers tell him what to do. He berated the ministers for their involvement in social issues instead of "spiritual matters" and proceeded to insult the whole black community with stereotyped statements about how "you people are lazy," and how Negroes prefer to be on welfare than to work. Although the investigating committee reported this incident to the Steering Committee on March 18, no action was taken until March 25, when an "action committee" was appointed to make some recommendations about how to respond to Country's Delight and to another company which had not cooperated. The "action committee" met on March 29, and reported their recommendation to the Steering Committee on April 1, 1966, that the ministers of Operation Breadbasket launch a "selective buying campaign" against Country's Delight products beginning the following week. The Steering Committee approved the recommendation, and scheduled a meeting on April 6 to work out details of the campaign strategy. The ministers decided to picket several stores that carried Country's Delight products in the black community until they received the information requested, until they had a meeting with company officials to discuss job demands, and until the company made a commitment to fill the jobs requested by the ministers. Picket lines marched in front of several Certified stores on Good Friday, 1966, and on Saturday. On Easter Sunday, Breadbasket ministers discussed the company's disrespect of black consumers and asked their congregations not to buy Country's Delight products. On Monday, the ministers received word that the officials of the dairy and the Board of Directors of Certified Grocers of Illinois were ready to negotiate. The first meeting did not resolve the conflict, but by Thursday, April 14, 1966, Country's Delight officials and the ministers of Operation Breadbasket sent a joint statement to Certified store owners indicating their commitment to hire forty-four additional Negro employees in a variety of job categories within thirty days. With this agreement, Operation Breadbasket announced its first victory in Chicago.

While the negotiation with Country's Delight was a victory, it also revealed some weaknesses in Breadbasket's procedures. In the Steering Committee meeting on the day following the agreement, the main topic of discussion was how to mobilize action more quickly and how to make a boycott more effective. In some ways, it would have been hard to lose a battle against a dairy company, since the low proportion of black workers was a clear issue,[12] and since milk cannot be sent back to the cows if people do not buy it for a period of a few days. The negotiating skills of the ministers had been effective, but needed to be sharpened. The Steering Committee needed to develop more effective ways of communicating quickly with larger numbers of ministers who would make pulpit announcements. They needed to develop ways to contact and mobilize picket teams more rapidly. The ministers also needed a means of paying for the expenses of leaflets and picket signs for such actions. In the two days of picketing Certified stores, the ministers had accumulated expenses of $1,353.73. At the Steering Committee meeting on April 15, 1966, less than two hundred dollars was collected to pay for these costs. A "finance committee" was appointed to discuss such matters with the Chicago Freedom Movement, the umbrella under which Breadbasket was working. On April 22, 1966, this committee recommended that the Steering Committee send a letter to all ministers who had expressed some interest in Operation Breadbasket or the Chicago Freedom Movement appealing for contributions to cover direct-action expenses. They also recommended that an account for Breadbasket be opened in a Negro bank, specifically Seaway National Bank, and that a treasurer and chairman of the finance committee be appointed. This procedure, which the Steering Committee approved, conflicted with the "loosely organized" nature of the program as it functioned elsewhere, particularly in Atlanta. Even though the National Director of Operation Breadbasket, Rev. Fred Bennett, recommended against an established treasury, no satisfactory alternative for paying expenses was offered. A bank account was opened, but it is not clear how satisfactory this arrangement was since the minutes of the Steering Committee meetings after April 29, 1966, contain no further reports on finances. Apparently the Southern Christian Leadership Conference and the Coordinating Council of Community Organizations assumed responsibility for the costs of the Country's Delight campaign and for subsequent actions, with contributions for Operation Breadbasket going into the general treasury of the Chicago Freedom Movement.

Rev. Bennett made another recommendation that altered the internal procedures of Breadbasket in Chicago. He suggested that the ministers focus their activity within one industry at a time. The Steering Committee agreed with this idea, and reorganized the committee structure. The four committees for the milk, soft-drink, bread and soup industries were realigned into three target committees for designated companies within the dairy industry. Two "call men" were appointed by the chairman, Rev. Jesse Jackson, to head each committee, for Hawthorn-Mellody Milk Company, the Borden Company, and Wanzer Dairy.

Although the finance committee was visibly dropped at this time, another committee which had been appointed on March 11, 1966, continued to function. This group, called the "Money and Finance Committee," was established to look into "finding ways to overcome the barriers churches and businesses in the Negro areas face when they want to borrow money, the interest rates that have to be payed [sic.] for loans, the whole problem of credit ratings."[13] Although five ministers had been appointed to the committee, only two, Rev. H. B. Brady and Rev. Jesse Jackson, actually met. They reported at the April 29 meeting about their discussion with the Chairman of the Board and the President of Seaway National Bank. They agreed to continue acting as an *ad hoc* committee to gather information about loans and credit arrangements in the Negro community.

During May of 1966, the new target committees began functioning. Both Borden and Hawthorn-Mellody delayed in providing the necessary information, and telegrams were sent to spur their responses. When these two companies and Wanzer had turned over their information, the evaluations showed that they all had failed in about the same way in hiring and upgrading black employees. For example, one company had only twenty-three black workers out of a total work force of 435 employees, for an overall black percentage of 5.3%. Furthermore, nearly all of the twenty-three were in the bottom three categories of work. The company had no black managers out of a total of fifteen, no black auto mechanics out of twenty-one, no black dairy production workers out of fifty-eight, and no black retail delivery salesmen out of 142. At the Steering Committee meeting of May 20, 1966, the ministers decided to present their demands first to the Borden Company. Three meetings were held with Borden officials to discuss the request for sixty-four additional black employees. During the meeting the ministers modified this figure to twenty in view of the company's program to eliminate all their retail delivery routes. On June 7, the ministers of Operation Breadbasket announced their second victory, this time without a boycott.

With the experience of Borden and Country's Delight, and with the new committee structure, Operation Breadbasket began to develop a rhythm of success. On June 10, 1966, the ministers decided that a "selective buying campaign" was necessary against Hawthorn-Mellody. Several National Tea and Del Farm Foods stores were picketed starting June 15. On June 21, the officials of Hawthorn-Mellody agreed to hire fifty-five more black workers to integrate every category of the company's operations in all four of its plants. The ministers met with Wanzer Dairy executives to discuss their request for seventy more Negro workers. This figure was modified to forty-three because of recent changes in the company's management and new employment practices. On July 5, the ministers announced Wanzer's commitment to hire an additional forty-four black employees. The ministers of Breadbasket announced another "selective buying campaign" on July 15, this time against Dean Foods and Bowman Dairy products. The Steering Committee had presented their request to Dean Foods in a letter sent March 4, 1966, and had sent another letter on April 15, expressing the ministers' dissatisfaction with the company's minuscule progress in increasing their minority employment. Action against Dean Foods had been postponed, however, because of the merger of Bowman Dairy into Dean Foods, a process delayed by court actions and union problems. In July, however, the ministers decided that the time for action had come. On July 21, Breadbasket announced another victory: Dean Foods had agreed to hire an additional forty-five black employees in a wide variety of job classifications.

Operation Breadbasket's string of victories was welcome news to the black community of Chicago, which suffered from an unemployment rate of 8.9%—far above the city average of 2.9%. In some areas, unemployment reached as high as 40%, a figure which did not even account for many unemployed men who were so discouraged and frustrated that they were no longer seeking jobs and thus did not show up in the official unemployment rate. More and better jobs for the black community were very much needed.

Along with the urgent need for jobs for Negroes, there was a feeling among the ministers of Breadbasket that perhaps the jobs were coming too easily, that the executives were making quick commitments in order to get the pressure off the company. On July 1, 1966, the Steering Committee appointed a "Follow-Up Committee" to make certain that companies were fulfilling their commitments. The committee was to maintain contact with the various companies to monitor their progress, to work with the Chicago Urban League which was serving as a referral agency for the job openings, and to make contact with black employees to check on the quality of the new employment situation within the companies. The effect of the work of the Follow-Up Committee was to close the gap between the agreement to fill jobs and the actual placement of Negroes in new jobs.

Counting the agreement with Dean Foods, the Steering Committee had negotiated commitments for 208 new jobs for black workers from the five largest dairy operations in the Chicago area. On July 22, 1966, the Steering Committee decided to move into a new industry. There was some discussion of negotiating with retail food chain stores, but the consensus was to stick with food products. The soft-drink industry was selected as the next focus of attention.

The Steering Committee already had some information from a few companies, since the old soft-drink target committee had sent letters requesting information to several companies in April. The Pepsi-Cola Bottling Company had provided some very inadequate data and was refusing any additional information. By August 5, the ministers had formulated a request of fifty-eight new jobs from Pepsi-Cola. Pepsi officials balked, and the ministers announced another boycott on August 9. At the same time, a request was given to Coca-Cola Bottlers, Inc., for thirty-five jobs for Negroes. Simultaneous with these negotiations, everyone's attention was focused on the demonstrations and marches for open housing in Chicago. In the midst of the larger Movement activities, Breadbasket picketed Pepsi-Cola outlets for two weeks. On August 22, 1966, the ministers announced the conclusion of the Pepsi campaign. Pepsi-Cola agreed to hire an additional thirty-two Negroes. Three days later, the ministers announced another victory, without a boycott, with Coca-Cola, who agreed to hire thirty more blacks. The next day, August 26, 1966, the open-housing marches ended with the signing of the "Summit Agreement," a potentially far-reaching program to end housing discrimination in the Chicago area.[14] These events converged in the hot Chicago summer as a summary of the Chicago Freedom Movement, SCLC's first activity in the urban North.

After the climactic events of the last week of August, Operation Breadbasket took a brief rest to review its course. At the Steering Committee meeting of September 16, 1966, there was a discussion of the basic guidelines for determining what request for jobs should be given a company to help it move toward a level of justice in its employment practices. Although the black community represented over 30% of the metropolitan population, a basic guideline of 20% in each of a company's job classifications was reaffirmed by the Steering Committee. The ministers left unresolved a further question of whether this proportion should be increased for a company's facility located in a predominantly black neighborhood. There was some discussion of the need for additional office space, since the Breadbasket staff, composed at this time of Jesse Jackson and David Wallace, was borrowing a small amount of space in the offices of the Coordinating Council of Community Organizations. Another SCLC staff member was introduced, Rev. Charles Billups, who was to work with the Follow-Up Committee in making certain that the jobs opened by the negotiations were actually filled with black workers. At this September meeting, the ministers also discussed strengthening their relationship with the Chicago Freedom Movement. Dr. Martin Luther King, Jr. had expressed a desire to keep the ministers more closely informed about the activities of the Movement, and the ministers were interested in meeting with him on a regular basis. In the following Steering Committee meeting there was more discussion of some kind of a "church committee" to meet with Dr. King. It was decided that the whole Steering Committee should participate in these meetings, so regular meetings with Dr. King were scheduled as part of the Steering Committee meetings at 1:00 p.m. on Fridays. Also on the agenda for discussion at the Steering Committee meeting of September 23, was the question of fund-raising for the Chicago Freedom Movement. The ministers of Breadbasket were urged to participate in some systematic fund-raising program, since they were an integral part of the Chicago Freedom Movement.

Even with these various organizational issues to discuss, the ministers continued with the business of opening more jobs for the black community. Negotiating teams evaluated employment from Seven-Up and Canfield soft-drink companies, and prepared requests. At the September 23rd meeting of the Steering Committee, the ministers confirmed their agreement with Seven-Up for fifty-seven new jobs, and scheduled a meeting with Canfield during the first week of October to discuss the request for twelve more black workers. Canfield's agreement was announced on October 6, 1966.

Some additional organizational issues were discussed at the Steering Committee meeting on September 30, 1966. There had been rumors for several weeks of difficulties with the way the Urban League had been handling potential employees referred by the Breadbasket ministers for the negotiated jobs. As it turned out, the ministers who had visited the Urban League to talk about the situation reported that there had been some problems in communications between the Urban League and Breadbasket, and between the Urban League and the people referred by the ministers. The crux of the problem seemed to center on the inability of the Urban League to do more than refer an applicant to a potential job. Breadbasket insisted that the companies hire "qualifiable" applicants who were available and who could be trained to be "qualified" according to company standards. However, the companies retained the final decision on who was to be hired, which left considerable room for frustration among people who expected to be hired without difficulty.

The Steering Committee also discussed the need for some kind of written documentation of the commitments made by companies for new black employees. Up to this point, there were not even letters from all the companies confirming the negotiated agreements. The Steering Committee agreed that companies should confirm in writing their commitments, not as legally binding contracts but as expressions of the covenant between the company and the black community. The growth of the staff at this time helped ease the problem of written documentation. In addition to Jesse Jackson and David Wallace, there was a secretary, Carol Griffin, and another program worker, Gary Massoni, who had been involved during April, May and June of 1966, as a student at Chicago Theological Seminary, and who joined the staff officially in October, 1966, as an intern from The Urban Training Center. Dr. Alvin Pitcher of the University of Chicago Divinity

School had been deeply involved with the development of the program of the Chicago Freedom Movement and was now spending considerable time with Breadbasket's negotiations.

At the September 30 meeting, the Steering Committee also considered the question of new targets, since most of the major soft-drink companies had, by this time, agreed to improve their employment practices in specific and measurable ways. Supermarket chains were discussed and selected as the next target industry. In addition to improved employment, the Steering Committee decided to add two other dimensions to the company's commitment. One was the matter of upgrading conditions and services in their stores in the black community. There was a general suspicion among black shoppers that they paid more for the same merchandise than shoppers in white areas and that stores in black neighborhoods were not as well managed and maintained as stores of the same chain in white areas. The chain-store executives always denied such allegations, but the ministers verified many such discrepancies during random inspections. The other new feature to be included in the negotiations was securing the cooperation of the chain stores in removing from the shelves any products subject to a selective buying campaign by Breadbasket. Such a concession would have been a significant leverage over product manufacturers, although the risk of restraint-of-trade violations made the demand practically impossible.

Four new target committees were formed, with new "call men," to gather employment data from Jewel Food Stores, National Tea Company, Great A&P Tea Company, and Red Star Stores. At the Steering Committee meeting of October 28, 1966, two other companies were added to the list. The minutes of that meeting listed the target companies in the order in which the ministers planned to negotiate: (1) High-Low Foods, (2) Grocerland, (3) A&P, (4) National Tea, (5) Red Star, and (6) Jewel. As the negotiations progressed, Red Star and Grocerland were dropped from the list, and National Tea preceded A&P.

Through correspondence with officials of High-Low Foods, the ministers had been able to get some preliminary employment data, but had not been able to get any interest in agreeing to a specific number of new jobs for black employees. In a letter presented to High-Low on November 1, 1966, the ministers requested 183 new jobs from the company, the largest request to that date. Although about 12% of High-Low's employees were Negroes, 88% of these black workers were either cashiers, stock clerks or security guards. The company had several categories that reflected severe discrimination. For example, High-Low had only one Negro store manager in their fifty-four stores (1.8%), and only ten Negro journeymen butchers out of 383 (2.6%). Because of the lack of cooperation by High-Low officials, a press statement was released announcing a "don't buy" campaign against High-Low stores on November 2. However, no pickets were dispatched, since the company quickly agreed to reconsider their response to the demand for 183 jobs for black workers in eight broad categories from truck drivers and store managers to more clerks and butchers. They also responded to an additional demand discussed in the November 1 negotiating meeting, which was to stock the products of Negro businessmen. A third demand was also discussed, but High-Low made no response until later to the request that High-Low stores make deposits in Negro banks. At the Steering Committee meeting of November 4, the three areas of demands on High-Low Foods were summarized: (1) increase employment by 183 Negro workers; (2) place Negro manufactured products on store shelves in the black community; and (3) place the accounts of stores in the black community in black banks. Several more meetings were held between High-Low and Operation Breadbasket, until on November 19, 1966, they issued a "Joint Statement from Operation Breadbasket and High-Low Foods, Inc."[15]

The agreement with High-Low Foods, Inc., was a crucial turning point for Operation Breadbasket. For the first time, specific steps were included for the development of business institutions in the black community. By channeling the capital resources of major white businesses into black-owned banks, the ministers of Breadbasket had a potentially significant means of increasing the flow and circulation of capital in the black community. Although only seven products were involved in the High-Low agreement, the success in breaking through the barriers of discrimination that excluded Negro-produced products from the shelves of major retail outlets quickly drew the attention of other Negro businessmen who had also been locked out of the market even in their own neighborhoods. It was at this point that Breadbasket made the concrete shift from finding jobs to a broader program to develop a strong economic base for the black community.

THREE

Business Development

The thinking about economic development in broader categories than jobs actually came earlier than the High-Low covenant. As early as March 11, 1966, Rev. Jesse Jackson raised the problems of credit and financing for Negro businessmen. The "Money and Finance Committee" formed at that time met several times with officers and directors of local Negro banks and provided a direct channel of communication about problems of Negro businessmen. Since a couple of product manufacturers and distributors were among these banking contacts, the committees discussed problems other than capitalization, such as exclusion from distribution in chain stores. From the relationships developed in this context, Rev. Jackson began meeting with a small group of black businessmen in the fall of 1966. Some specific ideas were developed in this group about how to deal with broader problems of healthy economic institutions in the black community.

In a memorandum to Dr. Martin Luther King, Jr., dated November 2, 1966, Rev. Jesse Jackson discussed "Fund Raising in the Context of Economic Development." Rather than considering fund-raising a program in itself, Rev. Jackson described it as an offshoot of a major, national economic development program. The idea was to use the charismatic appeal of Dr. King to draw together various elements of black community leadership in several cities into a "corporation of finance and fellowship" which would be the nucleus of systematic leadership for financing and guiding the economic development of their community. The starting point would have been a construction program using federal funds for 221-d-3 housing as a way to help black contractors get started on major jobs. In his description of the program, Rev. Jackson drew on much of the "Talented Tenth" theory of leadership and the primary importance of economic power for Negroes which W.E.B. DuBois had outlined in his autobiographical book *Dusk of Dawn*.[16]

Some of the ideas that came to expression in the memorandum on fund-raising were crystallized not only in the covenant with High-Low Foods, but also in Dr. King's appointment of Rev. Jackson as "Director of Special Projects and Economic Development" for SCLC on November 18, 1966. In this new role in SCLC, Rev. Jackson was to be responsible for continuing to expand employment opportunities for Negroes, for developing programs to stimulate Negro businesses, and for raising funds for SCLC.

Following this informal definition of Rev. Jackson's role, Operation Breadbasket developed along parallel lines. The negotiations continued to open new jobs for Negroes in 1967, but the primary emphasis in the negotiations began to shift more toward business development, with the question of national expansion emerging as the basic focus of activity later in the year.

The ministers of Operation Breadbasket signed a covenant with National Tea Company on December 9, 1966. The format of this agreement was similar to the one with High-Low Foods, except that the demands for the distribution of black-manufactured products and for banking in black-owned banks were expanded. In two more covenants with super-market chains, the employment demands remained essentially on the same basis but the business development demands were further elaborated. The creative energies of the staff and ministers directed toward what white companies could do to assist the growth of black businesses resulted in additional demands in the Jewel Food Stores agreement, announced on April 28, 1967. Jewel agreed not only to transfer some store accounts to black banks and to distribute the black products, they also agreed to establish a "Market Advisory Council" within their management group to advise Negro businessmen on ways to improve their marketing and general business skills. Jewel also agreed to use the services of Negro businessmen in the areas of garbage collection, pest exterminating and janitorial maintenance, and in the construction of new stores. On May 26, 1967, a similar covenant was signed with the Great Atlantic and Pacific Tea Company (A&P), which included additional demands for the use of black businessmen in the areas of advertising, employee training, and professional services such as law, accounting and insurance. The A&P covenant also called for the assignment of an A&P executive to develop additional programs of advertising and marketing for the black products. [See pages 326-327 for copy of the covenant.][17]

While the agreements with National Tea, Jewel, and A&P were by far the most significant employment commitments reached, they were more remembered for what they did for black business development. Although National Tea promised 377 new jobs, Jewel promised 512, and A&P promised 770, Breadbasket publicity emphasized the aspects of business growth and economic development. These expanded business demands were considered so important that the ministers carried the later demands back to

National Tea and to High-Low. National Tea cooperated and arranged for contracts with Negro scavenger services by the first of April, 1967, and broke ground on May 11, 1967, for the first major chain store to be built by black contractors in Chicago. Dr. King attended the ground-breaking ceremonies and announced the nation-wide significance of this event: it was the first such major construction job by black contractors anywhere in the country.

High-Low was not so cooperative in either the business development or the employment categories when progress was evaluated and the new demands discussed. Of the 183 jobs promised by the company, only fifty-six had been filled by May of 1967, with the largest shortages in the demand for journeymen butchers, managers and grocery clerks. Of the seven products the company agreed to distribute, they balked at selling three: Baldwin Ice Cream, Joe Louis Milk, and Diamond Sparkle Wax. The ice cream conflicted with their own brand, Roney Ice Cream, for which they wanted to restrict the market. They claimed that the shelves were too crowded to introduce another brand of wax, and that the addition of another brand of milk would cut into their profits too much. When the family-owned company refused to consider the new business demands and the revised employment demands, Breadbasket announced a "withdrawal of patronage" from High-Low stores in the black community. Picket lines and leafleters were dispatched to several stores on June 9, 1967. The campaign continued until High-Low responded on June 20, with an effort to obtain a court injunction against the boycott. The ministers of Breadbasket agreed to suspend picketing if they could continue passing out "informational leaflets" and if High-Low would "bargain in good faith." Circuit Court Judge Walker Butler was to decide on the merits of High-Low's allegations that Breadbasket was forcing the company to violate fair employment practices laws by discriminating in favor of Negroes. This and other issues never reached the stage of legal, precedent-setting opinion by the court, however. High-Low agreed to a new covenant on July 7, 1967, just before the final hearing on the motion for a permanent injunction.

As business development became the central theme of the negotiations, it also began to expand as a program in itself. From the small group of businessmen who were meeting during the fall of 1966, came the idea of increasing the assets of the black-owned financial institutions—both banks and savings-and-loan associations—through appeals to both the community at large and to governmental agencies that could make substantial deposits of public funds. This idea tied in with the urban renewal controversy in the Englewood area which involved some of the SCLC staff from the Chicago Freedom Movement, since one of the major supporters of the urban renewal project was the president of the white-owned Chicago City Bank, which stood to gain a great deal from the removal of housing units to provide room for expanded parking and shopping facilities in the renewal area. In November of 1966, Breadbasket and the Englewood protestors had urged Negroes to withdraw their accounts from Chicago City Bank and open accounts in the black banks which were sensitive to the needs of the black community. This "bank-in" action had an encouraging, though not overwhelming, response. The idea of "banking black" was developed and interpreted as part of the content of "black power": an account in a black bank was more meaningful evidence of concern for the black community than an Afro hairdo. The "banking black" program was extended when the Steering Committee agreed on January 20, 1967, to send telegrams to several government officials asking that public funds be deposited in black banks as a means of strengthening the economic base of the black community. Although Chicago's Mayor Richard J. Daley and Cook County Treasurer Edmund Kucharski ignored the request, Illinois State Treasurer Adlai Stevenson III responded. After forming a new state policy for the investment of public funds, he announced substantial deposits in Seaway National Bank and Independence Bank of Chicago on May 3, 1967. This high-level affirmation of the importance of economic development for the black community helped confirm Breadbasket's role as a program for black economic growth.

As concern for the development of Negro businesses increased, the meeting of businessmen that had started in the fall of 1966 grew in importance. In December of 1966, the main content of the meeting was the problem of distribution which the Negro businessmen, numbering less than ten at the time, faced in the chain stores. By January, 1967, the group had grown to include a variety of other kinds of businessmen, such as scavengers, exterminators, advertising specialists, building contractors—essentially the range of businesses represented in the negotiated covenants. As the size of the meeting grew from about a dozen, counting the Breadbasket staff that attended, to about thirty in several months, the content of the meeting changed too. Less and less of the agenda dealt with specific problems of individual businesses; more and more of the meeting was directed toward expounding the vision of Operation Breadbasket and how the businessmen of the black community needed to reorient their concerns from simply profit for themselves to the total economic development of their community. The preaching about healthier relationships among black businessmen and connecting social concern with business growth struck responsive chords among the struggling black entrepreneurs. They brought their friends to the meeting, and in just a few more months the group had grown to around 300, taxing the capacity of the Hales Student Center cafeteria of the Chicago Theological Seminary. With the addition of a small group of musicians who were faced with discrimination in securing major engagements, some special guest celebrities and eventually a youth choir, the once-small meeting of businessmen grew into an event in its own right. This was the genesis of the regular "Saturday morning meeting" of Operation Breadbasket which, after the assassination of Dr. Martin Luther King, Jr., mushroomed into a major weekly mass meeting attracting approximately 3,000 people at its peak.

Operation Breadbasket exhibited its primary focus on business development by sponsoring a "Trade Exposition and Seminar on Negro Businesses" on March 3 and 4, 1967. The purpose of this event was to make people, primarily white business leaders, more aware of the existence of Negro businesses, and to bring together a variety of resources to discuss, clarify and point to some solutions of black business problems. The main conclusion of the seminar was that "Negro businessmen are particularly excluded from access to capital for business growth and investment."[18] Several businessmen, both white and black, considered this problem and suggested some kind of a "pool of capital" available to minority businessmen on a more lenient basis than was possible through regular lending institutions. By July, 1967, Operation Breadbasket staff members were organizing a "Small Business Investment Corporation" to meet the investment needs of black entrepreneurs. Although subscriptions were solicited for the SBIC, and federal matching funds were assured, the program never materialized, primarily because of disagreement over how much control Operation Breadbasket should retain over the business decisions of the corporation.

The Business Seminar also focused on another weakness of Negro businesses: their general inability to advertise their products or services. Once a black manufacturer placed his products on the supermarket shelves, the problem was getting the consumer interested in purchasing them. This concern led to the formation of "Consumer Clubs" [See pages 291-303 for the Guide for Consumer Clubs.][19], which served not only as a means of effective person-to-person advertising but more importantly as a network of communication within the black community about the goals and programs of Operation Breadbasket. Formed primarily around the black businessmen, consumer clubs were groups of ten people organized by a "captain." This captain would attend a weekly meeting to learn about Breadbasket's latest activities and receive the consumer club assignment for that particular week. The assignment might be to buy a specific black product, such as Grove Fresh Orange Juice or Diamond Sparkle Wax. The assignment might also indicate to buy these products at a certain store or chain of stores, giving the consumer clubs a forced-marketing effect, so that no chain could claim that there was no demand for particular products. About once a month, all the consumer club members would attend a mass meeting to hear the effects of their activities on the growth of Negro businesses and to gain some inspiration about their role in the economic development of their community, which appeared to be fairly significant. Most of the product companies showed great increases in their sales volume, some doubling and one expanding by six times its previous volume.

The consumer clubs used organized consumer power not only to reinforce black businesses but also to picket and withhold patronage during selective buying campaigns, such as against High-Low Foods during the summer of 1967. The consumer clubs eventually added other consumer concerns to their activities, such as uniform pricing within a chain, the conditions of stores, and most importantly the quality of meat and produce. Several stores were picketed because of over-priced and spoiled meats.

As a form of organization within Breadbasket, the consumer clubs faded out of existence by the end of 1967. Some activity over the quality of meats continued well into 1969 on a rather sporadic basis, but even this ceased. The support generated through the consumer clubs was channeled into other programs, such as the Poor People's Campaign, which will be discussed later.

With the concentration of attention on Negro businesses, the group of businessmen meeting on Saturday mornings grew rapidly with many people wanting to become "members" of Operation Breadbasket. Like SCLC, Breadbasket was not a "membership" organization with dues and membership cards identifying those who would benefit from the negotiations. The only form of membership Breadbasket had was participation: if a person took part in the programs of Breadbasket, he was considered a "member." In dealing with the many businessmen who wanted to reap benefits from the negotiations, however, this vague concept of membership was problematic. Rev. Jackson appointed a committee to consider possible requirements for

214

the businessmen's group: was attending the Saturday meeting sufficient, or should other criteria or standards be applied? On May 2, 1967, a group composed of four Breadbasket staff members (Jesse Jackson, David Wallace, Gary Massoni and Al Pitcher), and four black businessmen (Cirilo McSween, Lester McKeever, Ernest Lafontant and Jerry Bell) met at the home of a University of Chicago Business School professor, Robert McKersie, to draw up some recommendations. The group agreed that there should be some standards developed and applied to businesses that wanted to be part of Operation Breadbasket, and that these might help the staff of Breadbasket provide the kind of help that a businessman might need at a particular stage of business development. Some general agreement that a black businessman wanting to join actually had a functioning, legitimate business was the first criterion. The group then agreed that some general standards of quality and safety were necessary in terms of evaluating a given product. The most important criterion, however, was some sense of cooperation with the goals and programs of Operation Breadbasket. In discussing the meaning of this cooperation in concrete terms, four specific criteria emerged: (1) each business "member" must bank in a black bank; (2) each businessman must organize a consumer club; (3) each businessman should participate, if possible from an economic point of view, in the program of "Movement Advertising," which was a program for cooperative advertising by the businessmen organized by the Breadbasket staff in November of 1966; and (4) each businessman should share in some regular program of contributions to the Southern Christian Leadership Conference. For this latter point, the unresolved question was whether contributions were to be considered assessments on the growth of the business or simply voluntary contributions out of a spirit of cooperation. Although various formulas were later considered, none was applied, so that the contributions never became thoroughly systematic but remained free-will donations.

These four criteria for membership, plus a broad fifth point about cooperation with any new Breadbasket program, became the standards for evaluating a businessman's community concern. The task of assessing this orientation for social concern became the function of the membership committee which came to be known as the "Attunement Committee," with Cirilo McSween as chairman. This committee met regularly to consider various issues related to the participation of businessmen in Breadbasket and to determine if particular businesses should be considered "members" and listed in the Operation Breadbasket "Directory of Black Businesses."[20] The committee soon developed a backlog of over thirty applications because of the difficulty—if not impossibility—of determining the "attunement" of a person. There was a tension within the committee over having a relatively open fellowship in which the members grew in their attunement as opposed to a relatively circumscribed group composed of those whose attunement to Breadbasket's way of thinking was clear and definite. This issue was never resolved satisfactorily, and the backlog grew to nearly 100 as the committee considered a variety of other important issues relevant to Breadbasket's program of business development. By the end of 1968, the Attunement Committee effectively ceased functioning as a "Commercial Division" was organized among the businessmen with a different structure for internal control.

FOUR

National Expansion

While business development was the central focus of Operation Breadbasket's activities early in 1967, the theme of national expansion began to dominate the program by the end of the year. In following through with negotiations in the retail food industry, the attention of the staff and ministers centered mainly on strengthening and expanding Negro businesses. Once the major chains were covered, however, the selection of new targets was guided primarily by consideration of the potential for a nation-wide campaign. Some of this national perspective was involved in the A&P negotiation in 1967. In later negotiations with Continental Baking Company, Hammond Organ Company and Walgreen Drug Stores, national potential clearly became a decisive factor. The only exception to this extended view was a negotiation with Certified Grocers of Illinois, concluded on November 17, 1967, which was partly a follow-up on the agreement with Certified's dairy subsidiary, Country's Delight, and partly an extension of the business demands to Certified's individually-owned stores.

The perspective of nation-wide action was developed early in Breadbasket's history but did not come to expression in any significant way until the local program in Chicago reached a relatively sound position, thus affording Jesse Jackson greater latitude in his travels and interest in organizing support for Breadbasket in other cities. The national scene was in view in November, 1966, when Dr. Martin Luther King, Jr. appointed Jesse Jackson "Director of Special Projects and Economic Development" for the Southern Christian Leadership Conference. Part of this job was to raise funds for SCLC, which immediately involved drawing on resources outside of Chicago. The staff at that time consisted of Jesse Jackson, Dave Wallace, Gary Massoni, Carol Griffin, Al Pitcher, and Jack Finley, an SCLC photographer and communications technician. In addition to the simultaneous activities of pursuing the program of negotiations and organizing the Negro businessmen, this staff began developing a fund-raising program called "Support a Worker" (SAW). The essence of the SAW program was to help large contributors, especially churches which had contributed to SCLC in the past, feel more directly related to the workers in SCLC's programs and thus encourage them to increase and regularize their contributions. A brochure was designed with the assistance of two black advertising men, Larry Shaw and Vince Cullers. Jesse Jackson then began to seek out commitments from potential contributors. Since he conceived of fund-raising as a secondary facet of an economic development program, he travelled to several cities to organize support for SCLC and Operation Breadbasket and got commitments to the SAW program as an extra benefit. The interest generated in SCLC's northern thrust, particularly in the successes of Operation Breadbasket in Chicago, made the SAW program a fair success as long as the staff in Chicago kept up with the necessary contact to remind the contributors of their commitments. The SAW program eventually faded out because of insufficient staff resources to keep it functioning.

In March of 1967, Dr. King prepared his recommendations to the SCLC Board for a thorough reorganization of SCLC's programs and structure, putting the highest priority on the "massive job of organization to gain economic and political power for Negroes," and stressing that "the achievement of long term objectives requires that movement activity be undergirded by organizational structure and stability."[21] Part of his recommendations were to expand the activities of Operation Breadbasket and to make Rev. Jesse Jackson the "Northern Director" of Operation Breadbasket, with Rev. Fred Bennett as "Southern Director." Dr. King also proposed a "national conference of clergymen" as a means of "launching a nation-wide Breadbasket program." The conference was to be composed of five ministers from twenty cities. When the conference was held at the Chicago Theological Seminary from the tenth to the twelfth of July, 1967, 155 ministers from forty-two cities attended. This conference solidified nation-wide support for Breadbasket and created a strong network of communications.

Unfortunately, neither SCLC nor Operation Breadbasket took seriously enough the need to organize systematically this unprecedented potential for economic power for the black community. After the conference was over, three target companies were announced, including General Motors, without any information about them and without any later follow-through on the announcement. Even after Dr. King appointed Rev. Jackson to be "National Director" of Operation Breadbasket during the SCLC convention in August, 1967, and a budget was submitted for the national program, significant commitment simply was not evident except in the rhetoric. The proposed budget for the Chicago operation called for a total of eight staff members, while the national program budget called for only four, two of whom were to be secretaries. Neither the Chicago nor the national staff reached these proposed levels until much later. In spite of the limited resources for a national program, however, the projections continued.

Toward the end of 1967, Rev. Jackson's travelling schedule outside Chicago was increasing as he visited various cities that were possible areas for the development of Breadbasket programs. Without staff undergirding, however, none of these other programs realized their potential.

Also toward the end of 1967, Dr. King and other leaders of SCLC were making plans for the "Poor People's Campaign." All of the SCLC staff was to be involved, either totally or at least partially, in this major assault on the system that trapped millions of people in poverty. Much of Rev. Jackson's time in the first months of 1968 was devoted to promoting support for the Poor People's Campaign. The staff in Chicago, which had now grown to about a dozen counting some key volunteers, generally continued with the programs of business development and negotiations, though some of their energy was also directed toward SCLC's larger program. Occasionally, Chicago staff members were called on to assist the organizing in other cities. When Dr. King was in Memphis, Tennessee, to assist the organizing of black garbage workers for better wages and conditions, Rev. Jackson and Gary Massoni were called on to coordinate a state-wide boycott to support the demands of the garbage workers and to focus attention on other categories of unorganized and underpaid workers. These plans were cut short by the assassination of Dr. King on the balcony of the Lorraine Motel in Memphis on April 4, 1968.

From this point, Jesse Jackson was primarily involved in the Poor People's Campaign, as was David Wallace who assisted him with his duties in Resurrection City. Rev. Ed Riddick, Breadbasket's Director of Research, focused much of his attention on developing a nation-wide campaign against P. Lorillard, a diversified company that made its fortune in the tobacco industry. The basic operations of the Chicago program were in the hands of Rev. Calvin Morris, Associate Director. Gary Massoni split his time between working with the black businessmen and the negotiations, including the national projections. Rev. Willie Barrow spent some time with a group of businessmen, but mostly worked on organizing action against stores that were selling rotten meat. With attention focused on the Poor People's Campaign and its demonstrations with Resurrection City in Washington,

D.C., Breadbasket in Chicago did not achieve anything significant during this period except attempting to involve the hundreds of people who thronged to the Saturday Morning Meetings after the death of Dr. King asking what they could do to help realize Dr. King's "Dream."

Once the first phase of activities of the Poor People's Campaign was over, Jesse Jackson began to project a national Breadbasket program again, and to stimulate again the local negotiations. With more staff time available, the negotiations began to move again. Several new companies were approached in order to get the necessary employment information, and all of the companies with whom Breadbasket had previously made agreements were asked for a progress report. From previous reports and meetings, and from the new reports, A&P turned out to be the most striking potential target.

In twelve months, A&P had hired only eighty-three additional black employees, and most of these were not in the more significant classifications outlined in the covenant that called for 770 new black employees. In two of the most crucial categories that Breadbasket wanted to see improved, A&P had even lost some of the blacks they had had. The businessmen were also having problems with A&P, and to add insult to injury, the executives of A&P refused to make any new commitment to increasing their minority employment. On July 6, 1968, Breadbasket began picketing several A&P stores. When A&P made no response, the picketing escalated to several more stores. Eventually whites who wanted to support Operation Breadbasket began picketing several suburban stores. The picketing seriously affected A&P's business in the whole Chicago area, yet they remained unwilling to make any commitment to improving their relations with the black community.

By the middle of September, it became clear what was holding the A&P executives back: they had not perceived the meaning of Breadbasket's concerns and had too little creativity to come up with a program proposal. Sensing that if given a concrete program, A&P might respond, the ministers of Operation Breadbasket appointed a committee to draw up a set of specific program proposals to present to A&P. With other chain stores, such specificity had not been necessary; the executives were generally able to devise a program that met the concerns expressed by Breadbasket in the negotiations. A&P, however, needed something more concrete; so on September 23, 1968, the negotiating team presented nine pages of "Proposals for A&P's Action."[22] Several more days of negotiations were necessary, but finally on October 5, 1968, A&P signed the most comprehensive covenant

Operation Breadbasket had ever designed.[23] Although it called for only 268 additional black employees, it included provisions for two black executives for A&P, selected with the approval of Operation Breadbasket, to work within the company to make certain that the letter and the spirit of the covenant became company practice every day. One of these executives was to oversee the improvement of A&P's black employment pattern, to develop training programs for blacks, and to hold seminars for white supervisors to make them aware that racist behavior was against company policy. The other black executive was to supervise the implementation of the expanded demands for minority business development.

During this three-month campaign against A&P, Breadbasket was launching something approaching a national campaign. During the SCLC convention in August, Breadbasket staff members led workshops on Breadbasket's program and the situation with A&P. After the convention, several other cities opened campaigns against A&P. Even though there was support for the Campaign in Indianapolis, Cincinnati, Philadelphia, Madison, Wisconsin, New York and the state of Virginia, no truly national negotiation took place and no nation-wide agreement was signed. Local covenants were signed in Chicago and Indianapolis, but elsewhere the action fizzled with no concrete results.

The Breadbasket staff was not unaware of the national significance of the A&P campaign, but no mechanism had been worked out to coordinate local and national issues and thus fashion a comprehensive form of agreement. The possibility of such a national victory was also hampered by the lack of staff resources at the national level. Rev. Ed Riddick and Gary Massoni prepared "Guidelines for the Organization of Breadbasket Outposts" [Reproduced in this volume, pages 305-326.],[24] but there was insufficient staff available to organize chapters in other cities in a systematic way and to provide sufficient communication and instruction in the procedures and orientation of Breadbasket. By the end of 1969, Breadbasket was claiming active chapters in New York, Los Angeles, Cleveland, Atlanta, Houston, Cincinnati, Milwaukee and Indianapolis. However, these local operations were functioning only sporadically, primarily due to the lack of assistance from the national office of Breadbasket and the lack of coordination.

FIVE

Program Proliferation

With Rev. Jesse Jackson spotlighted as a national leader by the news media, reinforced by his role in the Southern Christian Leadership Conference and by his own projections, Operation Breadbasket experienced a profound transformation. So closely identified were the leader and the operation that as his interests and responses to issues expanded, so did the programs of Breadbasket. As Rev. Jackson envisioned activity in areas beyond the basic negotiations for employment and business development, the programs of Breadbasket proliferated beyond the scope of the original conceptual framework.[25]

Cultural Events

The first new thread of interest was in the direction of greater cultural development. In late November, 1968, Rev. Jackson announced that Chicago would have a "Black Christmas," described as "an affirmation that black people are beautiful, proud and productive." The primary thrust of Black Christmas, with its own black "Soul Saint" dressed in a dashiki of the colors of Ghana's flag, was to create new psychological imagery for the black community, to inject some new cultural content into the popular "black consciousness." Black Christmas was also to be a means of emphasizing the spiritual dimensions of Christmas in ways especially relevant to the black community. There was emphasis placed on developing new relationships within the black community to break down some of the alienation that separated blacks from each other. Some of this was to be realized by the black Soul Saint who made special visits to schools, prisons, and hospitals. The main approach to these new relationships involved the material dimension of Black Christmas, namely shopping at black businesses and giving black products as gifts. In this sense, Black Christmas was an extension of the theme of black business development tied to a cultural event. The second Black Christmas, in 1969, reflected the commercial element even more clearly as dozens of Negro businesses set up sales counters inside the Operation Breadbasket Black Christmas Center in the old Fuller's South Center department store. The main impact of Black Christmas, however, was in its cultural qualities as it reinterpreted the traditional Christian festivities in terms of the experiences and needs of black Americans.

Early in 1969, shortly after the first Black Christmas season was over, Rev. Jackson announced a similar "Black Easter" program. Again there was the material dimension which stressed the importance of buying black products and shopping in black stores. Again, too, the dominant emphasis was cultural. For the Easter season of 1969, Good Friday fell on April 4—one year to the day following the assassination of Dr. Martin Luther King, Jr. Thus one aspect of Black Easter was to celebrate the life of Dr. King and to reaffirm the efforts that continue to help make his "Dream" come true. Part of the program was a parade on Easter Sunday to honor black leaders, to "resurrect the lives of our black heroes." Part of Black Easter in 1969 and again in 1970 was the production of the "Passion Play" written by Willa Saunders Jones, as an expression of support for a black-produced theatrical presentation.

Later in 1969, Rev. Jackson announced a third quasi-cultural event, a "Black-Minorities Business and Cultural Exposition," which came to be known simply as "Black Expo." For this event, the cultural dimensions were secondary, though there was an exhibit on the history and cultural heritage of Negroes and there were many black entertainers expressing the contemporary black culture. Some of the goals of the Expo were to educate the public about black businesses, to demonstrate that Negroes were not just consumers but were also producers of goods and services, and to show that blacks were not apathetic and lazy but were creative and innovative. The dominant aspect of Black Expo, however, was commercial, both for the black businessmen who had booths to exhibit their products or advertise their services and for Breadbasket which benefited from the sale of tickets to the display area and to the entertainment. The results of the first Black Expo were beyond expectations. Over 600,000 people passed through the exhibit area during the three-day period of October 3 through 5, 1969. So successful was Black Expo that plans were started for an even larger and longer exposition in 1970. Black Expo '70 was to be more national in scope, drawing black businessmen from around the country to promote their enterprises along with Chicago businessmen. Black Expo '70 was also to pull together other segments of leadership in the black community, such as politicians and physicians, to engage in discussions about the future of blacks in America. In November of 1970, the second Black Expo was held, coming close to the projections made for it. Black political figures, businessmen, entertainers, doctors, and lawyers from several cities gathered to discuss problems and issues in their own areas.

Closely related to these cultural events was the development of the Operation Breadbasket Band and Choir. Part of the interest in this area came as a result of problems faced by black musicians in their efforts to be included in major musical events. For example, the Chicago Symphony had no black musicians even though some of the major concert artists were being coached by black musicians who were musically qualified to join the orchestra. Likewise, black musicians had difficulty in being fairly represented by their union which generally gave significant and long-term engagements to white performers and low-paying, temporary "gigs" to black musicians. The "Music Department" of Operation Breadbasket was established as a way to begin dealing with such problems as well as to help locate and develop other musical talent in the black community.

Though the Music Department was formed in early 1969, there had been an Operation Breadbasket Band since 1967 when a few musicians began attending the Saturday morning meetings at the Chicago Theological Seminary. They brought their instruments and played a couple of numbers at the Saturday meetings as well as at other rallies for Breadbasket. Shortly after the assassination of Dr. King, the "Operation Breadbasket Orchestra" produced a record album entitled "The Last Request," based on Dr. King's request that the band play "Precious Lord, Take My Hand" at a mass meeting in Memphis scheduled for the night of April 4, 1968. Shortly after the album was released, efforts were made to organize a large choir to sing at the Breadbasket meetings. During 1969, and into 1970, both the band and choir were significant groups, numbering about twenty musicians and nearly one hundred vocalists, and added significantly to many activities including fund-raising affairs and political rallies.

Commercial Division

Operation Breadbasket continued to work on the problems of business development by organizing, late in 1968, a "Commercial Division" for the black businessmen who wanted to be part of the program. Although some general meetings of black businessmen were held sporadically in 1968, the structure of the Commercial Division with its own internal mechanisms was not worked out and implemented until early 1969. On January 28 and 29, 1969, five businessmen (Cecil Troy, Rual Boles, Celious Henderson, Charles Crockett and Daryl Grisham), one business school professor (Fred Allvine), and one Breadbasket staff member (Gary Massoni) met to draw up the structure of the Commercial Division. This group was expanded to become the Planning and Coordinating Committee, with Mr. Henderson as chairman, to be responsible for the implementation of the division's programs and for the content of the larger Commercial Division meetings. On February 18, 1969, a prestigious "Business Advisory Council" was convened as the basic policy group. However, many of the members of this group were unable to follow through on their commitment to serve on the Council, so that the Planning Committee, after considerable time had passed, became the *de facto* policy and executive group.

The Commercial Division became an important source of support for Breadbasket's many other involvements. The businessmen provided major support for the Black Easter program, including sponsoring floats in the "Resurrection Parade." They were the prime organizers of the Black Expo displays and managed the overall affairs of the exposition. They provided important assistance during the extended activities of the Illinois Campaign Against Hunger in the summer of 1969, and for the subsequent Breakfast Feeding Program. Several businessmen of the Commercial Division formed a group to sponsor the broadcast of the Saturday Morning Meeting of Operation Breadbasket, beginning in March of 1969.

In addition to participating in other Breadbasket activities, the Commercial Division also had its own programs, such as workshops on business problems and a campaign to advertise and promote black businesses. Through the efforts of Al Pitcher, who was spending considerable time organizing the black contractors to increase their capacity for larger construction projects, and several contractors in the Commercial Division, the Board of Education of the city of Chicago awarded a black contractor the right to build a new high-school, the first such project to be awarded to a black construction company.

Among the product manufacturers, a sales organization called United Distributors was organized to solidify their distribution in the Chicago market and to expand their distribution to other Midwestern cities, and eventually across the nation. The Planning Committee also considered an expanded format for this kind of business solicitation program for service businesses. However, by the end of July, the Commercial Division as a whole began to focus all of its attention on the Black Expo for 1969. By the end of the year, the Commercial Division was being transformed into a different structure, called the Breadbasket Commercial Association, Incorporated, under the direction of Noah Robinson, a graduate of Wharton School of Business and Jesse Jackson's half-brother. The Commercial Association developed a staff of its own, and provided several consolidated services to the black businessmen.

Hunger Campaign

Another thread of Breadbasket's activity was the "Illinois Campaign Against Hunger," an extension of the Poor People's Campaign into 1969. The Hunger Campaign was partially a continuation of Rev. Jackson's national role in SCLC's program to eliminate poverty, but the campaign took on a character much its own as it drew on the resources of the Breadbasket staff in Chicago. Even though staff members were also working on other projects, such as organizing businessmen or preparing for Black Easter and the production of the Passion Play, all of the staff was involved to some extent in the Hunger Campaign.

The first goal of the campaign was to raise the issue of hunger to the consciousness of the general public and second to stimulate action to eliminate hunger from Illinois, one of the richest states in the nation, and thus set an example for other states to follow. After a brief effort at organizing neighborhood "hunger hearings," the first major event of the campaign was an effort to block the passage of a bill in the state legislature that would have cut $125,000,000.00 from the welfare appropriation—about 30% of the total. Breadbasket organized a mass demonstration on May 14, 1969, in Springfield, at the state capitol, and brought sufficient pressure to have the Speaker of the House, Rep. Ralph Smith, drop his own bill to cut the welfare budget.

Speaking before the "Committee of the Whole" of the Illinois General Assembly on May 14, 1969, Rev. Jackson presented his position paper on "Human Subsidy," which sought legislation aimed at "stopping all hunger and malnutrition in this state and removing the scourge of poverty and destitution from its people." [Reproduced in this volume, pages 331-340.][26]

The concept of "human subsidy" was proposed as an alternative to the degrading system of "welfare" that trapped people at the bottom of the economic scale. The distinction was already established in the minds of legislators who had no trouble voting considerable subsidies to businesses to guarantee them some degree of survival protection and decent standard of profit but who balked at hand-outs to poor people to assure them some decent standard of living. Applying the concept of subsidy to human beings was an attempt to open constructive means for people to rebuild their lives in the midst of an affluent economy that left no room for the poor. The position paper on human subsidy called for legislation on the following points:

(1) That the State will declare hunger a disaster destroying human lives.
(2) That slums will be declared illegal.
(3) That the state and federal governments will raise the subsidy level for all people.
(4) That the Means test will be removed since it compels people to make embarrassing public disclosures of their possessions in order to receive money for food and shelter.
(5) That the Food Stamp Program be abolished as it stigmatizes persons when their real need is for money to purchase necessities of life.
(6) That the state (and federal government) will establish emergency job training programs for unemployed and hungry people. This should be done in much the same way that job training programs were developed to meet the emergencies of war.[27]

The first three points of the human subsidy proposal were the creative challenges to the legislators and the governor's administration. Under certain agricultural legislation, an area of widespread hunger could indeed be declared a "disaster area" and thus entitled to federal aid to ameliorate conditions. Through legislation to protect the rights of tenants and through tougher housing codes and more vigorous code enforcement, many aspects of slum conditions could be eliminated by becoming both illegal and unprofitable to unscrupulous landlords. Raising the "subsidy level" for all people in the state to a "decent standard of living" would be a key step in eliminating poverty in Illinois and in the rest of the country. Neither the state legislature nor the federal Congress, however, has yet come to grips with these issues.

After the successful demonstration in May, Breadbasket began to organize another mass demonstration in Springfield as the culmination of a tour of several cities in Illinois to underscore the extent of poverty and hunger throughout the state. Beginning in Rockford, the "Hunger Trek" gained the support of local community groups, walked through the town's poorest areas to expose the conditions to the public, and held a mass rally to arouse support for the final march on the state capitol. This pattern of activity was repeated in Peoria, Decatur, Aurora, East St. Louis, Carbondale and Cairo, Illinois. On June 26, 1969, the caravan of the Hunger Trek returned to Springfield along with supporters from all over the state, this time with the purpose of supporting some positive legislation to end hunger. Representative Robert Mann had proposed a bill increasing the state's school lunch programs which was being considered by the legislature at the time. Due partly to the demonstration of widespread support for this school lunch program bill by the Hunger Trek, the legislature approved Rep. Mann's bill. Strong support from within the legislature came from the new "Coalition of Black Legislators" which Rev. Jackson had helped form among the eighteen black elected representatives in Springfield.

After this effort to eliminate hunger at the state level, Breadbasket took the Campaign Against Hunger back to Chicago to stimulate action at the metropolitan level. Mayor Richard Daley appeared to respond when he promised that no one in Chicago would go hungry and then opened several "emergency food distribution centers." His system, however, only aggravated the plight of poor and hungry people by deducting the value of the emergency food from subsequent welfare payments. In July, Breadbasket began planning a free-breakfast program as a way to meet human need directly while at the same time demonstrating the fact that governmental agencies were not taking sufficient responsibility to "promote the general welfare." On August 6, 1969, Breadbasket opened two free-breakfast centers on Chicago's south side. These "Hunger Breakfast Feeding Program Cells" were open to anyone who wanted to eat breakfast—no questions asked. The food for the program was gathered through donations, largely from suburban whites who wanted to support Operation Breadbasket in some way. The centers were manned by volunteers, except for overall supervision by Breadbasket staff. In a matter of days, the first two locations were feeding over a hundred people, and within a few months more locations were opened which served several thousand meals each week.

Political Activity

Breadbasket's efforts for human subsidy legislation point to a significant turn toward political action to affect the "public economy" as distinct from the negotiations within the "private economy." Breadbasket's interest in politics stemmed from an early awareness that economic power and political power go hand-in-hand, that black independent politicians could not go far without an independent economic base of support in their own community. With its early successes in gaining jobs for blacks and opening new markets for growing minority businesses, the foundation seemed to have been laid for increased political action. In 1967, Rev. Jackson provided some support for Richard Hatcher in his campaign for election as Mayor of Gary, Indiana. In 1968, Rev. Jackson made his concerns in the political field clear when he endorsed Richard Ogilvie, the Republican candidate for Governor of Illinois, and Hubert Humphrey, the Democratic candidate for President of the United States. The basis of these endorsements was to stimulate a more healthy tension between the two major political parties for the benefit of the poor and the blacks who were generally forgotten by both parties. Some of the Breadbasket staff became involved even more directly in other political campaigns, such as the reelection bid of Carl Stokes in Cleveland and the campaign of Kenneth Gibson in Newark. In both cities, Jesse Jackson, a few other staff members and the Breadbasket Band helped stir up support for the candidates and generate a greater turnout of voters. In Illinois, Breadbasket was directly involved in Al Raby's campaign to be a delegate to the Illinois Constitutional Convention, in the November 18, 1969, election. In January, 1970, Breadbasket organized a "Political Education and Voter Registration Division," which was essentially an attempt to get people involved in political activity. The division developed a training program to prepare workers for political campaigns and voter registration drives.

At a staff retreat on August 25 and 26, 1970, Rev. Jackson announced that Breadbasket's primary thrust would be political action, with economic concerns—including negotiations for jobs, the hunger campaign, and business development—as the secondary thrust. In terms of priorities, resources, and the assignment of staff, Breadbasket was moving directly and primarily into political activity. However, the political focus was questioned by some of the staff partly because a shift in priorities meant draining staff attention from other programs, and partly because such a shift into politics came a little late to have much effectiveness, at least in Chicago's political situation. Breadbasket would have barely seven months to have an effect on the mayoral campaign, and even less than that for the aldermanic elections. In spite of the hesitation, however, Breadbasket turned its attention to political action. Ostensibly, the strategy was to organize in several selected wards to win the aldermanic election and thus build toward a coalition party to shake the Regular Democratic Organization in the mayoral election in April, 1971.

Jesse Jackson intended to run for mayor himself as the chief architect of the platform for the coalition of independent candidates. However, partly because other strong black leaders had made motions in the direction of running for Mayor of Chicago, Rev. Jackson did not declare himself a candidate until several weeks into 1971, and then it was a guarded announcement. The strategy changed to be simply a matter of getting an independent on the mayoral ballot. Rev. Jackson filed a suit in the circuit courts to have his name placed on the ballot with only a few thousand signatures on his nominating petitions, charging that the election laws unfairly discriminated against independent candidates by requiring a far greater number of signatures than were required for regular party candidates. The case went to the United States Supreme Court, with the hope of getting emergency relief in time to have Rev. Jackson's name placed on the ballot. The Supreme Court refused to take emergency action, thus cancelling any hope of his name being on the ballot. However, Rev. Jackson, expecting the Supreme Court to rule in his favor, had not worked out an adequate alternative strategy for the election, by this time only days away. Since no significant ward organizing had been done, Breadbasket had little noticeable effect on the aldermanic elections, and no effect on the mayoral election. Rev. Jackson's endorsement of the Republican-backed candidate Richard Friedman on the day before the election had no apparent effect on black voters on April 6, 1971; Mayor Richard J. Daley was reelected to his fifth term by an overwhelming margin.

Negotiations

Simultaneous with programs of cultural enrichment, political action, business development and hunger protests, Breadbasket's negotiations continued, though on a rather sporadic basis and in a de-emphasized fashion in relation to the overall operation. After the major success against A&P in October of

1968, the next negotiating effort was with a small chain of grocery stores located exclusively in the poorest black areas of the city. This chain of Red Rooster stores had the unenviable reputation as the worst stores in the ghetto: high prices, low quality products, spoiled meat and continual "errors" of overcharging at the cash register. The customers, most of whom lived in public housing and who survived on meager public assistance, could ill afford such practices. However, there was little competition from the major chains, most of whom had retreated far from the poorest sections of the black community. Also, the stores' marketing strategy was to offer bargains on some basic item such as bread or chicken or occasionally milk. While even these bargains were suspect (for instance, one batch of chickens at $.19 per pound was alleged to have been frozen for several years and chemically treated to obscure its taint), they nevertheless provided poor people, with no other alternative, some food for their tables. On several occasions, local neighborhood groups had protested against their nearby Red Rooster store, but with little success. Even city enforcement of freshness standards and weights-and-measures standards seemed to get lost in the courts. In November, 1969, some of the Breadbasket staff and ministers from the Steering Committee began to gather the complaints against Red Rooster from all over the city. On February 29, 1969, a meeting was held with Red Rooster to present the combined demands of the various community groups along with the usual Breadbasket demands for black business opportunity and improved employment for blacks. As it turned out, all of Red Rooster's employees were black except for the key executive positions, which were held by the owners. The main buyer and the day-time store managers were also white and also partners. Shortly after the first negotiating meeting, Red Rooster appointed a black night-manager as a "vice president," and later during a boycott and picketing campaign "promoted" this same man as a figurehead "president."

These empty promotions did not take the pressure off Red Rooster stores, however. The boycott continued until officials of the chain agreed to resolve the grievances and meet the demands of the community groups and Operation Breadbasket on March 15, 1969. This victory did not amount to much, however, for within a few months the owners of Red Rooster stores found themselves in federal court on tax delinquency charges. They attempted to sell their store operations to some black investors, and eventually went out of business. The significant part of the campaign and victory was the cooperation that occurred among the community groups which led to the formation of the "Coalition for United Community Action." Although Breadbasket had originally brought the concerns of the various groups together against Red Rooster, the conclusion of the campaign was really in the hands of the Coalition's own leadership.

After the Red Rooster agreement, the Coalition stayed together and grew to include nearly sixty organizations of various sizes from three or four people to hundreds of members. The Coalition moved to protest the lack of community involvement in the Model Cities program in Chicago, and then turned to attack discrimination against minority workers in the building trades unions and the whole construction industry. As a member-organization, Breadbasket continued to be involved in these activities, including the mobilization of marchers around some building sites and the symbolic reconvening of the SCLC convention in Chicago (after adjourning in Charleston, S.C.) as an expression of national support for the Coalition. The campaign for greater justice in the construction industry climaxed with the signing of the "Chicago Plan" on November 6, 1969. The Coalition, however, did not follow through on enforcing the agreement which was soon accepted by the leaders of the building trades unions and the construction companies. The leaders of the Coalition turned their attention to creating a "think-tank" for black community development called the "Black Strategy Center," which dissolved early in 1971.

For its part, Operation Breadbasket had not continued with other negotiations in 1969, after the Red Rooster campaign. A few of the ministers continued with occasional follow-up meetings with some of the supermarket chains, but there was nothing in the way of new negotiations. During a special meeting held on April 20, 1970, the ministers discussed the problems of the negotiations program with Rev. Jesse Jackson. He reassigned a staff person to work with the ministers on the negotiations as a concrete step to revive the program.

By the end of April, 1970, the ministers reestablished contact with Walgreen Drug Stores to pursue the negotiations initiated in 1968. Officials of Walgreen balked at making any specific, concrete commitment to improving their employment pattern. Like most other companies, Walgreen had their black employees in the lower-paying jobs and almost no blacks in the higher-skilled and higher-paying positions. There were no black workers at all in most departments of the company's national headquarters, and very few in the district level of supervision. By the middle of May, 1970, it was clear that Walgreen would be the target of a selective buying campaign. On

June 3, 1970, the boycott was launched with a letter sent to Breadbasket's supporters throughout the Chicago metropolitan area asking them not to shop at Walgreen Drug Stores until an agreement was reached. Several Walgreen stores were picketed on June 6 and June 13. More picketing was planned for June 20, but was suspended when Walgreen displayed a new spirit of cooperation. After a series of meetings to finalize an agreement, on June 27, 1970, Mr. Charles R. Walgreen, Jr., was present at the Saturday morning meeting to sign the covenant with Operation Breadbasket.

Several new issues were incorporated in the Walgreen covenant[28] having to do primarily with the means of recruiting and hiring black workers and of monitoring Walgreen's progress in fulfilling the agreement. The meetings that followed the new procedures proved to be fairly effective in finding the company's weak areas in implementing the covenental agreement, and thus resulted in greater effectiveness in improving the employment situation within Walgreen.

Other Divisions

While these various programs and activities were going on, the number of sub-groups within Operation Breadbasket was growing. For many issues that Breadbasket touched, additional sub-divisions were attached to the operation. At one point there were over forty such auxiliaries of various sizes and stages of development. Over a period of time, these groups resolved themselves into about twenty groups representing the spectrum of Breadbasket's interests. While the staff of Breadbasket did not always spend much time with many of the groups, they all were considered somehow related to Breadbasket.

Breadbasket began to call all of these sub-groups "divisions," some of which were functioning programs that developed early and some of which were only recently formed groups with no particular program. The ministers Steering Committee became known as the "Ministers Division," or sometimes the "Negotiations Division" according to its main function. The black businessmen were part of the "Commercial Division" which later became the "Breadbasket Commercial Association." The Breadbasket Band and Choir formed the "Cultural Development Division." Black school teachers became the "Teachers Division." Black union organizers and labor leaders worked together through a "Labor Division," while doctors and nurses organized a "Health Division." The voter registration and political education activities came under the "Political Education Division." A school to teach key-punch skills and computer programming was organized under the "Data Processing Division." The issue of hunger was continued under the "Special Projects Division." Several scattered fund-raising activities were consolidated under a "Fund-Raising Division" which operated with almost no relationship to the Breadbasket stuff. The development of support among whites in the suburban areas around Chicago proceeded through the "Suburban Alliance Division."

Functioning as a part of the ministers' group was the "Prison Outpost," coordinated by the Rev. Jessie "Ma" Houston, to maintain a creative relationship with prisoners in the city and county jails and the state prison in Joliet. Several young women formed the "Models Guild" which provided hostesses for such events as Black Expo. A group called the "Skills Bank" was organized to inform newcomers to Breadbasket about the operation and channel their skills into the appropriate division. In the summer of 1970, a group of black men formed "Black Men Moving" as a way to maximize the participation of men in Breadbasket's activities. Perhaps a dozen other groups appeared and disappeared between late 1969 and late 1970. Most of these never really functioned and so will not be named here.

SIX

Disintegration
of the Threads

During 1970, Operation Breadbasket's effectiveness began to suffer as a result of the proliferation of programs, the accumulation of so many auxiliaries, and the disintegration of the various program threads. The Campaign Against Hunger, which had been so much in the forefront during 1969, seemed to be holding strong when Breadbasket presented "A Hunger and Health Manifesto" on February 26, 1970, which called for a variety of state and city governmental programs to "declare hunger illegal" and assure all citizens adequate food and health care. Within a few months, however, Breadbasket brought no further public pressure to bear on the state or city administrations to act on the proposals of the manifesto. After a few minor protests against inadequacies in the city's free-breakfast program, Breadbasket began terminating its own feeding program. By the middle of 1970, the program against hunger was limited to distributing bags and boxes of donated food to poor people on an emergency-demand basis and through occasional food "give-outs" in various neighborhoods, including a rural area in southern Cook County. By the beginning of 1971, the Campaign Against Hunger was, for all practical purposes, a program of the past.

The program for black businessmen also seemed to be gaining momentum in the first months of 1970. The Commercial Division had grown to a fair size and was developing a variety of programs to help the businesses grow with more stable support. With the arrival of Noah Robinson, a relative of Rev. Jackson who had earned a Master of Business Administration from the Wharton School of Finance and Commerce, to head up Breadbasket's business development programs, prospects looked good for a strong thrust in this area. As soon as the "Breadbasket Commercial Association" was incorporated separately, however, tensions developed within the operation. There was confusion about the relationship of the new Commercial Association to the rest of Breadbasket, and how its problems and needs fitted into the needs and directions of the other programs. The most specific conflict was between the Commercial Association and the ministers who were negotiating for increased opportunities for black businesses to penetrate the retail chain store market. It was not clear whether the ministers were to negotiate business concerns in general terms, with the Commercial Association following with more specific contracts to negotiate, whether the two groups simply negotiated together, or whether the ministers did all the negotiating and the Commercial Association served as a monitor on progress in the business development areas of covenants. Although there were several efforts to deal with this issue directly during June and July of 1970, the problems were not resolved. For the Walgreen covenant, the ministers handled the uneasy situation by consulting with the Commercial Association about the kinds of business development issues that ought to be included and then proceeding to do the negotiating themselves, hoping that the implementation would be monitored by the Commercial Association. Although the Commercial Association was not satisfied with the Walgreen covenant, the staff did not offer any alternative approach and made no further effort to develop a cooperative relationship with the ministers. The tension between the quasi-autonomous Commercial Association and the rest of Operation Breadbasket increased to the point that, by the fall of 1970, the Commercial Association was no longer considered an integral part of Breadbasket. During the first few months of 1971, many of the key black businessmen in the Commercial Association became disenchanted with the strained relationship with Operation Breadbasket, which they had supported since 1967. Several of these businessmen also felt that the dues and commissions they were paying the Commercial Association were not producing an adequate return in terms of market expansion. Consequently, some of the main black businessmen pulled out of the Commercial Association and began an effort to reorganize another Commercial Division within the main body of Breadbasket.

The ministers who carried on the program of negotiations also went through what seemed a hopeful period. After the negotiations with Red Rooster as part of the Coalition for United Community Action in March, 1969, the negotiations were essentially idle until early 1970. Several ministers who wanted to reactivate the negotiations called a special meeting to discuss the situation with Rev. Jackson. At a meeting on April 20, 1970, Rev. Richard Lawrence, as spokesman for the sixteen ministers present, raised four issues for Rev. Jackson's attention: (1) the need for some form of "council" to tie together the various programs of Breadbasket and to work out priorities; (2) the need for a staff person to be assigned to work with the negotiations on a full-time basis; (3) the need for some clarity about the relationship between Operation Breadbasket and the Commercial Association; and (4) the need for some process for the ministers to share in the planning of national negotiations and the coordination of various local activities. Rev. Jackson responded only in general terms to three of the points, but he did assign a staff person to work on the negotiations without interruptions from other programs. This was the first time since 1967 that any staff member had been assigned to work exclusively with the negotiations, which were supposed to be the core of Breadbasket's operation. The ministers moved ahead with the negotiation with Walgreen Drug Stores, even though the question of the Commercial Association's role was left unresolved, and concluded a covenant on June 27, 1970. The ministers then turned their attention to National Food Stores, with whom a covenant had been signed in December, 1966. In meeting with National Food Stores officials to review progress on the 1966 covenant, it became clear that the company had come nowhere near trying to fulfill the agreement for more black employees in the significant job classifications, and that the company had no clear commitment to improve opportunities for minority businessmen. After an unusually long period of negotiations—due largely to the tensions within Breadbasket over how decisions about negotiations were to be made—the ministers announced a selective buying campaign against National Food Stores on November 6, 1970. Because of the internal problems, however, Breadbasket as a total organization did not take decisive action against National in support of the negotiating ministers. With attention focused primarily on political activity, Breadbasket mustered only shabby support for the boycott. The campaign dragged on over the winter at a relatively weak verbal level. To complicate this situation, a nationwide boycott of A&P Food Stores was announced by Rev. Jackson on the basis of a meeting with some Breadbasket ministers in Brooklyn, New York. By not consulting the ministers in Chicago about the A&P negotiation, and by not supporting the boycott against National Food Stores, Breadbasket and Rev. Jackson effectively discouraged many ministers from further action in the negotiations program. Over the first few months of 1971, there was some discussion of how to finish the National campaign and how to respond to the nationwide A&P campaign. As of May, 1971, however, no further action had been taken on these two campaigns, and the primary issue of how decisions should be made, and by whom, remained unanswered.

Breadbasket's political impotence in the 1971 mayoral election has already been discussed. In spite of the ineffectiveness shown in April, Breadbasket continues to push in the direction of political action. This thrust is essentially Rev. Jackson's projection and has not as yet involved the rest of the Breadbasket staff in any significant way. His most recent direction is toward developing a "third political force" for the 1972 presidential elections, hoping in some way to have an effect on at least the Democratic platform and selection of candidates. Except for some discussions with a few black elected politicians, the concept of a "third political force" remains at the level of rhetoric and may well remain an illusion unless some concrete organizing undergirds the idea.

The decline in effectiveness of Breadbasket's programs is reflected in a decline in attendance at the Saturday meeting, which is a kind of program in itself. While Breadbasket once boasted of attendance of over 3,000 people, during the first months of 1971 the attendance was closer to 1,500 people a week, many of these being visitors from white suburban areas seeking some contact with the rhetorical inspiration of the black community. The band and the choir, which once were a unique attraction and gave definite character to the Saturday meetings, are also losing their impact. The band has all but disappeared due to disagreements over the role of the musicians in the operation, and some members of the choir are critical of the "circus" atmosphere of the meeting which seems to have lost its focus on programs and action.

Internal Tensions

In addition to the proliferation and subsequent disruption of Breadbasket's major program threads, and the unwieldy accumulation of auxiliaries, the operation has suffered from increasing tensions within various segments of the programs and especially within the staff. Most of the internal turmoil seems to center around the questions about the decision-making process.

As early as May of 1967, during a retreat for staff and ministers at the Tower Hill Retreat Center, there was some discussion of how the Breadbasket staff dominated the decisions so that the ministers of the Steering Committee felt as though they had no responsible role in determining the program of negotiations. To a great degree, the staff, particularly Rev. Jackson, did dominate the decisions. This was partly due to the heritage of the Southern Christian Leadership Conference, which is a staff-operated organization, and not a constituency-based operation. As a department of SCLC, Breadbasket remained consistent with the style of the parent organization. This was also partly due to the charismatic qualities of Jesse Jackson, who was generally able to evoke support for his ideas. Whatever the reasons, the effect was some sense of estrangement among the ministers in relation to the process of making decisions. A "reflection-fellowship" group which met weekly for several months during 1967 helped bridge some of the gap between the staff, some of the ministers and a few of the businessmen. The issue, however, remained unresolved at the structural level.

Until early 1968, the ministers' Steering Committee remained, in theory, the primary structure for making decisions, even though the staff actually dominated this group and made many decisions apart from the Steering Committee in matters not directly related to the negotiations. At an extended staff conference in March, 1968, however, Rev. Jackson announced a new organizational structure which included an "Executive Committee" as the basic decision-making group. This Executive Committee, to be appointed by Rev. Jackson, was to determine the policy of Breadbasket, and to validate the "recommendations" of the Steering Committee. The shift in the role of the Steering Committee from making "decisions" to making "recommendations" was to be a safeguard on the validity of the actions of the Steering Committee. Since the Steering Committee meetings were open to any minister who wanted to participate, there was some fear that such an open-membership made the operation susceptible to infiltration from hostile organizations. Though the Executive Committee was to be primarily a protection for the negotiations program, it soon was described as the source of direction for the whole operation. Thus, the Executive Committee was to establish policy, review program recommendations, and assign staff as it determined.

The Executive Committee was composed of nine persons, four of whom were staff, four were ministers, and one was a businessman who within a few months became an SCLC official. Since the non-staff persons had many responsibilities outside of Breadbasket, they were not always so fully informed as the staff members, so that they often relied on the recommendations of the staff members on the Executive Committee. There were two main consequences of this situation. First, since only part of the program staff members were on the Executive Committee, a gap developed between those on the Executive Committee and those not on it. There was a sense among some of the program staff that their ideas and program needs were not being fairly presented and interpreted to the whole committee, and thus that they were not participating effectively in the decisions. The second consequence was that the staff continued to dominate the decision-making process, only in a more limited manner. The Executive Committee, and thus the whole operation, was under the direction of a very few people.

By the end of 1968, the Executive Committee had become a source of great friction within Breadbasket. Having assumed the role of reviewing all program activities and ideas, the Executive Committee became overloaded with problems to consider. Decisions were not made on many program questions; though operational issues were discussed, few were resolved. The time required for the meetings made it increasingly difficult for the non-staff members to participate. Before long, the Executive Committee faded into the background. Rev. Jackson, two staff members and the SCLC official continued to make the decisions.

With the deterioration of the Executive Committee, Operation Breadbasket started 1969 under structured staff domination. Rev. Jackson was the "National Director," giving him final and overall control of the operation. Rev. Calvin S. Morris was "Associate Director," to be considered the director in the absence of Rev. Jackson. On an informal but effective basis, Rev. Morris gathered around him a "cabinet" composed of Cirilo McSween (the SCLC official) and Rev. Willie Barrow, one of the other staff members from the Executive Committee. With Rev. Jackson out of the city regularly, this group became the decision-making structure for the Chicago operation.

This new "cabinet" also became a source of tension within the operation, particularly among the staff members. While staff reports to the directors were required from the program staff, many of the issues and questions raised were not answered or even considered by anyone. Although there were weekly staff meetings, these were mainly report sessions; there was no regular means for consultation between the program staff and the Associate Director or National Director. Part of the program staff felt increasingly alienated from the decision-making process. These tensions were compounded during this period by personality conflicts and differences in expectations and styles which were not dealt with directly and resolved. There were also tensions between blacks and whites on the staff. Although SCLC as a whole was committed to having an integrated staff, and though Rev. Jackson often talked of needing an integrated staff in a racist society as "an oasis of hope in a desert of despair," it was nevertheless not easy to have a smooth-functioning integrated staff during the period of popular "black consciousness" and "black power."

Besides the staff, other segments of the operation felt cut off from the decision-making structure. For most of the program areas, the problem was even more acute, since some programs did not have a full-time staff person even trying to be heard. A "Workers Council" was formed to help draw the staff and other workers in programs closer together, to have them share in the planning of forthcoming actions, and to coordinate activities among various areas. Part of the hope of the Workers Council was to develop additional secondary leadership by keeping more people informed and involved in the planning of activities. The high hope for this group soon faded, however, when the meetings became nothing more than reporting sessions from the directors. The workers only occasionally made reports and rarely had any role in planning activities.

By the beginning of 1970, there were serious divisions within Breadbasket, especially within the staff. Partly as a result of the lack of coordination and close consultation between the program staff and the directors, programs were lagging. At the end of March, 1970, there was a surge of activity around the Hunger and Health Manifesto, the one-time showing (March 24) of the documentary *King: a Filmed Record . . . Montgomery to Memphis*, and the second "Black Easter" and production of the "Passion Play." Early in April, however, the problems within the operation were acute. Everyone was exhausted from the weeks of preparation for the events of the last days of March. Rev. Jackson was seriously ill and went on an enforced vacation to recover some health. The office closed for a period of time. There was great uncertainty about the future, since almost nothing was happening in the way of program activities. The Associate Director left for a vacation, and rumors circulated among the staff—with confirmation from Rev. Jackson—that Rev. Morris had resigned.

Faced with an absence of active leadership and feeling acutely the frustrations of the previous months over the inadequacy of the decision-making process, part of the program staff raised several issues with Rev. Jackson in California. These issues included: (1) a complete review of programs to evaluate what Breadbasket should do and how programs should be administered; (2) revamping the decision-making structure to invest responsibility and authority for planning and implementing Breadbasket's operations in a "strategy board" composed of the staff members and other key actors from the major program areas; and (3) improvement of the economic benefits for the staff, who were considerably underpaid and enjoyed no fringe benefits, not even reimbursement for automobile expenses.

Rev. Jackson's response to the proposals was positive. He agreed with the concept of the Strategy Board, and agreed that its first assignment should be the total program review. He promised to work out the salary raises and fringe needs himself (which he did by August, 1970). Thus, the Strategy Board, which at this point consisted only of staff members, was launched during the meetings with Rev. Jackson on May 2 and 3, 1970. The first part of its task was to formulate an organizational structure according to some evaluation of the current and potential programs, and then to bring in other non-staff representatives from the various program areas. Before the Strategy Board had gone very far, however, conflicts arose within the staff about the purpose of the group. Although most of the program staff conceived of it as a means to be fairly represented in the organization's decision-making process, some perceived it as a threat to their autonomy within their program areas. Also, the Associate Director, returning to dispute the reports of his resignation, perceived it as a direct threat to his position. Consequently, even though the Strategy Board was dealing with one level of Breadbasket's structural problems by being more inclusive of the program staff and by moving toward involving other important volunteers, it failed to deal with the divisions that persisted within the staff. It promoted cooperation among part of the staff, but aggravated the tensions among others. Primarily because of the lack of trust, the Strategy Board disintegrated by August, 1970.

With the disbanding of the Strategy Board, Breadbasket's decisions again centered on the directors, primarily on Jesse Jackson. Although he was more decisive than the previous methods of deliberation, some of the basic organizational issues remained. It was still unclear what the limits were for a staff person to make decisions in his program area without referring a recommendation for a decision. There was still no way for staff members or other program leaders to participate in the ordering of priorities for Breadbasket's action. There was no way to draw together the concerns of the various program areas except through one person: Jesse Jackson.

The problems over the structure for decisions in Breadbasket were compounded by a diminishing clarity of vision and purpose among the staff. Without a defined role in determining the operation's direction, many staff members found themselves being quite busy while accomplishing little. The staff expended a lot of energy, but too much of it was random motion, and as Rev. Jackson once phrased it, "all motion is not progress."

As Operation Breadbasket moved into 1971, it faced a difficult situation. With cloudy goals, an inadequate system for arranging priorities, deteriorating structures and internal turmoil, Breadbasket had to resolve some basic organizational issues before it would be able to forge an effective role for itself in the future. A more thorough analysis of Breadbasket's organizational structure and internal dynamics would be in order as a step toward suggesting how Operation Breadbasket can meet its primary challenge.

Part II

Organizational

Perspective

Modes and Forms
of Authority

Having reviewed the historical development of SCLC's Operation Breadbasket in Chicago, two related elements stand out as significant in relation to organizational structure. The first is the expansion of the operation from a relatively simple program to negotiate for more and better jobs for Negroes into a relatively complex, multi-program approach to the development of the black community. This has meant an increase in the size of the staff, in the range of the programs and in the scope of the vision that inspires both the staff and the programs. All of this growth has not been without problems and frustrations, and has challenged the staff to develop more effective means of operation and administration. Having grown beyond the capacity of a single person to control, Operation Breadbasket has required the development of structural forms for guiding its functioning. As the historical survey has suggested, however, Breadbasket has not been completely successful in developing a viable decision-making structure.

The second significant feature of Breadbasket's development is the rather unique person of Rev. Jesse L. Jackson, the National Director. Jesse Jackson was a key element in the formation of the nucleus group that started Breadbasket in Chicago, and a key factor in guiding Breadbasket's programs and projecting its goals and purposes. The personal power of this individual has been the most crucial component in shaping the character, genius and power of Operation Breadbasket as it has been and, no doubt, as it will be in the future.

At one level, the expansion of Breadbasket and the role of Rev. Jackson are complementary. Though the growth of the operation is partly due to needs and circumstances within the black community, the extension of the programs has paralleled the extension of his vision and understanding and analysis of what ought to happen. At another level, however, these two factors have been in profound conflict. This tension is between the need, on the one hand, for systematic organization to fulfill specific, defined goals and to cope with the requirements of an expanding operation, and on the other hand the need for immediate response to the creative ideas and spontaneous directives of the inspirational "leader." Systematic efforts to accomplish particular goals or to maintain some continuity in programs has frequently been broken by the direct intervention of the leader by reassigning staff or by creating an entirely new program thrust. On the one hand, Breadbasket attempts to become a significant organization which exercises power to achieve particular, concrete results in terms of community development. On the other hand, Breadbasket remains a kind of charismatic movement under the direct, personal control of the leader.

This kind of tension between "charismatic inspiration" and "systematic organization" is not unique to Operation Breadbasket. History contains many examples of the effect of exceptional personalities on the growth of organizations which attempt to embody their thinking. One of the most thorough and useful discussions of the factors involved in this type of organizational dilemma is found in the writings of Max Weber. A review of his topology of "legitimate authority" and his description of the "routinization of charisma" should be fruitful in establishing a clearer perspective on Breadbasket's organizational problems and what might be suggested for the future of the operation.

Weber's analysis focuses on what holds an organization together and how the basis of cohesion affects the structure and style of organization. Weber proposes the concept of "legitimate authority" as the strongest force in binding an organization together. Weber defines "authority" as "the probability that a command with a specific content will be obeyed by a given group of persons."[29] This is not the same thing as "power," which Weber defines as the "probability that one actor within a social relationship will be in a position to carry out his will despite resistance, regardless of the basis on which this probability rests."[30] Power is a more general concept which relates to any kind of social relationship, whereas authority specifically involves the response to "commands" within some set of formalized relationships of a structured group. This group is generally designated as the "administrative staff" of an organization, defined as "a system of continuous purposive activity of a specific kind."[31] The authority that binds the administrative staff in obedience to the commands of their superiors (or superior) can be based on a variety of things, including custom, calculation of material advantage, ideal motives and personal devotion. Weber asserts, however, that these factors "do not, even taken together, form a sufficiently reliable basis for a system of imperative coordination. In addition there is normally a further element, the belief in legitimacy."[32] Legitimacy essentially means the acceptance of authority in a situation as binding, so that the people involved orient their actions according to their belief that the formal structure of power is valid or legitimate.

Weber proposes a classification of organizational types, indicating that "according to the kind of legitimacy which is claimed, the type of obedience, the kind of administrative staff developed to guarantee it, and the mode of exercising authority, will all differ fundamentally."[33] Weber distinguishes three "pure-types" of legitimate authority according to the basis of the claim to legitimacy:

> 1) Rational grounds—resting on the belief in the 'legality' of patterns of normative rules and the right of those elevated to authority under such rules to issue commands (legal authority).

> 2) Traditional grounds—resting on the established belief in the sanctity of immemorial traditions and the legitimacy of the status of those exercising authority under them (traditional authority); or finally,

> 3) Charismatic grounds—resting on devotion to the specific and exceptional sanctity, heroism or exemplary character of an individual person, and of the normative patterns or order revealed or ordained by him (charismatic authority).[34]

It should be noted that Weber intends these to be understood as "pure-types" which may not be found in any historical situation in any exact or complete way. Rather, he is attempting to delineate the logically coherent characteristics of each type for purposes of clarity. This form of analysis can be useful in making sense out of the confusions and contradictions of historical reality as found in the conflicting tendencies within an organization such as Operation Breadbasket.

Traditional Authority

At this stage of history, traditional authority is not decisive for understanding Operation Breadbasket. The claim to legitimacy of a "traditional" order is based on the sanctity of traditionally established relationships and powers of control as they have been derived from the past. Further, the person or persons exercising authority are designated according to traditionally transmitted rules and claim personal obedience by virtue of their traditional status.[35] As yet, Breadbasket does not appeal to the sanctity of traditions or to traditionally transmitted rules as the basis for decision-making. In fact, Breadbasket often emphasizes its newness and its discontinuity with a variety of established standards and patterns. Tradition, privilege, and status-honor do not regulate relationships in Breadbasket in any primary way as they do in a traditional order. The loyalty of the administrative staff to the leader is not based on his traditionally hallowed dignity as in a traditional system.

Although a traditional basis of authority is not primary for Breadbasket's authority, there are some elements of this type that are relevant to the operation's development. These have to do mainly with Breadbasket's relationship to the religious traditions of the black community. There is a degree of acceptance of Breadbasket's decisions among many people in the constituency on the basis of deference to the patterns of the black religious heritage. This acceptance reflects the generally authoritarian pattern of black preachers in black churches, and the significance of black churches in the social organization of the black community. E. Franklin Frazier points out that "organized religious life became the chief means by which a structured or organized social life came into existence among the Negro masses."[36] He goes on to describe the particular situation within the Baptist churches (in which the majority of blacks have always been concentrated) which allowed greater opportunities than other churches for self-assertion and leadership. "This naturally resulted in a pattern of autocratic leadership which has spilled over into most aspects of organized social life among Negroes, especially in as much as many forms of organized social life have grown out of the church and have come under the dominant leadership of Negro preachers."[37] Although the influence of the black church has been greatly reduced by the forces of modern urbanization, Frazier concludes that the black church is still an important institution in the black community since blacks have generally been excluded from other opportunities for organizational participation and experience. "Since, as we have seen, the pattern of control and organization of the Negro church has been authoritarian, with a strong man in a dominant position, the same pattern has characterized other Negro institutions."[38]

This authoritarian pattern of organization has been carried over into Operation Breadbasket, too, and provides the basis for some people to accept its leadership. This similarity to black churches is not entirely accidental on the part of the Breadbasket staff, which has been aware of the significance of the church in the life of black people. Breadbasket's inception in Chicago was within a religious context: Rev. Dr. Martin Luther King, Jr. addressing an assembly of clergymen. Breadbasket's motto follows a religious theme: "Your Ministers Fight for Jobs and Rights." The operation is often referred to as "the church in action." When Breadbasket took its first step beyond employment opportunity and began to deal with business opportunities for minority entrepreneurs, the Saturday morning breakfast meeting was established. As this meeting grew in size, the character of the meeting changed from a gathering of businessmen to become a form of worship service complete with singing, praying, and, of course, preaching. Some respect and deference was given to the status of the "Country Preacher," as Jesse Jackson came to be called, and the ministers on his staff. This religious sanctity was cultivated from time to time in various circumstances to enhance the prestige and validity of Breadbasket's activities, not only among churches but also with the news media, by emphasizing the title of the *Reverend* Jesse Jackson or other members of the Breadbasket staff such as the Reverend David Wallace, the Reverend Calvin Morris, the Reverend George E. Riddick, the Reverend Gary Massoni, etc.

Breadbasket has drawn upon the black church traditions and the broader black culture experience for some other elements of its style. The Breadbasket Band and Choir have been used very effectively to reaffirm the richness of the black musical heritage, to provide people with opportunities to express their creativity in the field of music, and to gain an additional measure of acceptance for the operation through its appeal to the common cultural legacy. The special programs of Black Christmas, Black Easter and Black Expo are efforts to reinterpret traditional events in ways which are more relevant to the "black experience," and thus to stimulate meaningful new traditions for the black community.

Operation Breadbasket is also beginning to develop some traditions of its own, both in terms of its form of organization and in the content of its vision. Reflecting the authoritarian character of the Negro church, which generally includes a strong central leader, Breadbasket shows some tendency to solidify this pattern in its internal structure. Much effort is spent reinforcing the importance of the position of the director and, in his absence, the associate director. Although deference to these positions is expected partly because of the wishes of the leader, some "respect for the office"—not necessarily the persons—is expected because of the inherited pattern of a central authority-figure which is gaining the force of tradition.

Some value-orientations in Breadbasket have also developed some effect of their own apart from the charismatic inspiration that formulated them. Primary among these is the acceptance of each person regardless of social circumstances. This is expressed in a litany repeated at every Saturday morning meeting, "I Am Somebody," which affirms the importance of each individual even though he or she might not be respected by the general society:

> I am somebody
> I may be black
> But I am somebody
> I may be poor
> But I am somebody
> I may be on welfare
> But I am somebody
> I may be in jail
> But I am somebody
> I may be uneducated
> But I am somebody
>
> I must be respected
> I must be protected
> I am God's child
> I am somebody

While this openness to everyone has some effect on strengthening relationships within Breadbasket and developing greater unity in the black community, it is somewhat modified by another value which can also be seen as a tradition within Breadbasket. This is the idea of participation and contribution. While everyone is accepted as "somebody," more appreciation is accorded those who take an active part in the operation's programs. Such involvement becomes a means of gaining status based not on rationally evaluated performance but on enduring support and continuing effort. This is often expressed in terms of what a person "brings to the banquet table." To achieve status in Breadbasket, a person has to come with "more than an appetite," and must participate in the programs and be attuned to concerns for community development as more important than personal gain.

In some ways, then, Breadbasket does have some emerging elements of tradition which help determine to some degree the relationships within the operation. As yet, however, these aspects of traditional authority are not primary.

Rational-Legal Authority

Although Breadbasket is developing some traditions of its own and nurtures its continuity with the black religious and cultural heritage, the major tension within the operation is between the characteristics described by Weber as "rational-legal" and "charismatic." As already suggested, this tension is partly the result of the growth of the operation and the increase in the number of functions and programs encompassed by Breadbasket. This expansion necessitated some division of labor among the staff with some rough definitions of areas of responsibilities. These developments have given the staff of Operation Breadbasket some of the characteristics which Weber attributes to the administrative staff of an order claiming rational or legal authority.

Weber's first characteristic of rational-legal authority is that there is "a continuous organization of official functions bound by rules."[39] The essential elements here are the delineation of functions, the arrangement of these functions into a coherent order, and the elaboration of rules or abstract principles for the execution of the functions. The first element has been thrust upon Breadbasket by the sheer size of the operation; any given member of the staff is no longer able to do every function all the time, so that specific functions have been sorted out and assigned to specific staff members. Thus, there has been the development of "divisions" or "departments" within Breadbasket which tend to be synonymous with major programs or functions. There are, among others, the Ministers Department which carries out the negotiations program, the Special Projects Department which operated the Campaign Against Hunger, and the Communications Department which handles press relations, news releases and other forms of information distribution. This delineation of functions, however, is not sufficiently comprehensive to handle adequately the second element: the arrangement of these functions into a coherent order. Several functions have been defined but have not been placed in the framework of "departments" or "divisions" with any consistency. A major example is the execution of direct action campaigns, especially picketing. On one occasion this function will be the responsibility of the Ministers Department, at another time of the

Special Projects Department, and yet another time of "Black Men Moving," which is not even a division but a semi-autonomous group. Where the responsibility for picketing falls is usually a matter of the personal preference of the director and not a matter of a rational determination of the appropriate placement of the function within a logical order. Breadbasket also falls short of Weber's definition in terms of the third element: that the execution of functions is bounded by rules. Breadbasket has no established set of rules to guide the operation. Partly this is a matter of the inadequate arrangement of functions and partly a matter of the staff's orientation to freedom and creativity as opposed to rules and regulations. The absence of a set of procedural rules is also related to Breadbasket's relative youth as an operation; too little time has elapsed for many such rules to be formulated. Some operating guidelines have begun to emerge out of past experience, which is helpful, but which still misses Weber's point that these rules are generally intentionally established.

The second characteristic Weber suggests for rational-legal authority, related to the specification of functions, is "a specified sphere of competence" for members of the administrative staff. This involves: (a) a sphere of obligations to perform specified functions as part of a systematic division of labor; (b) the necessary authority to carry out these functions; and (c) the necessary means of compulsion, which are clearly defined and subject to definite conditions, to enforce the authority exercised to fulfill the defined functions.[40] Although the Breadbasket staff has been forced into the beginnings of a systematic division of labor, providing the various staff members with the necessary authority to carry out their responsibilities has been a recurring problem. In spite of the large size and complexity of the organization, the essential authority structure of Breadbasket has changed little from the centralized control by the "leader."[41] Thus the delegation of authority has not kept pace with the delegation of responsibility. Likewise the means of compulsion have remained concentrated within the sphere of the director so that the head of a department has relatively little sanction over those under his supervision. Since the necessary authority and means of compulsion have not been distributed throughout the operation, the development of departments has proceeded only so far as the informal power of individual staff members has made possible. In spite of the pressures for a more rationally coherent and efficient mode of organization, Breadbasket has not moved significantly toward the deliberate organization or ordering of functions characteristic of rational-legal authority.

The third characteristic of rational-legal authority is that "the organization of offices follows the principle of hierarchy; that is, each lower office is under the control and supervision of a higher one."[42] Within Operation Breadbasket, this characteristic is absent. As mentioned above, there is no fully-developed arrangement of functions into a coherent order, and no distribution of authority and sanction within the operation. Thus, all of the departments and the other unordered functions are essentially on the same level, with only the position of the director above them all relating directly to each one. This, of course, has meant an extreme burden on the schedule of the leader. At various points, an intermediary has been appointed to relieve some of the pressure on Jesse Jackson and to meet some of the needs for directing various segments of the operation. However, these assignments of responsibility have not carried the appropriate level of authority, and have often been undermined by the direct intervention of the leader. This method of ordering and arranging the operation has thus proved relatively useless. One area in particular underscores the problem of "hierarchy" within Breadbasket: the relationship between the "national" program and the "Chicago" program. In a hierarchically ordered structure, one would expect to find a staff person or department responsible for the national program, to which would be responsible in some way the various "local" programs including the "Chicago project." At the present time, Breadbasket has no such differentiation of staff or departments. One staff member carries the title of "National Coordinator," directly under the "National Director." However, a major part of his activities are within the "Chicago project," though he carries no particular authority over Chicago programs. There is, in effect, no ordering of the various responsibilities involved in national and local functions, and no hierarchy of supervision or control.

It should be noted that there is a definite resistance to the idea of "hierarchy" within Breadbasket, stemming from the dominance of charismatic authority which projects an image of a "community of organizers" in direct relationship with the "Country Preacher." This emphasis on "community" within the operation tends to weaken any tendency toward the hierarchical arrangement of functions and authority.

Weber's fourth characteristic of rational-legal authority has to do primarily with the preparation of a staff member for performing a specific function. Weber says that "the rules which regulate the conduct of an office may be technical rules or norms. In both cases, if their application is to be fully rational, specialized training is necessary."[43] As Breadbasket encompasses more and more functions, the need grows to find staff members with particular skills of a fairly specialized nature. For example, the relatively new and ambiguously-related "commercial association," designed to assist the growth of minority businesses within Breadbasket, depends on staff trained in economics and business management. Breadbasket is thus beginning to embody another characteristic of rational-legal authority. The extent to which this is carried will depend on a great variety of factors, not the least of which is the degree to which Breadbasket conceives of itself as a "movement" with a charismatic leader or as an "institution of power" organized around ordered functions to achieve specifically defined goals.

The fifth characteristic offered by Weber is that "it is a matter of principle that the members of the administrative staff should be completely separated from ownership of the means of production or administration."[44] This seems to be the case within Breadbasket, since the operation depends primarily on contributions from the community at large for its support and has no endowments. The ownership of the property where the offices are located could potentially conflict with this principle if the members of the administrative staff who are on the "finance board" play a dominant role in relation to the non-staff "trustees" on this board.

Finally, Weber notes that in a system of rational-legal authority, "administrative acts, decisions and rules are formulated and recorded in writing, even in cases where oral discussion is the rule or is even mandatory."[45] Within a few months of its inception in Chicago, there was a definite orientation within Breadbasket to keep written documentation of major events, such as "covenants" from negotiations. However, there are no general regulations for the operations, and only rarely have written rules been distributed within the staff. Most decisions are communicated within the staff meetings, or directly between the leader and individual staff members affected. It would be impossible to reconstitute the history of Breadbasket on the basis of recorded decisions.

Weber extends these general characteristics into a discussion of "the purest type of exercise of legal authority . . . which employs a bureaucratic administrative staff."[46] Although it is probably impossible to avoid the negative connotations of the word "bureaucratic," the meaning in this context simply has to do with the arrangement of offices, or "bureaus," and their specified functions into a continuous organization. While it will not be necessary to review Weber's detailed discussion, there are three additional characteristics of this mode of operation which are relevant to the situation of Operation Breadbasket. First of all, members of the administrative staff in Weber's "pure-type" are "remunerated by fixed salaries in money, for the most part with a right to pensions."[47] Although the staff in the early days of Operation Breadbasket was relatively insecure from an economic point of view, the relationship to the Southern Christian Leadership Conference helped stabilize this situation with fairly regular salaries. There was usually some difficulty having someone working for Breadbasket as a volunteer put on the SCLC payroll, but once the arrangement was made the SCLC salary was generally dependable. The staff received salary increases in August, 1970, paid from funds in Chicago, providing them with generally adequate salaries, although with no prospect of pensions. Secondly, in Weber's "pure-type" the "office is treated as the sole, or at least the primary, occupation of the incumbent."[48] This describes the general situation within Breadbasket, although there have been occasional exceptions. One recent exception was a person who had been given the title of "Program Director," a very crucial role in such a centralized operation. His continued role as minister of a church raised the questions of which was his primary occupation, and how well he would perform his role in Breadbasket. As it turned out, this person was unable to cope with being only a part-time Program Director. Because of this as well as some personal reasons, his position was terminated in March, 1971, and he returned to his pastoral duties on a full-time basis.

Finally, Weber points out that in the purest form of rational-legal organization, a member of the administrative staff considers his occupation a "career," with a "system of 'promotion' according to seniority or to achievement or both."[49] Because the operation does not have a long hierarchical range (i.e.: most staff members are in relatively direct contact with the leader, and thus on approximately the same level as one another), the question of promotion is not clear. There is no hierarchy of positions through which a person could be promoted. However, most members of the staff do consider their activity a "career," in that they foresee remaining with Operation Breadbasket for an unspecified length of time.

Even though Operation Breadbasket embodies to some degree several of the characteristics of Weber's category of rational-legal authority, a very fundamental element is missing. Operation Breadbasket does not claim "legitimacy" for its authority on the basis of rational organization or legal constitution. The absence of this essential quality accounts for the relative weakness of the characteristics of rational organization in relation to the predominant characteristics of charismatic authority. Breadbasket does not

259

base its validity on being a "legal" or "legally established" organization. In fact, Breadbasket's leader often points to the "supralegal" nature of the operation, emphasizing that at many points it stands in opposition to established laws. Breadbasket does not base its claim to leadership on any form of "enactment" by the black community, or even by any segment of the black community. Jesse Jackson occasionally reminds the people attending the Saturday morning mass meeting that "there won't be any voting here." Furthermore, Breadbasket does not establish its "norms" on grounds of "expediency or rational values or both."[50] The operation does follow some general norms or standards, but these are more of a moral or "visionary" nature coming directly from the charismatic leader, and do not reflect the kind of rational calculation suggested by Weber. On this point, Breadbasket's staff generally opts for "principle" instead of "expediency" in their rhetorical statements and in their operational style.

Finally, Breadbasket does not depend on an orientation among its constituents or within the staff toward acceptance of a "body of law" which "consists essentially in a consistent system of abstract rules which have normally been intentionally established," so that the process of administration "is held to consist in the application of these rules to particular cases."[51] While Breadbasket is guided by some general values, such as "justice," "freedom," and "economic development for the black community," these are not of the nature of "abstract rules" which are applicable to concrete situations. The embodiment of these principles depends upon the interpretative vision of the charismatic leader who proposes programs to be implemented and refined. More importantly, Breadbasket does not depend upon the acceptance of "abstract rules" among its supporters. In this light, Breadbasket's director often appeals to the "newness of what we are doing," to the uniqueness of the operation and the lack of precedent for its activities and decisions. A "body of law," even of a general nature, is alien to this attitude of discontinuity.

From this discussion of Weber's category of rational-legal authority, it should be clear that Operation Breadbasket bears only little resemblance to the "pure-type" at significant points. It should be equally clear, however, that Breadbasket does embody to an increasing extent several other important characteristics of this type of authority. As the tendency toward rational organization and authority increases, so the conflict within Breadbasket increases as the adequacy of the predominant charismatic authority is tested in the daily operation of a complex organization. A careful evaluation of the charismatic authority in Operation Breadbasket should thus prove helpful in determining what is in store for the future of the operation and how Breadbasket might take a greater and more informed role in guiding its own course.

Charismatic Authority

The distinguishing factor in charismatic authority is the concept of "charisma," which Weber describes as follows:

> The term "charisma" will be applied to a certain quality of an individual personality by virtue of which he is set apart from ordinary men and treated as endowed with supernatural, superhuman, or at least specifically exceptional power or qualities. These are such as are not accessible to the ordinary person, but are regarded as of divine origin or as exemplary, and on the basis of them the individual concerned is treated as a leader.[52]

Since the concern here is with the effect of charisma on forms of organization, a complete analysis of the psychological dynamics will not be attempted. However, a few points should be raised which suggest why authority based on charisma would be so potent. There are three elements to note in Weber's definition. First, charisma is applied to a person who is recognized or treated as a leader who stands in some kind of personal relationship with his followers. This very personal dimension carries a sense of immediacy and allows for more intense devotion than would be possible in relation to an impersonal system. Secondly, Weber points to the "non-ordinary," superhuman or strikingly exceptional qualities of the charismatic person. The extraordinary characteristics or special powers of the charismatic person generate a more intense admiration, respect and loyalty than could be expected in an "ordinary" situation. Thirdly, these exceptional qualities or powers of the charismatic person are considered to be in some sense "divine" or particularly purified. It is this "divine" element which is the primary basis for the intense strength or charismatic authority. Devotion to the charismatic leader is not simply a matter of "good ideas" or even "moral excellence"; it is a matter of religious commitment and participation in a realm of ultimate meaning and purpose to which the charismatic leader offers direct and personal access. In this way, charisma is a "revolutionary" force which demands an internal value reorientation, and may produce a "radical alteration of the central system of attitudes and directions of action"[53] of a person in relation to his life in the world.

While the transcendent dimension tends to characterize charisma, the concern here is with the effect of this mode of authority on concrete organizational structure. For this aspect, "it is recognition on the part of those subject to authority which is decisive for the validity of charisma."[54] In other words, the effectiveness or legitimacy of charismatic authority depends upon acceptance by the followers of the leader's charisma. Such acceptance rests on the idea that "it is the *duty* of those who have been called to a charismatic mission to recognize its quality and to act accordingly."[55]

The acceptance of the charismatic leader—the complete personal devotion to the possessor of charismatic gifts—must be undergirded constantly by "proof" of the effectiveness of the leader's "gift of grace." "If he is for long unsuccessful, above all if his leadership fails to benefit his followers, it is likely that this charismatic authority will disappear."[56] Consequently, even though charisma can demand extremely intense devotion and obedience, charismatic authority is also very unstable. The charismatic leader might feel his gifts failing him and give up, or his followers might abandon him because his powers are insufficient to help them. Such instability is inherent in charismatic authority "because pure charisma does not know any 'legitimacy' other than that flowing from personal strength, that is, one which is constantly being proved."[57] As long as the leader gives evidence of his continuing powers, "obedience is given exclusively to the leader as a person, for the sake of his non-routine qualities, not because of enacted position or traditional dignity."[58] Thus, the finitude of the charismatic leader, especially in terms of his health or his available time, is a threat to charismatic authority.

The qualities of charismatic authority just described are relatively apparent in Operation Breadbasket. The foremost factor is the charisma of Jesse L. Jackson. His charismatic qualities establish his authority with all members of the staff and with the active constituents. Consistent with Weber's definition, his power and appeal flow from purely personal qualities which are beyond the range of ordinary people. These qualities have to do with his particular abilities in rhetorical preaching, projecting a "vision," developing strategy, and using his insight into human behavior to involve people in his programs. He is able to command obedience because of the recognition of these personal qualities, not because of established or elected position (as in rational-legal authority) nor primarily because of traditional dignity and status (as in traditional authority). The acceptance of his charismatic authority is considered by the staff and regular volunteers as a kind of "spiritual duty" for those who accept the "call" to work toward fulfilling "the Dream" which Rev. Jackson projects. These elements of charismatic authority were quite intense in the early days of Operation Breadbasket in Chicago. Some of the original force has diminished with Rev. Jackson's frequent absences from Chicago for speaking engagements and "organizing" elsewhere and with the increasing size of the operation. Nevertheless, his personal authority still predominates.

As with traditional authority and rational-legal authority, there are forms of organization that are characteristic of charismatic authority. Primary among these characteristics is the composition of the administrative staff:

> The corporate group which is subject to charismatic authority is based on an emotional form of communal relationship. The administrative staff of a charismatic leader does not consist of "officials"; at least its members are not technically trained. It is not chosen on the basis of social privilege nor from the point of view of domestic or personal dependency. It is rather chosen in terms of the charismatic qualities of its members. The prophet has his disciples; the war lord his selected henchmen. . . .[59]

The staff relationship at Breadbasket's inception in Chicago were strongly "communal" in that mutual assistance had no clear limits. Personal lives and organizational lives become one. The members of the staff would as quickly wash the car of the charismatic leader as they would organize a picket line or write a press release for him. This situation has changed considerably, especially within the last two years. There is now a clearer distinction between "Breadbasket business" and "personal affairs" in terms of how staff members spend their time. Also, there are too many staff members to have a single "communal" relationship; instead there are sub-groups within the staff formed of members who relate to each other outside the office. This has resulted in "cliques" within the staff rather than a cohesive staff community.

Until recently, members of the staff were chosen for reasons other than technical or other specific skills or training. As mentioned earlier, only with the expansion of the business development program and the formation of the Breadbasket Commercial Association has there been any primary consideration for particular skills and training.[60] Otherwise, staff members have always been selected on the basis of commitment, enthusiasm, and ability to carry out some of the charismatic functions of the program, such as speaking engagements and organizing groups. Even the clerical staff must qualify in terms of commitment to a greater extent than clerical ability since extended working hours are often demanded without additional payment. In this sense, doing the job is considered its own reward.

Weber suggests that for pure charismatic authority, "there is no such thing as 'appointment' or 'dismissal,' no career, no promotion. There is only a 'call' at the instance of the leader."[61] This is largely true within Breadbasket, although most staff members conceive of making Breadbasket—or at least working with Jesse Jackson—a career. Although several staff members have left on their own decision, no staff member was ever dismissed or fired until recently. This is due partly to the lack of specific definitions or responsibility for which a staff members can be held accountable, and partly to the "communal" quality of most relationships within the staff. However, as the operation tends to become more rationalized in its operations, and if it continues to expand and encompass additional areas of functions, then particular qualifications will become increasingly important, and means of evaluation for appointment and dismissal will soon be developed. The actual tendency in this direction is confirmed by the "notices of termination" given to several staff members in March, 1971. Dismissing these persons was explained as due to "budgetary considerations." Although finances were a major factor, questions of performance were also involved.

Weber further points out that under charismatic authority:

> There is no hierarchy; the leader merely intervenes in general or in individual cases when he considers the members of his staff inadequate to a task with which they have been entrusted. There is no such thing as a definite sphere of authority and competence, and no appropriation of official powers on the basis of social privileges. There may, however, be territorial or functional limits to charismatic powers and to the individual's mission.[62]

As discussed before, there is some tendency toward the definition of areas of responsibility within Breadbasket. However, these areas do not, as yet, carry with them the commensurate authority necessary to fulfill the responsibilities. This is evident in the way the leader intervenes in the operation to reassign staff at his own discretion and initiates new programs without regard for the continuity of existing programs.

Another characteristic of charismatic authority is the absence of standardized procedures:

There is no system of formal rules, of abstract legal principles, and hence no process of judicial decision oriented to them. But equally there is no legal wisdom oriented to judicial precedent. Formally concrete judgments are newly created from case to case and are originally regarded as divine judgments and revelations.[63]

It is in this context that the leader of Operation Breadbasket often asserts the newness or uniqueness of the program, and the lack of precedent for particular decisions. Guidelines for decisions are in terms of very general principles of justice and/or considerations of strategy (i.e.: assuring success). The "non-ordinary" character of charisma is thus reflected in the "non-ordinary" character of the operation. Weber illustrates this in distinguishing charismatic authority from both traditional and rational-legal authority:

> Both rational and traditional authority are specifically forms of everyday routine control of action; while the charismatic type is the direct antithesis of this. Bureaucratic authority is specifically rational in the sense of being bound to intellectually analyzable rules; while charismatic authority is specifically irrational in the sense of being foreign to all rules. Traditional authority is bound to the precedents handed down from the past and to this extent is also oriented to rules. Within the sphere of its claims, charismatic authority repudiates the past, and is in this sense a specifically revolutionary force.[64]

While Breadbasket does not conform perfectly to the "pure-type," charismatic authority is clearly the dominant form of authority for the operation. One final characteristic of charismatic authority will confirm its dominant role in Operation Breadbasket, as well as suggest how this form of authority is being modified. Weber contends that "pure charisma is specifically foreign to economic considerations"[65] in the sense that it "rejects as undignified any pecuniary gain that is methodical and rational."[66] A charismatic structure depends upon purely voluntary "support by gifts, sometimes on a grand scale involving foundations, even by bribery and grand-scale honoraria, or by begging."[67] In general terms, Breadbasket is not an "anti-economic force," since a major emphasis is precisely the economic development of the black community and the increasing participation of blacks in the rich economy of America. However, in terms of its internal organization, economic considerations tend not to be rational and systematic. Breadbasket's relationship with the Southern Christian Leadership Conference made it possible for the program to avoid the full force of financial questions until very recently. SCLC paid the staff salaries and most of the office expenses.

265

Monies for additional operational expenses were raised locally through individual contributions. Even in terms of the attitudes of the staff, economic problems, though important, tend not to be decisive for joining or leaving the staff, or for dedication to the job. This de-emphasis of economic matters, however, is changing at the structural level. The Breadbasket program in Chicago has been given a new status under SCLC; it now functions as a "chapter" with greater financial autonomy. In August, 1970, the operation raised staff salaries, and in November, 1970, moved into new office facilities, which are being purchased rather than rented. These factors have increased the financial burden of the organization, and thus have brought financial questions into greater prominence. In spite of these increased responsibilities, though, the operation still depends primarily on voluntary contributions. As a mark of the growing importance of financial matters for the operation, one staff member was assigned at the end of 1970 to work primarily—though not exclusively—on special fund-raising projects, such as benefit concerts. This reflects not only the new significance of financial considerations, but also the continuing influence of the charismatic leader, whose personal intervention is responsible for getting performers to donate their talents for the benefit of the operation.

Routinization of Charisma

The categories of authority discussed here tend to sound like static forms. Actually, Weber was quick to point out the dynamic quality of authority, and discussed the process by which a particular style of authority changed. Relevant to the situation of Operation Breadbasket, Weber described the transformation of charismatic authority into other forms of authority. He called this process the "routinization of charisma." Since charismatic authority is inherently unstable, according to Weber, the transition to a more stable form of authority is necessary if there are to be sustained, effective results from charismatic inspiration. In any case, the process is inevitable because of the finitude of the charismatic leader. According to Weber:

> In its pure form charismatic authority has a character specifically foreign to everyday routine structures. The social relationships directly involved are strictly personal, based on the validity and practice of charismatic personal qualities. If this is not to remain a purely transitory phenomenon, but to take on the character of a permanent relationship forming a stable community of disciples

or a band of followers or a party organization or any sort of political or hierocratic organization, it is necessary for the character of charismatic authority to become radically changed. Indeed, in its pure form charismatic authority may be said to exist only in the process of originating. It cannot remain stable, but becomes either traditionalized or rationalized, or a combination of both.[68]

In discussing the "routinization of charisma" in more detail, Weber points to the continuing needs of the staff and the larger constituency of followers as the essential force behind this transition of authority:

The following are the principal motives underlying this transformation: (a) The ideal and also the material interests of the followers in the continuation and the continual reactivation of the community, (b) the still stronger ideal and also stronger material interests of the members of the administrative staff, the disciples or other followers of the charismatic leader in continuing their relationship. Not only this, but they have an interest in continuing it in such a way that both from an ideal and a material point of view, their own status is put on a stable everyday basis. This means, above all, making it possible to participate in normal family relationships or at least to enjoy a secure position in place of the kind of discipleship which is cut off from ordinary wordly connections, notably in the family and in economic relationships.[69]

These factors are apparent in the growth of Breadbasket and in the shift toward a more systematic structure. The black community, the primary constituency, has both ideal and material interests in the continuation of Operation Breadbasket. In a material sense, Breadbasket means more and better jobs and more business opportunity through its negotiations, or the chance to sell merchandise at the Saturday morning meetings, or some other similar specific benefit. Beyond this material interest, many people find ideal concerns satisfied by the existence of Breadbasket, such as the chance to pursue Dr. King's "Dream," or the chance to engage in action for community development, or to participate in uniquely "black" cultural events, or to share in a community that emphasizes the worth of each individual in spite of social circumstances. These interests of the larger community have meant an increasing sense within the staff of Breadbasket of the obligation to meet a greater variety of needs for an increasing number of people. This growing sense of obligation to meet the needs of the community is part of the ideal interest of the staff, along with their more intense interest in actualizing such ideals as "service," "justice," "brotherhood," etc.

Weber indicates that the material interests of the staff are also quite significant. Family relationships for nearly all of the members of the

267

Breadbasket staff have been under severe stress. One family has already separated and completed divorce proceedings. Another family finds itself in a very tenuous situation, and yet another finds the shift from a previously stable pattern of life troubling to the point of physical illness. This is not to say that these families would not have had marital problems if they had not been involved in Breadbasket. This is to say, however, that under the conditions of involvement in Breadbasket, with its demands for long hours and low pay and high devotion to the charismatic leader and to the ideals of the operation, such marital problems become more difficult to resolve than would be true in other contexts. Though a staff member would feel that he wanted to have a stable, well-grounded family life, the demands of Breadbasket posed conflicts which made choices in favor of the family difficult to make. Likewise, personal financial considerations have been significant for members of the staff. Weber points out that very few followers or disciples are willing to make the necessary economic sacrifices to participate in the charismatic mission on an extended basis:

> The great majority of disciples and followers will in the long run 'make their living' out of their 'calling' in a material sense as well. Indeed, this must be the case if the movement is not to disintegrate.[70]

Thus, consistent with Weber, much of the pressure to put Breadbasket on a more rational and routine basis comes from such needs among the members of the staff for greater financial stability and greater opportunity to engage in normal family activities. In order to meet the economic needs of the staff and of the operation as a whole, Operation Breadbasket has had to give more attention to its economic structure. This is, according to Weber, an indication of the transformation of charisma, when it adapts to "some form of fiscal organization to provide for the needs of the group."[71]

According to Weber, these interests of the staff and the larger group of followers become most evident when the question of the succession of the charismatic leader is faced. For the situation in Breadbasket, this is only partly relevant, since the operation does not immediately have to face the question of who will run it in the event Jesse Jackson is unable to. The question of how the operation is to be run in the absence of the charismatic leader, however, is relevant when he is absent from Chicago for long periods of time. During such absences, the structure of authority has not been clear. Some staff members continue to function on the basis of assignments directly from the charismatic leader, given either before or during his absence; some staff members cease to function effectively at all, particularly when they find themselves with insufficient authority to carry out their responsibilities; others assume authority beyond the scope of their assignments and thus undermine the development of an internal structure of authority appropriate to the assignment of functions. Thus, the temporary absences of the charismatic leader have underlined the need for a more stable and rational structure of authority in order to continue the work of the operation, and have allowed some initial vestiges of this development to take place in an informal way. The growth of this informal structure, however, has tended to be limited within "departments," and not among departments for the operation as a whole.

One final element suggested by Weber is simply the day to day needs of routine operation, in the "objective necessity of adaptation of the patterns or order and of the organization of the administrative staff to the normal, everyday needs and conditions of carrying on administration."[72] This adaptation involves some definite order in the organization of the staff itself, and some means of arranging economic considerations. One example of the effect of such needs within Breadbasket is in the way demands for printed materials, such as leaflets or brochures, are met. Until relatively recently, a decision to have a given piece of printing done was made on the basis of needing the printed piece. The decision was generally made by or consented to by the charismatic leader. Recently there have been too many printing needs within the various departments for the charismatic leader to handle directly. Decisions about printing have thus been left open to considerations of available money and persuasive lobbying within the staff by those of the department involved. Since departments have no budgetary independence, and since the responsibility for printing decisions was not located with one person or department, such as within the Communications Department or under the office administrator, an informal structure for decisions about printing has developed around the "keeper of the purse strings." Thus, a definite order is emerging within the staff for its internal organization based primarily on control of finances and only secondarily on program considerations.

This example illustrates not only the force of everyday economic pressures on the routinization of charisma, but also the conflicts that occur during this process of transformation. The lack of a rational basis for decisions about printing, aside from available money, is a source of conflict between those on the staff who seek a more systematic structure for decision-making and those who seek to appropriate authority in order to enhance their status within the operation. Add to this the force of the various personal relationships of the individual staff members with the charismatic leader, and the resulting tension becomes predictably high:

> As a rule the process of routinization is not free of conflict. In the early stages personal claims on the charisma of the chief are not easily forgotten and the conflict between the charisma of office or of hereditary status with personal charisma is a typical process in many historical situations.[73]

EIGHT

Authority and Function

The analysis of Operation Breadbasket's internal situation in terms of Weber's categories of legitimate authority could lead to the unfortunate conclusion that the leadership of the operation should opt for one mode or another, that Rev. Jackson and the rest of the staff should attempt to establish a purely charismatic group, or a bureaucratic institution, or a traditionally perpetuated set of programs. Such a conclusion would be not only impractical but nearly impossible for at least two reasons.

First, as Weber himself carefully pointed out, the categories of charismatic, rational and traditional authority are "pure-types" designed for purposes of clarity. Weber was delineating the components of distinguishable tendencies and not prescribing options for organizational perfection. Although, for example, a "purely bureaucratic type of administrative organization" is capable of the "highest degree of efficiency" and is superior to other forms of organization in terms of precision, stability and reliability,[74] it is not a perfect solution to questions of human organization. A highly disciplined rational organization tends to diminish the importance of individual action and responsibility.[75] In its pure form, this type of organization tends to suspend individual freedom, responsibility and creativity. Such consequences would not be consistent with some of the basic values and goals of Operation Breadbasket in terms of the importance of each individual. The pure form of charismatic authority, however, would not be desirable either, since the values and purposes projected need to transcend the limitations of an individual leader and become solidified in order to have sustained, effective impact. Likewise, a program established on a purely traditional basis would not be desirable, since such an operation would not be sufficiently flexible to respond to changing conditions and could lead to an insensitivity to actual human needs that were not being addressed by the inherited approaches.

Secondly, a deliberate choice of one form of authority would be impossible. Weber pointed out that in concrete, historical situations, the basis of authority is constantly subject to change. This is not to say that a group will be traditional one day and charismatic the next. The dynamic character of authority does mean that there is no static condition and that, in fact, elements of all three "pure-types" might be found in any particular situation. As the analysis here has already suggested, the basis of authority in Operation Breadbasket is predominantly charismatic, though both traditional and organizational elements are beginning to develop.

It should be noted, too, that it is not always easy to differentiate the various elements in a specific case. A particular action might be prompted by defined expectations within an organizational structure as well as by concern for following traditionally derived patterns. An order might be obeyed because the charismatic leader issued it as well as because the order made sense in terms of accomplishing specifically defined goals.

A more appropriate conclusion from this analysis would be that the various forms of authority somehow ought to be blended into a stable and workable foundation for Operation Breadbasket. Since Breadbasket is highly charismatic—a relatively unstable form of authority—some greater balance should be nurtured to include more traditional and rational-organizational elements. Although the leadership of Breadbasket cannot select simply one mode or another, the operation can be guided by conscious intentional effort toward a more stable internal cohesiveness.

The present task, then, is to make some suggestions or projections about the appropriate balancing of charismatic, traditional and organizational modes of authority within Operation Breadbasket. Although Weber points out that charisma in its pure form exists only in the initial stages of a group's activity, he does not suggest any appropriate balance of subsequent traditionalized or rationalized components. The appropriateness of such a blending cannot be determined by general rules, but must be considered in terms of the specific given context. To do this for Operation Breadbasket, it is now necessary to evaluate the effect of the three modes of authority on various operational functions. Although the set of functions to be used here is not totally comprehensive, it should be sufficiently inclusive for the purpose of suggesting some ways in which traditional and rational-organizational authority can be used consciously and deliberately to strengthen and revitalize Operation Breadbasket.

Goals and Values

The first function to consider is that of determining goals and defining values. Every organization has some specific set of goals through which it projects its understanding of itself and the world. For Operation Breadbasket, this self-conception is fairly complex and not sharply defined. The operation has long since grown beyond its motto: "Your Ministers Fight for Jobs and Rights." Breadbasket is usually described as an organization working for the economic and political development of the black community. Some of its values, however, carry it beyond even this general description. At times, Breadbasket projects itself as a prophetic assault-force against all kinds of injustices, and at other times it pretends to be a parapolitical institution for established control of the commerce and politics of the black community.

This profusion of purposes reflects the shifting basis of authority in Breadbasket; traditional, charismatic and organizational emphases are all influencing the operation's purpose and goal-orientation. As would be expected from the previous discussion, charismatic inspiration is the dominant force in delineating and projecting goals. In many ways, Breadbasket is identified with its director, Jesse Jackson. The basic analysis of community problems and projections of what ought to be done have come from the charismatic leader. The directions the operation has taken at various points have been determined largely by him. For instance, Rev. Jackson's interpretation of "black power" in terms of black unity and black cooperation (such as with black businesses) was a key factor behind several programs, especially in the area of business development. Rev. Jackson's differentiation of "power" and "influence" was the primary framework for the negotiations program, which depended on power as the "ability to cut off or supply the adversary's need" instead of influence or moral persuasion. The understanding of power as a way to change behavior and alter unjust structures, as distinguished from influence which affects only feelings and individuals, guided the negotiators in developing covenants with concrete demands on companies. Similarly, Rev. Jackson's emphasis on the theme of "I Am Somebody" has been part of the guiding understanding behind the Saturday morning meetings as a time when the "black community can come together" and people can share with one another their hope of overcoming the many problems they face as an exploited and disrespected minority.

The breadth of Breadbasket's concerns mirrors Rev. Jackson's vision. As he becomes interested in politics, Breadbasket moves into political action; as he becomes interested in issues of health care or education, so does Breadbasket.

Although Breadbasket's goals and values have come primarily from the wellspring of charismatic inspiration, some of this function is being influenced by the force of traditional elements. Some aspects of Breadbasket's identity are beginning to be related to an independent understanding of "blackness," such as concern for black unity, stimulating a stronger sense of black identity, affirming the black cultural heritage and nurturing a consciousness that every individual has a potentially significant contribution to make to the whole community. Through this connection with the "meaning of the black experience," some of Breadbasket's values and purposes are becoming rooted in the broader traditions of the black community. By emphasizing these connections, Breadbasket can draw further on the rich heritage of the black community for other goals to incorporate and thus establish its conceptions on a basis broader than just a single individual.

Organizational forces are also influencing Breadbasket's goals. The charismatic leader has described the importance of power for the black community and has discussed the need for the systematic exercise of power to solve social problems and establish justice. As Weber's analysis of the forms of authority points out, however, charisma is not a sufficient basis for sustained activity of this kind. Within Breadbasket, the formulation of some goals in terms of effective, rational organization has begun. Some of the concerns projected by the charismatic leader are being refined into goals with rational confirmation, such as the significance of economic stability or political empowerment for the black community. The implications of these broad goals are being considered in terms of establishing institutions of community control which do not depend on an individual leader for their success. Conscious decisions on the part of Breadbasket to accelerate the development of such mechanisms of power which are open to community participation would certainly enhance the development of more goals and specific directions growing out of the increasing ability of the community to determine its own destiny.

Programs and Structures

Another organizational function is to translate goals and values into concrete programs appropriate to actual conditions and to develop structures to support and sustain the programs. Broad value orientations are usually too vague and nebulous to guide everyday activities, and so must be converted into specific decisions. In Operation Breadbasket, the process of attaining goals has been guided mainly by the wisdom and insight of Jesse Jackson. The operation has functioned like a band of disciples following the inspired directives of the charismatic leader. For example, when Rev. Jackson conceived of the concept of Black Christmas near the end of November, 1968, as a means of expressing the meaning of "blackness" in the context of a traditional white holiday, the staff moved immediately to implement the programs announced by the director. In a matter of days, a Black Christmas Parade had been organized, a Black Christmas Center had opened to display and sell black-produced gift products, and a black "Soul Saint" appeared in a new outfit of the colors of the flag of Ghana. The same immediate response came when Rev. Jackson presented his concepts of Black Easter and Black Expo. The staff had to exercise great resourcefulness to pull everything together in very short periods of time with no extensive planning. Rev. Jackson also engineered the timing of most negotiations, at least until the A&P campaign in 1968. His sense of strategy set the pace for all activities in 1966 and for all major activities since 1967.

As Breadbasket grows in size, however, a single individual is less able to determine all activities. In some areas, charismatic authority is giving way to traditional patterns. For example, Breadbasket has projected a yearly "agenda for the black community" which includes celebrating the birthday of Dr. Martin Luther King, Jr., Black Easter, the anniversary of Dr. King's assassination, Black Expo and Black Christmas—along with the weekly Saturday morning meeting. This calendar of events represents a means of establishing some continuity of programs within Breadbasket. Beyond this internal effect, these activities are beginning to assume the status of "traditions" both for Breadbasket and for the black community. Some of the events already require less direct involvement of Breadbasket staff, except at the level of overall supervision, and do not depend totally on word from the charismatic leader. By reinforcing these activities and events as recurring patterns, Breadbasket can utilize the force of tradition to develop and implement other programs in this broadly cultural area.

For much of Breadbasket's activities, especially in the areas of economics and politics, rational organization is beginning to influence program development. The potential significance and effectiveness of the negotiations program is becoming a major factor in motivating the negotiating ministers in spite of the lack of attention and resources given to the negotiations by the director. Some of the ministers have been troubled by Breadbasket's internal confusions, especially those which make it difficult to get needed manpower and budgetary resources and to coordinate actions in relation to other Breadbasket activities. In spite of these difficulties, however, several ministers continue to work on the negotiations and the follow-up program. If Breadbasket nurtured this kind of rational-organizational development and provided the negotiations program with sufficient resources, especially staff manpower, and greater latitude to take action without being blocked by other kinds of activities, then this part of the operation would function on a considerably more stable foundation.

Closely related to the rational development of the negotiations is Breadbasket's research activity. So far, most of Breadbasket's research has been done to support the rhetorical statements of the director. Some research, however, has pointed out new areas of concern, especially in terms of industries to consider for negotiations. If Breadbasket would put more effort into research, and give it sufficient latitude to locate problems and issues on its own, this area could become a significant stimulant to the development of programs on a stable, rationally powerful basis. This would be especially true, for instance, in translating the concern for political empowerment into the most effective approach, whether it be voter registration, ward and precinct organizing, supporting candidates, or developing a third party. Thorough research could provide a substantial basis for immediate and long-range strategies in the political area. Research might also locate and help determine the most effective point of attack on other issues, such as health, housing and public education. By pinpointing specific injustices and locating opportunities for new programs, research can reinforce within Breadbasket the systematic translation of values and goals into programs and actions on an enduring basis.

Although Operation Breadbasket can consciously increase the effect of traditional and rational modes of authority on program development, it should not be concluded that there is nothing that charisma can contribute to the effectiveness of Breadbasket's programs. Even in the process of reinforcing the organizational and traditional aspects, charisma can maintain a high level of enthusiasm and commitment to the programs, and can maintain a crucial sensitivity to injustices that sometimes is dulled by everyday activities. The danger for the future, however, would be in letting charismatic authority continue to dominate every aspect of the operation's functioning and thus inhibit the development of programs with continuity and sustained effectiveness. The power of charismatic authority should be used intentionally to support the organizational and traditional developments.

The need for charismatic authority to support consciously the growth of the other forms of authority can be seen clearly in relation to Breadbasket's structures. Any operation with a variety of continuing programs needs to develop structures to support and coordinate these programs. So far, Breadbasket has depended primarily on the director to nurture the programs and to coordinate their various needs and directions. While this has worked well at times in the past, it is becoming decreasingly satisfactory for the future. The finitude of one person makes it impossible to spend sufficient time with each program in Breadbasket to maximize its effectiveness. Some of the burden of administration and coordination has been shifted to other positions, primarily to the associate director. However, this has been successful only to a limited degree. In a dynamic operation like Breadbasket, the pattern of centralized authority is not an adequate structure. A more adequate structure could emerge out of rational and pragmatic considerations. Since one key problem is the coordination of many programs, there should be some structure or mechanism that includes representatives from the major program areas. Although the Strategy Board, which was discussed earlier, failed primarily because of a lack of trust within the staff, something similar is still needed. If such a structure were developed and consistently supported by charismatic authority, then many of the problems of coordination and the allocation of resources might be alleviated. Some of the tensions over increasing autonomy and authority within various program areas while maintaining accountability to the overall direction of the operation might also be resolved.

Resources and Priorities

Once goals and values have been translated into programs and structures, organizations must deal with another set of functions which have to do with determining priorities and allocating resources. Some assessment of the relative importance of various goals must be made so that the operation can define in its own terms what it thinks is most important to do. This in turn affects how various resources, such as manpower, money and facilities, are distributed in order to carry out the programs and thus accomplish the goals in some order of priority. Determining priorities and allocating resources in Breadbasket has been done primarily on the basis of charismatic inspiration. Rev. Jackson's insight into what needed to be done at the time, what the staff was capable of doing and what other support could be developed for a program has guided all major activities in Breadbasket. The intense personal loyalty inspired by the charismatic leader, both within the staff and in the larger community, has made available talent which could not have been paid for. This arrangement has been relatively satisfactory in the past, but by itself is not a sufficiently stable basis for an enduring operation of the magnitude of Breadbasket.

The development of patterns within the cultural area of Breadbasket's programs is a means of establishing one level of priority on a kind of traditional basis. The repetition of Black Easter, Black Christmas and especially Black Expo has already begun to draw support and new resources to these events. The relationship of these activities to the meaning of "blackness" and the development of inherently "black" traditions definitely will be a strong attraction for some people to support and carry on the traditions. For these people, such cultural programs will be their top priority. This will ease the demand for attention and resources from the rest of Breadbasket so that other programs in other areas of importance can be strengthened.

Rational-organizational factors are also beginning to affect the resources and priorities of Breadbasket. At one level, the financial problems of the operation are starting to cut the size of the staff and what can be done. Financial limitations have seriously hampered some programs, but, as yet, have not meant the elimination of any, since an area of interest and concern can be continued at some level with volunteers. Such non-staff talent, however, should be nurtured to a more stable basis of involvement and motivation than charismatic appeal.

A more significant effect of rational considerations is in terms of the process of evaluation. Just as research can play an increasingly important role in program development, evaluation of past performance can be a crucial factor in planning the best use of resources in the future. In the context of community development and concern for economic development, for example, systematic means should be developed to evaluate what actual needs exist and then what needs could be met with available or potentially available resources. By measuring the effectiveness of previous use of resources, future allocation can be made on a more sound basis. Even though charismatic appeal should continue to draw additional resources, with the development of such organizational modes of operation, Breadbasket could project more effective programs, both in terms of immediate actions and long-range strategies.

NINE

Operation Breadbasket

as a

'Coordinating Center'

The above analysis of the effect of the different modes of authority on various organizational functions suggests that there are at least three "sub-communities" with differing orientations within Breadbasket. One sub-group is motivated mainly by direct, personal loyalty to Jesse Jackson. This group would follow the inspiration of the charismatic leader in whatever directions he projected. The second group participates mainly in Breadbasket's cultural events, including the Saturday morning meetings, largely because of their enthusiasm for the "meaning of the black experience" and for the content of the black cultural heritage. The third segment is motivated primarily by their concern for programs in whatever areas they perceive as crucial for involvement, such as employment opportunities or business development.

Although these sections of Breadbasket have differing orientations, they are not necessarily incompatible with one another nor with the development of a more viable and stably based organization. So far, the influence of the charismatic leader has maintained some degree of harmony within the operation. As discussed earlier, however, this is not a perfect and enduring solution. Unless the internal organizational tensions are somehow brought into balance, Breadbasket could deteriorate completely.

Breadbasket needs some new conceptual framework to blend the diverse elements into a cohesive operation. Following the previous analysis, such concepts as the "charismatic band of disciples" or the "bureaucratic institution" are not adequate for Breadbasket's situation. Perhaps a more useful framework would be to understand Operation Breadbasket as a "coordinating center" for black community development.

As presented here, the concept of a "coordinating center" is basically an elaboration on an idea which W. E. B. DuBois was developing through his writings and in his activities, especially during the 1930s and 1940s. As early as 1915, Dr. DuBois was working on this idea in the form of the first Amenia conference "which tried to unite the American Negro in one program of advance."[76] His hope was to bring about "as large a degree as possible of unity of purpose among Negro leaders" which would eventually develop into "some central organization."[77] When Dr. DuBois returned to Atlanta University in 1934, he proposed a quarterly magazine "to record the situation of the colored world and guide its course of development," and developed a "series of conferences looking toward a long-time program of Negro economic stabilization."[78] The conferences and the journal, called *Phylon*, brought to clearest expression Dr. DuBois's concern for a unified program for improving the conditions of black Americans, based on careful research and study. In 1941, Dr. DuBois linked this careful sociological study to specific action through the idea of a "national planning institute," which was to be a means for the "Talented Tenth," namely the educated Negroes, "to guide the great mass of our folk to desired economic and cultural ends."[79] Through a centralized office, relevant sociological information and interpretation would be gathered and published so that across the country local community leaders could "act, explore, experiment and build" according to a common program.

Although DuBois never fully developed his concept of central coordination, some other aspects can be elaborated for the present consideration of Operation Breadbasket. The basic role of such a coordinating center would be to raise problems and issues to the attention of the black community, to draw together various resources to plan creative responses, and then spin off autonomous programs to act on the problems. Breadbasket's traditional cultural events could be used, as the Black Expo is already beginning to do, to bring together a wide range of resources. Black leadership in a variety of fields, such as business and politics, could be brought together to meet with each other as well as with other intellectual resources who are researching various social, political and economic conditions. These people along with administrative and financial resources could work out particular programs of action and patterns of organization. The charismatic appeal of Rev. Jackson could be used effectively to attract the necessary variety of talent and to inspire them to greater unity of purpose and program. Through careful analysis and thorough discussion, the assembled group could reach rational decisions together about priorities and the best use of local resources for the coordinated thrust.

There is a potential conflict between this participatory decision-making structure and the spontaneous directives of the charismatic leader who would help bring the key resources together. Although this tension might never be resolved, it could be alleviated if the clear goals of the coordinating center were to develop new patterns of leadership for the black community and to stimulate new leadership oriented toward unified, carefully planned programs. The charismatic leader would have to make these goals his primary concern and place his own particular program ideas on a subordinate level. This would no doubt be difficult, especially for the charismatic person who is acutely sensitive to his "vision" of what is needed for his community. The coordinating center, however, requires a perspective that focuses on developing a strong core of capable leadership who can cooperate on building unified programs. To be effective, the coordinating center—and the charismatic leader—must see its role as being a resource for developing autonomous programs, and consciously utilize the force of charisma creatively without making the operation dependent on the charismatic leader.

While traditional and charismatic factors can be useful in starting the processes of the coordinating center, an orientation toward organizational effectiveness could be nurtured through the continuing need for evaluation and fresh study and planning. With a wide base of leadership involved in the decisions, the coordinating center could be a significant means of extending the range of rational-organizational authority.

This description of the concept of "coordinating center" is far from thorough. The intention here is only to suggest this as one conceptualization of Breadbasket's potential role in the black community. Although it is certainly not a perfect solution to the internal issues facing Breadbasket, this conceptual framework at least offers a starting point for the process of analysis and evaluation for the future of Breadbasket. It could prove to be a means of unifying the diverse—and sometimes divergent—elements in the operation. If Breadbasket could adjust its goals and purposes to define itself as a coordinating center, perhaps its organizational functions could be carried out with relative harmony, and perhaps the operation could forge for itself a creative and meaningful new role in the development of the black community.

Appendices

Consumer Club Guide

1967

WHAT IS OPERATION BREADBASKET?

Operation Breadbasket, an economic development program of the Southern Christian Leadership Conference, consists of Negro and white clergymen of all faiths who are working to build a solid economic base among Negro people. Increasing fair employment opportunities, expanding Negro businesses and developing sound financial institutions are the keys for overcoming the economic destitution which results in the physical and spiritual destruction of the Negro community.

DR. KING CONFERS WITH OPERATION BREADBASKET
L. to R. Standing: THE REV. STROY FREEMAN; DR. KING; THE REV. JESSE L. JACKSON; THE REV. H. B. BRADY; THE REV. CLAY EVANS; Seated: THE REV. JOHN L. THURSTON

WHAT HAS OPERATION BREADBASKET DONE?

OPERATION BREADBASKET

1. Has opened over 2000 jobs to Negroes — each job averaging over $120 per week amounting to over 15 million dollars per year in new income for the Negro community.
2. Is strengthening the economic resources in the Negro community through securing the deposits for the following institutions:
   a. Independence Bank of Chicago
   b. Seaway National Bank
   c. Hyde Park Federal Savings and Loan
   d. Illinois Federal Savings and Loan
   e. Service Federal Savings and Loan
   This process will make available to members of the Negro community money in the form of loans for business, education, housing, etc.
3. Has opened the market for products and services of Negro businessmen.

   As a result of the deprivation of a whole people, Negro businesses are small and largely inexperienced in the ways of business. These limitations must be overcome by continued involvement in business and through creative educational processes. Experienced consultants and advisors from leading business, financial, and educational institutions are invited to participate in solving the concrete problems of managerial decisions, finance, production, marketing, advertising, consumer education and other business concerns.

National Office
Atlanta, Georgia

Chicago Office
366 East 47th Street
Chicago, Illinois 60653
Telephone: 548-6540

Southern Christian Leadership Conference

Martin Luther King Jr., *President*   Ralph Abernathy, *Treasurer*   Andrew J. Young, *Executive Director*

Dear Friend,

There is something you can do immediately to help the Chicago Negro
Community progress.

As you can see by the enclosed press release, Operation Breadbasket has
embarked upon an economic campaign that promises benefit for the Negro
community as well as for the entire city.

We are appealing not only for the transferral of government funds to Negro
financial institutions but also for deposits in Negro banks by organizations,
churches, and individuals. If the Negro is ever to gain a voice in the life
of the city he must speak from an established economic base. Already
many individuals and corporations have recognized the justice and
economic necessity of this program by depositing money in the institutions listed
below.

Independence Bank of Chicago and Seaway National Bank of Chicago both offer
a full range of commercial bank services on terms that are competitive with
other financial institutions in the Chicago metropolitan area. The Federal
Deposit Insurance Corporation insures deposits in these banks with $15,000
maximum insurance for each depositor.

The Savings and Loan institutions that we feel serve the interests of the
Negro community especially are: Illinois Federal Savings and Loan
Association, Service Federal Savings and Loan Association, and Hyde Park
Federal Savings and Loan Association. Your savings in these institutions
are insured to $15,000 by the Federal Savings and Loan Insurance Corporation.

For further information, materials or speakers, contact Alvin Pitcher,
Gary Massoni, or Sara Wallace at 548-6540.

Sincerely,

Rev. Jesse L. Jackson
Northern Director-Operation Breadbasket

JLJ/sw

OPERATION BREADBASKET

SCLC

More State Funds Urged For Negro Banks

Operation Breadbasket Asks Increase

Chicago Daily Defender

MONDAY, JANUARY 23, 1967

In a telegram to State Treasurer Adlai Stevenson III; Edmund Kucharski, Cook County treasurer; and Mayor Richard J. Daley, the Steering Committee of Operation Breadbasket has urged that more Illinois funds be deposited in four Negro financial institution.

The telegram to the state, county, and city officials read, in part:

The institutions named were: Illinois Savings and Loan, 4619 S. South Park ave.; Service Federal Savings and Loan, 108 E. 51st st.; Independence Bank of Chicago, 7936 S. Cottage Grove ave.; and Seaway National Bank, 645 E. 87th st.

* Operation Breadbasket, an organization comprised mostly of ministers and administrated by the Coordinating Council of Community Organizations and has used the economic power of the Negro community to gain hundreds

* Hyde Park Federal Savings and Loan, 1508 E. 55th

of jobs for individuals and to promote the marketing of products manufactured by Negroes, a spokesman said.

"The ministers of Operation Breadbasket have launched a campaign to help the Negro community help itself economically. We hope to relieve our city of much of the blight that pours over into the unrest of the Jong and bitter 'hot summers.' We believe that the development of a strong economic program will instill in the disinherited and deprived a sense of dignity and worth.

"The Negro community has

disenchantment and hopelessness in its belief that the politicians were concerned about its destiny until election time. The Negro community wants to determine its destiny in positive and creative ways which will be the most effective rebuttal to intemperate charges by some of irresponsibility and a desire to subsist on handouts.

"It has been shown that Negro institutions can develop when given access to markets and to capital. But the despairing truth is that Negro businesses are systematically excluded from entering the mainstream of the economy by the absence of funds to launch creative ventures. Many financial institutions either re-

fuse to lead money to Negroes or stipulate almost totally nonnegotiably term.

It is clear that all of these denials of opportunity interact to put the Negroes one hundred years behind in their economic development. Therefore special efforts must be made to nullify the injustice and to extend economic opportunity. It is felt that the crushing pressure could be relieved if funds were provided in the Negro financial institutions which are fully accredited to handle fiscal matters.

"Encouraged by us, several corporations have already investigated and transferred of governmental funds to deep concern to achieve the

objectives of dignity and self-achievement for all individuals. We are confident that you will extend your best consideration in this matter of crucial importance.

"There is another side to this matter which should be mentioned. The moral and ethical imperatives are commanding ones. It is a crusade to expect, people to achieve self-determination when one of the basic ingredients — that of the 'self' assets — is missing.

"We are confident that you will take the lead with other governmental agencies in establishing a pattern for the use of governmental funds that will be a landmark in the struggle for justice and fairness."

National Office
Atlanta, Georgia

Chicago Office
366 East 47th Street
Chicago, Illinois 60653
Telephone: 548-6540

Southern Christian Leadership Conference

Martin Luther King Jr., *President*   Ralph Abernathy, *Treasurer*   Andrew J. Young, *Executive Director*

OPERATION BREADBASKET

Dear Consumer,

The aim of Operation Breadbasket is to create economic power and independence in the Negro community.

Negro businesses must be created and developed and given a chance by all stores to compete with other products on the market.

Negro banks and Savings and Loan institutions must grow to the magnitude wherein they have enough lending power to facilitate and participate in the growth of Negro businesses and the Negro community.

It must be understood that one basic obligation for any merchant in the ghetto is to bank in our banks and thus to allow Negroes a chance to participate freely in the capital market.

Major industries whose profit and loss margin is significantly affected by sales in the Negro community must express their respect for our consumer power not by giving Christmas baskets once a year but by hiring us proportionately and if necessary, preferentially, thus allowing us a basket a week rather than a basket a year.

We will no longer accept the excuse that we are unqualified. If major industries can cultivate our appetites with millions of dollars of advertising, they can cultivate our fingers for jobs with massive training programs.

If we are to send our children to school, we need money.
If we are to buy houses in an open city, we need money.
If we are to overcome long years of debt, we need money.
If we are to become producers after years of being excluded, we need money.
If our politicians are to become and remain decent and independent, we need a black economic base.

We must build our community. Though money is neither a total nor an ultimate solution to our many problems--for those it will not heal, it will surely kill the pain!

Sincerely,

Rev. Jesse L. Jackson
Coordinator-Chicago Operation Breadbasket

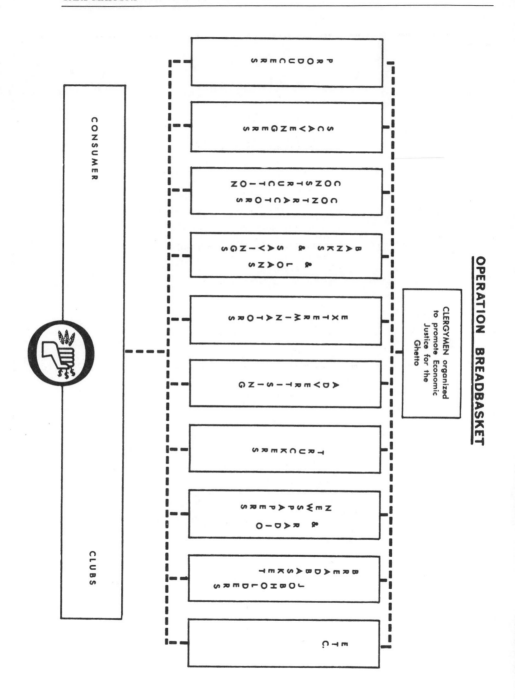

OPERATION BREADBASKET

CONSUMER

CLUBS

PRODUCERS

SERVICES

CONSTRUCTION CONTRACTORS

SAVINGS & BANKS
& LOANS

EMPLOYERS

GAS & OIL INDUSTRY

MARKETS

W & PAPER
PRODUCTS

BAKED GOODS
BEVERAGES JOBBERS

ETC.

CLERGYMEN organized to promote Economic Justice for the Ghetto

WHAT IS A CONSUMER CLUB

A Consumer Club is a group of organized consumers (people who buy goods and use services) whose goal is to develop power in the Negro community which would provide:

1. job opportunities for non-whites of the community
2. outlets for products produced by Negro businessmen
3. available money for loans from Negro banks and Savings and Loan Associations
4. information about Negro services that are available — scavengers, construction contractors, and tradesmen (exterminators, accountants, etc.)
5. information that tells the truth about all aspects of ghetto life and the freedom movement
6. a community of mutual concern in the ghetto.

The idea of Consumer Clubs originated from the need to advertise Negro products. It became clear that even though Negro producers gained shelf space so long denied their products it would be another matter to move those products from the shelves into the hands of consumers. It is impossible for Negro manufacturers so long denied the chance to grow to compete with the millions of dollars spent to advertise other products. Thus the Consumer Club conception evolved.

The Consumer Club will be a means of person-to-person advertising of the various products. At the same time they are developing into much more than an advertising agency. They are also conceived of as a community network for information and communication, a network by which consumer pressure can be exerted in economic areas where it is needed, a network that can supply cohesive strength in other areas affecting the Negro community. The Consumer Clubs could become a means of strength in developing the Negro community.

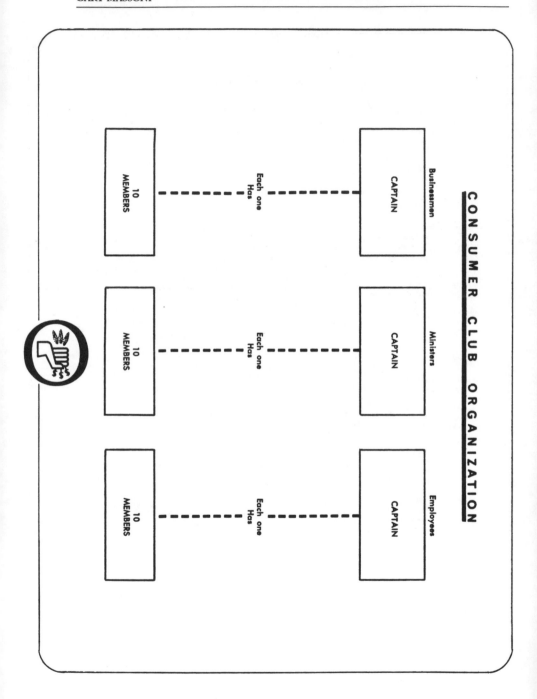

CAPTAIN'S INSTRUCTIONS

Captain's Responsibility

The primary responsibility of the Consumer Club Captain is to develop an allegiance to and a clear understanding of Operation Breadbasket and its economic program.

In order to organize a **successful** Consumer Club, the Captain must endeavor to do three (3) things:

1. Communicate
2. Educate
3. Motivate

Communication:

1. Plan regular meetings with your consumer club which will be training and informative sessions. Later, it will be necessary to keep close contact by phone.

. . . When you lose contact with your members, they lose interest AND DIE! . . .

2. Be Firm, be Kind, keep Business on your mind.

3. If you find yourself having difficuty keeping up with your club, perhaps you could find an assistant (wife, secretary, friend) to help with many of the details.

Education

1. Each captain should make sure he has tried the product before attempting to communicate the IDEA of consumer clubs to new members.

2. When you talk about banking and changing accounts, be sure you are a **living** example.

3. **Remember** — no one meeting can do the complete job of training. . . . The consumer club is a family affair.

4. Each and **every** member of you family should be made aware of the Negro products on the markets us well as of the Negro services.

5. When your members go to buy products, they should be able to relay the following information to you which you will in turn relay to the Operation Breadbasket office (458-6540):

    a. **Price of Product**
    b. **Display** (Good, Fair, Bad)
    c. **Quantity of the Product compared to competing products** (Ex. how many rows? Did you find the product where you expected to find it?)

6. If any of your members cannot find a product in the particular store, he should ask the **manager** of that store **why** the product is not on the shelf and **when** will it be there.

7. If you or your members need Operation Breadbasket information or materials, call the Operation Breadbasket office (548-6540). Ask for Sara Wallace, Brenda LeMay or Al Pitcher.

8. It is important to have well planned Consumer Club meetings. Note the enclosed agenda as a suggestion for your meeting.

Motivation

. . . Here is where you win or lose. You con teach a consumer everything but unless he wants to work, you have failed. . . .

1. The Consumer Club Captain must possess two (2) things:

    a. **ENTHUSIAM** . . . You must use the products, and when you do this, you do not have to pretend enthusiasm — it is inherent.
    b. **A positive attitude** about the whole economic program.

2. Make each member feel that he is a part of the operation . . . let him tell how he carried out his specific assignment and the approach he used.

3. **Be consumer oriented** . . . be interested in your consumer's future not in products alone. A genuine interest in his problems, his profits, his successes, and his growth will do more to motivate him and help you than all of the empty encouragement you can give.

. . . Sure it is a lot of work . . . a lot of detail . . . but it pays off!

In order to tell the story fo Operation Breadbasket and the significance of Operation Breadbasket Consumer Clubs, you will, perhaps, find this <u>sample</u> <u>agenda</u> useful in conduction of a Consumer Club meeting.

OPERATION BREADBASKET
COORDINATOR- Rev. Jesse L. Jackson
CONSUMER CLUB NO._____

SUGGESTED AGENDA

I. WHAT IS OPERATION BREADBASKET

II. WHAT IS THE SIGNIFICANCE OF OPERATION BREADBASKET
    A. WHAT IS YOUR INTERPRETATION
    B. WHAT IS THE INTERPRETATION OF BREADBASKET LEADERS

III. WHY IS THERE A NEED FOR CONSUMER CLUBS
    A. WHAT IS YOUR INTERPRETATION OF ITS NEED
    B. WHAT IS REV. JACKSON'S INTERPRETATION (You may want to use a tape given April 1 by Rev. Jackson)

IV. HOW ARE CONSUMER CLUBS ORGANIZED

    Who are Captains
    Who are Members

V. WHAT IS THE RESPONSIBILITY OF EACH LEADER

VI. WHAT CAN A CONSUMER CLUB DO- Suggestions for a program for Consumer Club No. _____
    A. Enlistment of Teams of 10 (women or men or both for a club)
    B. Enlistment of more leaders
    C. Education of Each Team.

    D. There should be regular reports to the office
    E. There should be a regular telephone net work to notify members quickly of important events for Consumer Clubs
    F. Teams should visit stores that have a good volume of business where Negro products are sold.
    G. There should be a continual flow of materials of Operation Breadbasket to the members in order that they may be kept aware of what is happening
    H. Members should be encouraged to transfer their funds to Negro financial institutions
    I. Other Suggestions
        1. Seek to put Joe Louis Milk in schools
        2. Get reaction to Negro products
        3. Report on the situation in stores
                Products absent
                Poor display
                Dirt on products
                Space related to other similar products
                Location of display (visible)

(SAMPLE)

OPERATION BREADBASKET CONSUMER
CLUB ASSIGNMENTS

Assignment No. III (New) beginning June 5, 1967

    A. To buy at Jewel Tea Food Stores
        OUTCLEAN DRAIN LIQUID OPENER
        METROPOLITAN SAUSAGE
    B. To write Edmund Kucharski (Cook County Treasurer, 118 N. Clark) strongly urging that Cook County help the Negro community by placing county funds in those Negro institution that will benefit the community.
    C. To subscribe to JET Magazine. Subscription Blanks are available at the Operation Breadbasket office — 366 East 47th St. 548-6540. Please Subscribe through OPERATION BREADBASKET.

Assignment No. II beginning May 8th

    A. To buy at National Tea/Del Farm
        GROVE FRESH ORANGE JUICE
        STEWARD'S BLEACH
    B. To send letters or telegrams to Adlai Stevenson III (State Treasurer, 160 N. LaSalle) congratulating him for placing state funds in Negro financial institutions.
    C. To send letters or telegrams to Edmund Kucharski (Cook County Treasurer, 118 N. Clark) and Marshal Korshak (City Treasurer, 121 N. LaSalle) urging them to place County and City funds into institutions that benefits the Negro community.
    D. To write Lloyd Webb at WAAF, 221 N. La-Salle protesting the change of the Jazz format to that of Rock and Roll.

Assignment No. I beginning April 24th

    A. To buy at National Teal/Del Farm
        MUMBO SAUCE (a choice of Original, Hickory, Tangy)
        RUAL'S DIAMOND SPARKLE FLOOR WAX
    B. To Bank and Save at the following Institutions:
        Seaway National Bank - 645 E. 87th St.
        Independence Bank of Chicago - 7936 So. Cottage Grove
        Illinois Federal Savings and Loan Association- 4619 S. Parkway
        Service Federal Savings and Loan Association - 104 E. 51st St.
        Hyde Park Federal Savings and Loan Association - 1508 E. 55th St.
(These assignments are for a one to two week period. If you are starting a new consumer club, start them on the assignment of that particular week. Then in the course of the building of the club, you can work in the other assignments.)

(SAMPLE)

CAPTAIN'S LETTER TO A
CONSUMER CLUB MEMBER

        4927 South Dorchester Ave.
        Chicago, Illinois 60615
        May 2, 1967

Dear Friend,
    Thank you for consenting to become a part of Consumer Club No. 14 of the S.C.L.C. sponsored Operation Breadbasket.
    As we previously discussed, the current project is to move onto and off of the National Tea Stores' shelves two Negro produced items: Rual's Diamond Sparkle Floor Wax and Mumbo Bar-B-Q Sauce.
    If you found that you could not participate as fully as you may have desired during the past week, please contact your 10 (or more) people to continue making inquiries and purchases of these two items especially during the period ending May 13, 1967; and subsequently to make them part of their regular purchasing pattern when needed.
    Please ask your contacts to:
      1. Note whether or not the items are on the shelves, if not, ask the Manager when they will be available.
      2. Note the price.
      3. Note manner of display.
      4. Approximate location of National Tea Store visited.

    It would be very helpful if the results of visits made by you and your contacts could be reported to me by Thursday, May 18, 1967. The best time to contact me is either evenings after 6 p.m. or mornings between 7-8 a.m. My telephone number is 283-4763. However, you may find it more convenient to send the results to me at the above address by mail. The enclosed form may be of some use in recording information. If there is any additional information you may need, please feel free to contact me.

        Sincerely yours,
        MARY S. EDELEN, Leader
        Consumer Club No. 14

In order to keep records concerning the products, the Operation Breadbasket office needs a report (regular) from the captains of consumer clubs. This is a suggested form for that report

OPERATION BREADBASKET
CONSUMER CLUB NO._____

Contact Person	Phone No.	Location of Food Store	Price of Items		Display (good, bad etc.)
			Rual''s Wax	Mumbo Sauce	
1.					
2.					
3.					
4.					
5.					
6.					
7.					
8.					
9.					
10.					
11.					
12.					
13.					
14.					
15.					

COMMENTS: _____

Guidelines for the Organization of Breadbasket Outposts

September, 1968

OPERATION BREADBASKET
SOUTHERN CHRISTIAN LEADERSHIP CONFERENCE

Reverend Jesse L. Jackson, *National Director*

NATIONAL OFFICE: 366 EAST FORTY-SEVENTH STREET CHICAGO, ILLINOIS 60653 AREA CODE 312/548-6540

GUIDELINES FOR THE ORGANIZATION OF BREADBASKET OUTPOSTS

   I.   National Organization: We Grow Through Good Communications

  II.   Guidelines for Operation Breadbasket Committees

 III.   The Five Stages of the Negotiation Process

  IV.   Principles for Selecting a Target

   V.   Procedural Steps of the Negotiation Process

September 1968

"Your Ministers Fight For Jobs and Rights"

OPERATION BREADBASKET
SOUTHERN CHRISTIAN LEADERSHIP CONFERENCE

Reverend Jesse L. Jackson, *National Director*

NATIONAL OFFICE: 366 EAST FORTY-SEVENTH STREET CHICAGO, ILLINOIS 60653 AREA CODE 312/548-6540

September 1968

Brothers:

The National Office sees this program as related
to a total community and not merely to forming
Operation Breadbasket Committees. This means
unity and discipline (not uniformity in detail).
We should see ourselves, in the words of the Apostle
Paul " as members one of the other.."

As we pursue the task of building economic viability
we need to realize national conciousness as growing
from authentic, througly cultivated localism; that
is, localism in the fullest sense of the word relative to participating in the total development of our
respective local communities and in the decisions
which determine the direction of those communities.

Building economic viability in the black community
shifts our focus from economic security to economic
independence. As this occurs we need to understand
that BLACK COOPERATION IS THE MOST EFFECTIVE EXPRES-
SION OF RESPONSIBLE AND MEANIFUL BLACK POWER that
is POSSIBLE FOR BLACK PEOPLE AND BLACK ORGANIZATIONS.
Our thrust if for economic and political equity as
consistent with our just claim to a share of the economic resources of the nation.

Finally, let us work together, pray together and we
should be able to STAY TOGETHER.

Respectfully,

Rev. Jesse L. Jackson
National Director
SCLC's Operation Breadbasket

JLJ/js

"Your Ministers Fight For Jobs and Rights"

NATIONAL ORGANIZATION: WE GROW THROUGH GOOD COMMUNICATIONS

The continued development of a national consciousness rests upon a functioning network of communications, sensitive to the overall needs and direction of the program of Operation Breadbasket.

We are hoping to achieve this by creating program machinery that will bring order and discipline while allowing flexibility for our operations.

The following matters will need your attention so that you will understand the organizational network which Operation Breadbasket is attempting to create:

1. The National Office in Chicago is the central headquarters of the network.

2. The network is composed of Strike Outposts.

3. Each outpost has been given a numerical designation (know your Strike Outpost number).

4. The headquarters of the Southern Christian Leadership Conference in Atlanta is Outpost number one (#1).

   The National office of Operation Breadbasket is Outpost number two (#2).

For Negotiations:

During negotiations at the national level, ministers from the headquarters of the target firm (i.e. the "home offices of the target firm) will make up the primary part of the negotiations team. They will be joined by members of the National Staff (designated by the National Director) and ministers from other areas that are strategic locations of major outlets of the target firm.

Other members of Minister's Committee of Breadbasket will be asked to send telegrams to the national offices of the Target Firm the morning any series of negotiations opens.

These wires or telegrams will serve as proxie votes on behalf of the National negotiations team.

The wires should be in the offices of the Target Firm no later than 9 O'Clock the morning of the negotiations.

Further Matters of Organization:

It is projected that the national office will decentralize its operations into Regional Divisions within the near future. This is done to facilitate movement of the program and to sustain a more effective network of communications and operations in the field.

NATIONAL ORGANIZATION: WE GROW THROUGH GOOD COMMUNICATIONS...page 2

A mid-western division of Operation Breadbasket will be organized
within the near future to provide a better liason with the central
states areas of the nation and to see that our program encompasses
the indurtrial hub of the nation.

We subsequently expect to form a Northern Division and a Southern
Division of Operation Breadbasket.

These divisional offices will be coordinated.and given.administra-
tive direction through the National Offices of Operation Breadbasket and will be accountable to those offices, though the
National Director, assisted by the National Coordinator.

Let us remember that unity and discipline are the key to a well
functioning apparatus.

You, who are in the field, will determine how far we move and
whether we accomplish the goal of bringing economic viability
to the black community.

August, 1968

GUIDELINES FOR OPERATION BREADBASKET COMMITTEES

The development of the type of national consciousness sought in Operation Breadbasket rests upon practicing discipline and relating to each other with integrity and to the goals of the organization with a sense of meaningful committment.

In this regard some basic guidelines have been established to provide a framework for activities of Operation Breadbasket Committees or "Strike Outposts."

1. Committees of Operation Breadbasket should be organized to include a Convenor and/or a Call Man and Chairmen for the following committees:

   A. Direct Action
   B. Research
   C. Legal Problems

   These officers should rotate often to keep the Committee flexible at <u>all times.</u>

   Committees are counseled not to have a treasury. The reason for this lies in the problem of a committee becoming liable in the event of a legal action on the part of a firm which has been selected as a target firm by the ministers of Breadbasket. An alternative would be to establish an account through the offices of the SCLC Affiliate in the city in which the committee is located.

2. <u>Communications are essential.</u> Therefore reports should be sent into the national office once per month at least, and during negotiations, twice per month. This gives the national office the kind of information needed to assist local committees and to make timely and sound decisions with regard to key negotiations.

3. Firms selected by Operation Breadbasket for negotiations will be know as <u>TARGET FIRMS OR COMPANIES</u>.

   The selection of these companies should take place only after careful evaluation of data on the companies and careful analysis of the jobs and benefits which the committee can reasonably expect from negotiations with the proposed <u>TARGET COMPANY OR FIRM.</u>

4. <u>Breasket Demands:</u> Basically the demands are for a percentage of the jobs comparable to numbers of black people in the city and the volume of business done in the black ghetto.

Guidelines for Operation Breadbasket Committees...page 2

1. In addition Operation Breadbasket Committees demand
    the following:

    1. Placement of black products on shelves in a
        competitive position with other products sold.

    2. Advertising in black journals or other news media
        (radio) oriented to the black community

    3. Banking in black banks and Savings & Loan Assoc.

    4. Use of black services (Scavengers for collection
        of refuse; janitorial for custodial and floor
        maintenance).

    5. Use of black accountants; and development of
        group plans with black insurance companies.

    6. Use of black constructionists and black sub-con-
        tractors in the building, redecoration; or general
        remodeling of stores located in the ghetto.

    7. Use of black advertising men, disk jockeys and other
        black opinion makers - along with black artists,
        printers, engravers, linotypists, etc.

5. Businessmen's Committees: Businessmen;s groups are
    valuable and essential to Operation Breadbasket. Such
    groups need careful planning and preparation before forma-
    tion. Thus they should not be formed prior to consultation
    and approval from the National Office.

    This request is made because the National Office wishes
    to make its resources useful to local groups. These
    resources can be useful only if the National Office is
    consulted about decisions to form businessmen's committees.

6. Arrangements for distributorships or franchises; or any
    other business arrangements and expansion programs should
    develop in concert with the program of Operation Bread-
    basket and should take place only after consultation and
    approval from the National Office.

7. All inquiries for information, speakers and materials
    concerning the national program of Operation Breadbasket
    should be channeled to the National Office of Operation
    Breadbasket, 366 East 47th Street, Chicago, Illinois, 60653.

    No person is authorized to speak or act on behalf of
    Operation Breadbasket without approval or clearance of
    the National Office.

Guidelines for Operation Breadbasket Committees....page 3

8. The National Director or persons whom he so designates are empowered to deal with any violotions of these guidelines;.or to make amendments to them when he so sees fit. Only those persons whom he approves or he, as National Director, should undertake this responsibility.

9. Operation Breadbasket is an interdenominational and inter-racial program. Committees should feel free to involve persons of other racial and other denominational bodies in their activites and in the overall program of the Breadbasket Committees.

10. The Information and Development forms from the National Office should be completed and sent into the National Office within fifteen (15) days (or sooner). Please get these forms in as this information is essential for establishing the kind of tight communications network and making our machinery function on a simultaneous basis on all major issues.

11. Committees should Keep Informed. Read the black press and keep aprised of information on business opportunities and the whole question of building economic viability in the black community. It would also be appropriate to keep informed of the major trends and events in the business section of your local newspapers.

311

OPERATION BREADBASKET -- The Five Stages of the Negotiation
Process

I Information

No negotiation can get maximum results without proper information
about the target and its market. Negotiators first of all need
knowledge of the retail stores in their "kingdom". This will be
of value in determining the vulnerability of both the stores and
the products they carry. An attached sheet shows some of the useful information to have. In different places this may need to
be revised, but the basics of store location, ownership and
products and services utilized are standard.

The most important information for negotiations is about the
target company. What the company does in terms of employment,
community service, advertising, banking, etc., is vital in de-
terming the substance of a new relationship between the target
company and the black community. The employment data will have
to be requested from the company itself, and **must** be in the hands
of the negotiators at least three days <u>before</u> the meeting with
the company. This amount of time is necessary in order to review
and evaluate the information sent.

An attached sheet shows what this information might look like.
While it should be as accurate and complete as possible, do not
get too involved in unimportant details. The following data is
essential:

(1) The total number of employees in each job classification.
      Use the classification the company itself uses.
      Form 100 of EEO (Equal Employment Opportunity) is not
      sufficient, but may be useful as a cross-check.

(2) Number of black employees in each classification.

(3) The salary range for each classification.

This information should be requested by letter. Do not depend on
telephone communication to make certain that everyone understands
what is happening. If a company is slow or refuses to answer a
letter, a visit to the company by a group of three of the ministers
might be necessary. This visit, however, should also be confirmed
by a letter. Documents are important.

II <u>Education</u>

Once the ministers have gathered their informatuon, they should
schedule a meeting to educate the top officials of the company
about the problems of the black community. This is basically
an educational session, and secondarily a preaching session.
Make certain the company officials understand the issues involved
and that repentance may cause some pain, that ressurection does

312

not come without crucifixion. The substance of this session
should be the economic problems black people face as well as
the problems of injustice and assaults on human dignity they face
every day. Local information on housing standards, unemployment
rates, median income levels, etc., is useful.

The plight of local black businessmen should be outlined too, by
indicating the inability of these men to get loans and to get a
market. The same is true for service companies as well as for
product companies: black businessmen have been excluded from substantial markets and denied access to operating capital. Local
businesses including newspapers can be used as illustrations.
For instance, black newspapers seldom get large advertising accounts
from businesses that make large profits in the ghetto.

The purpose of this educating session is to get the company
officials to understand the problems and realize their responsibility
as a company to help solve the problems. The aim is not to get
them as individuals to feel emotionally sorry, but to get them
actively involved in solving the structural problems. They shoud
be willing to share the pain of problem solving on their own
without a withdrawal of consumers.

III Negotiation

Once the ministers have gathered their information and have
attempted to educate the company officials, the ministers make
concrete requests based on the information about the company;
They should be challenging but should be possible for the company
to fulfill. The requests should be made according to definite
rationales in relation to the percentage of the population that
is black and how much business the company does in the ghetto.
Though employment should be raised to a "fair representation"
of black people, the employment demand should not be a straight
percentage. Asking for a "ratio" has some legal problems that
will make a meaningful negotiation impossible. The request should
be in terms of specific numbers of jobs in specific categaries.
The result should be a fair representation of black people in all
job classifications, including management positions.

The meetings to actually negotiate an agreement on a program of
economic justice should always be held with the company men who
have the power to make decisions. If the company sends members
of their public relations department, cancel the meeting and re-
schedule it to meet with the company president, general manager,
and personnel manager, and any other officials necessary.

IV. DEMONSTRATION

In many negotiations this step will not be necessary. Hopefully most companies will participate in a program of economic justice without the exercise of a consumer withdrawl. However, do not enter a negotiation without the ability to cut into the margin of the company's profit in the black community. Always be prepared to back up any demands made on a company with community support. The power of Operation Breadbasket is in the people of the community who respect themselves enough not to cooperate with evil embodied in companies that exploit the black community.

An effective demonstration is basically a task of educating the community about the disrespect the company expresses in its refusal to do justice and employ black people fairly. This process of education is carried out in several ways.

(1.)   All of the ministers associated with Operation Breadbasket should announce from their pulpits the withdrawl of consumer support of the company that refuses to cooperate. Every minister should know the story so that he can tell it effectively.

(2.)   Church members should tell their friends and families not to buy the products of the offending company.

(3.)   Retail outlets of the products of the company should be picketted and/or leafletted. Because of legal questions, it should be clear that the picket is about the target products, not the store unless the store itself is the target. Of course, the most effective picket is when no one goes in the store. The purpose here is to encourage the store to put pressure on the offending company.

V.   RECONCILIATION

The purpose of any demonstration is to overcome the barriers that divide man from man, company from community. Once the company knows that the community respects itself, the company will come to respect the community too. In this coming back together is the great joy of reconciliation.

Even if there is no demonstration, and the company agrees to the requests of the negotiators, there is still the joy of reconciliation that comes out of a new and renewed relationship between the company and the community.

This new relationship and reconciliation ought to be made specific in a covenant (not a legal contract) which summarizes the general intent and the specific steps the company will take to do justice. This event should be made public and announced to the press, so that everyone will know that past barriers have been broken down and the new community is being built.

BASIC RESEARCH INFORMATION ON STORES IN THE KINGDOM

NAME OF STORE_____

ADDRESS OF STORE_____

OWNER OF STORE_____

MANAGER OF STORE_____

PHONE NUMBER OF STORE_____

NUMBER OF CASH REGISTERS (Operating or not)_____

NAME OF SCAVENGER SERVICE_____

NAME OF EXTERMINATOR SERVICE_____

NAME OF FUEL OIL SUPPLIER_____

NAME OF BANK_____

       OTHER ACCOUNTS_____

BRANDS OF MILK_____

BRANDS OF BREAD_____

BRANDS OF ICE CREAM_____

NUMBER OF EMPLOYEES_____

COMMENTS ABOUT CONDITION OF THE STORE:

EMPLOYMENT INFORMATION: COLONIALIST FOOD STORES -- March 1968

Job Classification	Salary Range	Total	Black		Demand
Retail Stores		(2826)	(658)		(83)
Managers	8500--14,000	171	20		20
Assistant Managers	7200 - 8000	134	51		
Bonded Clerks	6500 - 7000	110	33		
Produce Department Heads	7200 - 7900	117	32		
Head Cashiers	6200 - 6500	123	26		5
Checkers	4600 - 5700	472	120		
Meat Department Heads	7800 - 9300	161	22		18
Meat Journeymen	7500 - 8500	323	38		40
Meat Apprentices	4800 - 6500	25	7		
Meat Wrappers	3600 - 4200	9	5		
Grocery Clerks	5200 - 6000	1181	304		
Grocery Warehouse		(149)	(20)		(18)
Supervisors	8000 - 11,000	11	0		3
General Office Workers	3700 - 6000	6	1		1
Carpenter/Electricians	10,000-12,000	6	0		2
Selectors	7900 - 9000	87	12		10
Equipment Operators	6500 - 7500	16	3		1
Other (E.O.D.)	6500 - 7000	20	4		1
Janitors	7100 - 8000	1	0		
Watchmen	6500 - 7000	2	0		
Meat and Produce Warehouse		(422)	(51)		(54)
Supervisors	8000 - 11,000	18	1		4
Buyers/Inspectors	8000 - 10,000	22	1		4
General Office Workers	3700 - 6000	56	3		11
Laborers	6500 - 7000	61	4		11
General Merchandisers	6500 - 8500	11	0		3
Selectors	7900 - 9000	149	33		6
Equipment Operators	6500 - 7500	6	0		2
Mechanics (maintenance)	6500 - 8500	6	1		1
Production Operatives	6000 - 7000	82	7		12
Janitors	7100 - 8000	7	1		
Watchmen	6500 - 7000	4	0		
Office		(363)	(26)		(65)
Officials	15,--- up	10	0		2
Professionals	7000 - 10,000	9	1		1
Auditors	6500 - 10,000	17	2		2
General Office Workers	3700 - 10,00	159	10		30
Secretaries/Stenographers	4000 - 6500	52	0		13
Office Machine Operators	3700 - 5500	27	5		2
Telephone/Messenger	3700 - 5000	5	1		1
Mailroom	3700 - 7000	14	4		
Tabulating	3700 - 5000	33	2		6
Order/Billing	3700 - 5000	37	1		8
Garage		(223)	(22)		(34)
Supervisors	8000 - 11,000	6	1		1
Drivers	9000 - 12,000	155	15		24
Helpers	7200 - 7500	16	0		4
Mechanics	8000 - 10,000	27	3		3
Dispatchers	8000 - 8300	8	0		2
Clerks	5200 - 5500	4	0		
Service	7200 - 7500	7	3		
TOTALS		3983	777		254

PICKET INSTRUCTIONS

1. Picket lines must be orderly and moving at all times.

2. Picket lines must use only 1/2 the sidewalk space, preferably the outer half.

3. Do not block the store entrance.

4. Do not talk with people not on the lines unless you are designated to answer questions by the captain.

5. Do no go inside store with picket signs or other materials.

6. If you get tired and want to drop out of the line, do not stand with picket sign in your hand.

7. Do not stack picket signs against the store wall.

8. Do no touch shoppers. If you hit anyone -- even in self-defense -- you will be charged with assault and battery.

9. Each line will have a Picket Captain who will serve as your spokesman.

10. Remember, look neat and stand tall.

CAPTAINS' INSTRUCTIONS

1. Call office frequently, at least once every half hour.
   Phone - 548-6540

2. Report on:

   a. What's happening in the store.
   b. Number of people in picket line.
   c. Need for supplies.
   d. How many cash registers and how many operating.
   e. Other problems, police or gangs, etc.

3. Report to office immediately all emergencies or significant changes.

4. Train others and delegate authority wherever possible.

OPERATION BREADBASKET -- Principles for Selecting a Target

There are many factors that need to be considered when selecting a target for negotiations. Some of the basic principles are listed here according to their relative importance. These are considered to be guidelines, not rigid rules. These have been helpful in the past and are basic considerations for finding targets.

CRUCIAL OR VERY IMPORTANT PRINCIPLES

(1.)   POWER OVER THE COMPANY: Breadbasket should have enough power over the company to gain what it seeks. This ability to back up demands is based on the amount of the company's business that can be controlled by Breadbasket. Black people should account for a high proportion of the company's business, at least 10% and ideally over 25%.

(2.)   POSSIBILITY FOR SIGNIFICANT GAINS: The situation of the company should be such that it would be worth the effort to negotiate. A significant number of jobs should be available. There should be some serious and visible deficiencies in the company's employment practices, so that the issues can be clearly communicated to people who will support a withdrawl of patronage.

(3.) VULNERABILITY TO LOSS OF BUSINESS: The company should be sensitive to a loss of business. This can be seen in two ways: (a) The company should have a low profit margin so that consumer withdrawl would have quick effect on the company's profits. (b) The company should have a number of strong competitors who would be a threat to absorb the market of the target company.

IMPORTANT (BUT SECONDARY) PRINCIPLES

(4.)   EASY TO IDENTIFY: The target company should deal directly with the consumer or should market a product that is known by a brand name and easily available to the average consumer. (For instance, steel is not a product that would not be recognizable enough to lend itself to an effective boycott).

(5) CONSISTENT WITH "KINGDOM THEORY": The "Kingdom Theory" essentially is to have developed relationships with retail outlets within the "ghetto kingdom." These relationships are power relationships which have been reached through negotiations with chain stores and large independents. By selecting target companies which have products in the major outlets with which the Breadbasket chapter has a "power rapport," It is possible to extend the basic consumer power by having the stores take the products off the shelves.

target selection.....page 2

OTHER HELPFUL PRINCIPLES

(7.) The narrower the ownership of the target company, the more vulnerable it will be. Such companies are more sensitive to economic pressures than broad-based stock corporations.

(8.) The more a company has worked to develop an image in the field of reac relations, the more sensitive it will be to adverse publicity.

(9.) The smaller the number of retail outlets for the products of the target company, the better. If outlets are too numerous, Breadbasket's power runs the risk of being too diffuse.

(10.) The target company's business should be transacted primarily in public and not by phone, mail order, or in the customer's home. These latter conditions make enforcement of a boycott difficult.

OPERATION BREADBASKET -- Procedural Steps of the Negotiation Process

1.   LETTER FOR INFORMATION: The initial contact with any given company
should be by a letter asking for employment information. This letter
should ask for the employment data from each of the company's locations
or departments. The data should inclued:

(1.)   list of all job classifications for each location and/or depart-
       ment of the company. This includes offices and management
       positions.

(2.)   the total number of employees in each of these job classifi-
       cations.

(3.)   the number of black employees in each classification.

(4.)   the salary range for each classification.

As a cross check on this information, the company should also send the
information used on the EEOC Form 100. This does not have useful categories, but the totals should correspond to the more detailed information
outlined above.

A specific period of time should be stated for the company to respond
in with the information. Seven to ten days is enough time for the company to get the information together if they consider the request important enough.

2.   INFORMATIONAL MEETING: Once the employment information has been
received,or if the company does not respond, a team of three or four
ministers should visit the company to verify the information and to get
any necessary clarity and to fill any gaps in the data. The ministers
should set the appointment up with a letter to the top men in the company. The ministers should be alert to any kinds of information that
might be useful in strengthening Breadbasket's demands on the company.

The ministers should keep clearly in mind that this meeting is not a
negotiating meeting, but purely an informational meeting. They should not
discuss anything pertaining to what Breadbasket will be demanding or what
Breadbasket will do. The only conversation should be about the information
that the company did or did not send. The only explanation necessary for
this is that the ministers cannot make any kind of a rational decision a-
bout what to do with the company without the necessary information.

Usually only one meeting will be necessary for all of the information
to be obtained. If necessary a second meeting is acceptable. However, the ministers should be certain that the company is not delaying
or stalling by being slow in gathering the information. Such a tactic
by the company is just as much disrespect for the black community as
overtly saying that it will not cooperate with black people.

3.   EVALUATING THE INFORMATION: Once the employment information is
complete, the ministers need to evaluate it carefully and try to understand what the figures mean in terms of how the company employs black
people. A typical conculsion might be that most of the black people
employed are in the lowest paying categories, and that the higher the pay

Procedural Steps...page 2

and the more responsibility, the fewer black people. In many cases a
company will have no black people in supervisory or managerial positions.
Most companies have few black office workers and few black sales people.
A careful look at the employment information will reveal these and other
possible d'ficiencies.

Once the deficiencies are determined, the ministers can begin designing
demands on the company aimed at getting a fair representation black employees in every job classification. The demands should be in terms of
specific numbers of new black employees in specified job classifications.
The specific numbers are determined on the basis of the ratio of black
people to the total population. For instance, if the black population is
20% of the population of the city, then 20% black employment would be a -
fair representation in the company. This might need to be modified, however, in view of two factors: (a.) the amount of business the company
does in the black community; and (b) the ability of the company to move
quickly enough to change employment patterns. First of all, if the company does an exceptionally large volume of business in the black community,
so that black people account for a major percentage of their business, then
the demands might need to be increased in proportion to the business. For
example, if the company does 30% of its business in the black community,
and even though the population is only 20% black, a guideline of 30% might
be a more appropriate basis for demands. However, if the amount of business in the ghetto is a percentage less than the black percentage of the
population, the population percentage still should be the basic guideline. The second consideration means that in certain circumstances, the
company is so far behind in black employment that they could not reason- -
ably meet the demands for a large increase in employment. This is difficult to determine, and the company will no doubt like to make the ministers
believe it is always the case that meeting significant demands would be too
difficult. Beware, however, for it is not often the case that this consideration will modify the demands in any way.

It is important to emphasize that the demands are not asking for a "quota"
of black employees. Rather Breadbasket is demanding that the company respect
black people by allowing them access to all jobs in the company. The only
true test of this new relationship is that a specified number of jobs be
filled with black people in a specified period of time.

The period of time is usually 30, 60 or 90 days. Only under unusual circumstances should this time be extended beyond 90 days.

Special consideration should be given to part-time and summer employment
so that youths can find work.

4.   RECOMMENDATION TO THE STEERING COMMITTEE: Once the ministers of
the information-gathering team have evaluated the information, they -
should describe the situation they found at the company and make a re--
commendation for demands to be taken to the company. The Steering Committee then should decide whether it wants to go ahead with that company or not, and if so whether the demands recommended are acceptable.
If this is agreed on, then the Steering Committee should select a team
of ministers to meet with the executives of the company for a educational
meeting.

procedural steps.....page 3

5.   EDUCATIONAL MEETING: Having evaluated the employment information
and knowing the company's deficiencies in employment, the ministers should
meet with company executives, <u>not to negotiate</u>, but to educate them a-
bout the problems that black people face, about economic exploitation,
and about the need for businesses to take an active role in trying to
slove these problems by changing the structures that destroy people and   —
perpetuate exploitation. The meeting should be aimed at getting the executives to understand the challenge before them to end racism in their company and to deal creatively with the problems of black unemployment and
underemployment.

Statistics from the local situation should be used to illustrate the
situation, and some local youth might be invited to "tell it like it is."

The ministers should plan to meet no less than an hour and a half before
the company representatives arrive. This "pre-meeting" is designed to
plan the strategy for the meeting with the company to discuss what ought
to be accomplished, and who will say what. One person should be designated
as spokesman for the session. He is in full charge of the meeting, and
everyone must submit to his decisions during the meeting even if they are
questionable. The reason for this is that the company would like to get
the ministers to argue and debate among themselves. In order to keep onto
the issues and maintain unity, everyone must submit to this discipline of
deferring to the spokesman. If it appears helpful, do not hesitate to
break for a caucus. This helps maintain the team's strength and unity.

The location of the meeting is fairly important. The educational meeting
and any negotiating meetings ought to take place in the ghetto. This is
disrepect if they are "too busy" or unwilling to come to the ghetto, which
is the scene of the economic "crimes" they commit daily.

The ministers must remember: this is an educational meeting. It is not
a negotiating meeting. No demands are to be presented yet, and discussions
about what demands might be should not take place.

When the educational meeting is over, the ministers should again meet   —
alone to evaluate what happended, and to decide if the company representatives understood well enough to procede with the demands, or whether they
need another educational session. If they decide another educational session
is in order, they should schedule it right away, within the following three
or four days. If they decide to proceed with the demands, they should
send the demands to the company in a letter, which asks that the company
be prepared to respond to the demands at a meeting which the ministers
should set up, indicating the time and place.

6.   NEGOTIATING SESSIONS: Once the ministers are satisfied that sufficient
time has been taken to educate the company executives, the next step is
working out an agreement on the details of the demands. As mentioned above,
the company should be sent a letter stating the specific demands, indicating
the number of additional black employees necessary in each category. The
letter should also state the time and place of the meeting, which would be
somewhere in the ghetto, preferably in a church. Again the ministers
should plan to meet not less than an hour and a half before the company
representatives arrive. This "pre-session" is extremely important in
getting the negotiating team to understand thoroughly the demands and how
the meeting will proceed. The spokesman should be designated, and his role
defined. He should open the meeting by calling on someone to pray. Then he

procedural steps....page 4

should go over once more the things covered in the educating sessions
(although more briefly) as an introduction to the specific demands. Then –
the company should respond. During the pre-meeting, at least two "hatchet-
men" should be selected. The hatchet men are never satisfied with anything. They should not say much, but what they say should be radical,
always pushing at the need to get more from the company than is being asked.

During the meeting with the company representatives, the basic procedure–
is not complex. After the prayer and the introductory statement summarizing what has happened so far and why there is a need for the agreement
between the company and the ministers of Breadbasket to be worked out in
detail, the company should be allowed to respond to the request. It is
important however, that they be kept on the point, and that they do respond.
Often they will try to stray from the point and get the discussion on to
some side issue. This must not be allowed. The ministers themselves need
to be aware that the primary issue is building the economic base of the
black community; specifically it means more and better jobs for black
people. No excuses are acceptable; it may cost the company more money to
hire and train black people, but it must be done. In the company's esti-
mation the black people may not be ready for the more skilled or responsible
positions. At this point the company heeds to do what is necessary to
accomplish the goals that form the basis of a new relationship between the
company and the black community.

During the discussions it is extremely important for the ministers to
allow the company to respond to each comment or question. One minister –
should never follow another with a comment; he should wait until the company has answered the first one before he states his own. Never let the
company get the ministers arguing among themselves.

It may take three or four meetings to work out the details of an agreement. The details of employment that need to be considered throughout
the process are: the number of employees demanded in specified categories,
the period of time within which to fill the jobs demanded and the recruiting and training programs that the company would need to implement
the necessary structural changes in employment.

7. REPORTING TO THE STEERING COMMITTEE: During the negotiations, the
ministers on the team must report any progress to the Steering Committee.
Even though an agreement seems likely or that an agreement seems to have
been reached, the negotiating team must report to the Steering Committee
for it to give the approval of the details of the agreement in the light
of any new information that might have been learned during the negotiations.
The negotiating team must remember that it does not have the final authority in accepting a agreement. They can only recommend to the Steering
Committee, which has the authority to decide on the agreement.

OPEIONS: If the Steering Committee approves the recommended agreement, then
the next step is a press conference in conjunction with the company to
announce to the community the new covenantal relationship. If the Steering
Committee does not accept the recommended agreement, then the negotiating
team needs to meet with the company again. If the Steering Committee
modifications are not accepted by the company, then the next step is to
demonstrate, to communicate to the community the disrespect and lack of
cooperation of the company.

procedural steps.....page 5.

8. DEMONSTRATION: the action taken against a company is, as the name indicates, a demonstration to the community of the lack of cooperation and lack of concern expressed by the company's refusal to enter into a covenantal relationship with the black community. The basic purpose is communication, to tell people what the issues are and to challenge them not to cooperate with evil as it is found in the target company. There are many possible techniques or strategies used to demonstrate the truth. The action the ministers take might include these:

(a.) announcements from the minister's pulpits about the need for people to respect themselves by not cooperating-with companies that disrespect them. Sunday morning services are primary places for these announcement and they should be part of the preaching so that people understand the importance of the campaign.

(b.) announcements over ministers' radio broadcasts.

(c.) letters to people who have expressed interest in supporting Breadbasket.

(d.) getting the support of community groups to announce through their own channels of communication the campaign.

(e.) letters to stores asking that they remove the products of target companies from their shelves.

(f.) picket lines and leafleting at the stores that still have the products on the shelves. These should be large volume stores, not simply every store that has the product.

(g.) statements and announcements to the press, primarily the black-owned newspapwes, about the campaign.

9. RECONCILIATION: the demonstration should continue until the company agrees to meet the Breadbasket demands. The ministers should not be in too much of a hurry to settle. If the company wants to go back to the negotiating table, the consume withdrawl should still continue. Only when the issues are settled is it possible for a new relationship to be established. This step of acknowledging that a new agreement has been reached and a new relationship has been established should be made public so that the community can share in the joy of reconciliation. A press conference should be called , with special emphasis on getting the black-owned press to attend. The press conference should be an event done in conjunction with the company. Both the ministers and the company should-read statements, the covenant, as it spells out the details of the agreement, should also be read. Any questions from the press should be answered only as they relate to the issues involved in the economic development of the black community and the moral necessity for businesses to share the burden of this effort.

10. FOLLOW-UP: every month the company should submit a report on progress made under the covenant. This should be an up-dating of the original information the ministers asked for. Simply the number of people hired is not adequate. It is important to have the number of black people currently employed in each category, and the total number of people employed in each category. Two or three ministers should meet with company representatives after having reviewed the information to raise any questions that might

procedural steps......page 6

need to be asked about the information or any reports from employees or
people who applied for jobs. Part of the follow-up task is establishing
contact with employees who can relate the inside story of conditions and
practices of the company. Occasionally an employee will be mistreated or
will think he has been mistreated, in which case the ministers have the
responsibility to try to find the source of the problem and resolve the
situation.

One of the issues that the company might raise during the negotiations
and during the follow-up process is their difficulties with labor unions.
The ministers must not involve themselves in the company's relationship
with the unions. Any problem will have to be worked out by the company
itself as it deals with the union. The only leverage the ministers of
Breadbasket have is over the company at the consumer level.

11.   REVISING THE COVENANT: Once the time period of the covenant is up,
the ministers might want to work out a new covenant with the company..
The hope is that the company will get the spirit of the covenant and will
not need the pressure of a new covenant. In many cases, however, a new
agreement will be necessary to make certain that the company remains committed to increasing employment opportunity for black people and to developing the economic base of the black community.

Sample Covenant

Covenant Between Operation Breadbasket And the Chicago Unit of the A&P Company

May 26, 1967

The Chicago Unit of the A&P Company enters into a convenantal relationship will the ministers of Operation Breadbasket through an agreement on a five point program of creative employment and business development aimed at ending the economic indignities and injustices which have ravaged the Negro people physically and spiritually.

The A&P Company, in defining a new, positive, and equitable relationship with Negro people, agrees to the following five specific programs:

I. A&P will open 770 positions to Negroes by upgrading present employees and by hiring new employees in the following categories:

Managers and Assistant Managers	41
Bonded Clerks	13
Produce Department Heads	11
Head Cashiers	11
Checkers	100
Meat Department Heads	28
Meat Journeymen	75
Grocery Clerks	175
Office	**100**
Officials	2
Professionals	
Eng., Draftsmen	2
Auditors	5
General Off	50
Sec. Sten. Typist	10
Office Machine Oper.	7
Tel. & Messenger	1
Mailroom	2
Tabulating	9
Order & Billing	12
Produce Warehouse	**72**
Supervisors	3
Buyers-Inspectors	5
General Office	16
Laborers	24
Gen. Mtc.	4
Selectors	17
Equipment Operators	2
Janitors	1
Garage	**64**
Supervisors	2
Drivers	44
Helpers	-
Mechanics	7
Washers	-
Dispatchers	2
Clerks	1
Meat Warehouse	**59**
56 plus 8 to be absorbed in any category	
Supervisors	3
General Office	3
Mechanics	2
Selectors	22
Production Operators	28
Janitors	1
Watchmen	-

Bakery	0
Grocery Warehouse	**21**
Supervisors	2
General Office	1
Carpenters-Electricians	2
Selectors	16
Equipment Operators	0
Other (E.O.D. work)	0
Janitors	0
Watchmen	0
TOTAL	**770**

In its effort to increase A&P's total employment of Negroes A&P will supplement its equal opportunity employment policy my aggressively seeking out and recruiting Negroes for all levels of its business in permanent jobs. In recognition of the problems of disadvantaged groups to compete, A&P will particularly concern itself with the employment and training of the disadvantaged Negro for whom the doors of employment are slowest to open by providing on-the-job training programs, and by giving special consideration in its pre-selection program. A&P will utilize its own facilities and the services of Marion Business College, plus other community groups for recruitment and preparation for training. To fulfill this goal A&P will seek to add 120 Negro employees per month between June and the end of November with the remaining 170 employees hired by December 31, 1967.

A&P will recruit and hire an additional 200 part-time Negro employees by July 15, 1967.

The hiring and the distribution of new employees will be handled in the two A&P employment centers located at:

849 W. 79th Street
2622 N. Pulaski Road

A&P will upgrade 20 Negroes, either those presently employed as Assistant Managers or others, to Manager or Co-Manager within 45 days and will upgrade 20 Negroes to replace them within 45 days.

A&P will furnish Operation Breadbasket with periodic progress reports of hiring and upgradings as a result of this agreement so that the minister may carry out their pastoring functions for the benefit of those affected and the A&P Company.

II. A&P will market products of Negro producers and suppliers in Metropolitan stores and will designate a particular staff member with adequate authority to work with the Negro suppliers in developing a creative program to provide advice for marketing. A&P will also:

1. Develop educational proms for middle management and store managers on all aspects of this agreement.
2. Price items competitively with appropriate promotions.
3. Give shelf space to Negro suppliers' products equal to national brands.
4. Develop special advertising through a planned sales schedule.
5. Insure that Negro suppliers' products are lisited in the regular goods order book appropriate to their products.

A&P'S "open door" policy lends itself to receiving products recommended by Operation Breadbasket and will be implemented as soon as A&P buyers and the representatives of the following companies recommended by Operation Breadbasket finalize the details. It is understood their products will be competitive in quality and the companies are responsible.

R. S. Boles — Rual's Diamond Sparkle Floor Pro.
Daryl Grisham — Parker House Sausage Co.
George Jones — Joe Louis Milk Company
Willard Payne, Sr. —
        Metropolitan Sausage Manufact. Co.
James Stamps, Sr. — Baldwin Ice Cream Co.
William Steward — Steward's Chemical Co.
George Johnson — Johnson Products Co.
Argia B. Collins — Argia B's Food Products
Clarence Rich — Dixie DeLuxe Sausage Co.
Cecil Troy — Grove Fresh Distributors
S. B. Fuller — Fuller Products Company
Dave Conway — Conway Soap Products Co.
James Watts — IMPAC Chemical Company
Graythorn Heard — Out Clean Corporation
Claude Grannum — Gran-Gay Import Company
John H. Johnson — Supreme Beauty Products

III.   A&P will utilize the services of emerging Negro businessmen. To implement this program, A&P will grant scavenger and exterminator service accounts from a minimum of forty (40) A&P stores to Operation Breadbasket for distribution to the alliances of scavenger and exterminating companies. Additionally in consultation with Operation Breadbasket, A&P will increase Janitorial services to a minimum of 40 stores. The contracts, three to five years, will state a fair price that is reasonable for each service, and will provide for annual reviews of prices, if requested by either the service or A&P, and will contain double-option responsibility and protection for both the service companies and A&P.

A&P will add the Chatham Citizen to those Negro papers now being used to advertise and communicate to Negro people about its concrete and creative program among Negroes. A&P's Advertising Department will meet with representatives of Vince Cullers Advertising Agency, Poly-Graphics Associates, and Galaxie Press Incorporated in an effort to use those services when local ad services are needed. Through all of these efforts A&P will encourage positive images of Negro people.

A&P will also seek to use the services of other Negro business and professional men and women such as in law, accounting, and insurance. Operation Breadbasket will offer consultation in such other services.

IV.   A&P will transfer the banking transactions from a minimum of forty (40) stores to the two banks which are sensitive to the problems of the Negro community. Substantial balances will be maintained in the Independence Bank of Chicago and Seaway National Bank. A&P will also seek to place other funds, such as Federal withholding taxes in these two institutions to fulfill its own banking needs, while at the same time using its funds in a constructive manner for the economic development of Negro people and institutions.

V.   As A&P projects it construction and refurbishing of buildings throughout metropolitan Chicago, especially in the Negro community, it will, after consultation with Operation Breadbasket, provide emerging Negro building organizations and related trades in the construction industry opportunity to work on stores constructed or refurbished by A&P. A&P will also provide the Negro financial institution working with Operaton Breadbasket the opportunity to furnish the interim and long term financing of such work.

The ministers of Operation Breadbasket agrees to communicate to their congregations and to the Negro community at large that the A&P Company has adopted a substantial and far-reaching program aimed at solving the problems of economic deprivation, unequal employment, and lack of economic development of people and institutions within the Negro community.

The ministers of Operation Breadbasket agree to assist A&P by referring potential employees for new jobs and by working with the businessmen in points II, III, IV, and V in providing programs of continuing education in the different aspects of business. Operation Breadbasket joins with A&P in a cooperative effort to build healthy and economically viable people, to develop creative and productive businessmen, and to structure sound and strong economic institutions for the mutual benefit of the total life of the city.

This agreement between Operation Breadbasket and A&P is a demonstration to all men of good will that business institutions and ministers can join together with the belief that the economic and social future of the Chicago metropolitan area is dependent upon the economic and social uplifting of the Negro communities within that market. Operation Breadbasket and A&P intend to play a vital role in overcoming the deep social tensions that now keep the fabric of our society frayed.

Human Subsidy

A Position Paper by

Rev. Jesse L. Jackson

Southern Christian Leadership Conference
366 East 47th Street
Chicago, Illinois 60653

Poor Peoples Campaign,
Phase II
May 1969

Human Subsidy

A Position Paper by

REV. JESSE L. JACKSON

Introduction

Famine is perhaps non-existent in this state and in the nation, but there is hunger throughout the land.

Hunger is a present reality in some 40 Illinois counties where 25% or more of the households are plagued with it each day. Cook County has at least 54,000 households on the hunger rolls—and even the more affluent DuPage, Winnebago and Lake counties have in excess of 12,000 households in which hunger is a fact of life.

In light of these facts the Ministers of Operation Breadbasket of the Southern Christian Leadership Conference have conceived a Human Subsidy Bill which has as its aim "stopping all hunger and malnutrition in the state and removing the scourge of poverty and destitution from its people."

The proposed legislation will include the following points:

1. That the State will declare hunger a disaster destroying human lives.
2. That slums will be declared illegal.
3. That the state and federal governments will raise the subsidy level for all people.
4. That the Means test will be removed since it compels people to make embarrassing public disclosures of their possessions in order to receive money for food and shelter.
5. That the Food Stamp Program be abolished as it stigmatizes persons when their real need is for money to purchase necessities of life.
6. That the state (and federal government) will establish emergency job training programs for unemployed and hungry people. This should be

done in much the same way that job training programs were developed to meet the emergencies of the war.

The following is a "Position Paper" on the issue of hunger and poverty and the need for altering the very conception of welfare in this society.

Not Welfare, but Subsidy

America is caught in deep internal conflict. Though the nation is the richest in the world, it allows a fifth of its population to languish in poverty. As a blessed nation, we have a surplus of food. But we also have starvation in the midst of surplus. The nation's ethic allows the rich to readily receive subsidies for the maintenance and explosion of the economy, but the poor are stigmatized with welfare payments. Subsidy and welfare both come from government funds, though one is viewed as constructive and the other destructive. These conflicts plague America deeply as it struggles with the question affecting the nation's attitude and behavior toward all citizens.

The conflicts cannot be resolved, however, until America admits the truth to herself.

America is a land in which the rich are subsidized, aided and upgraded, while the poor are compelled to live on subsistence. It is absolutely inconceivable that hunger should touch over 10,000,000 in this nation; 629,000 households containing 2 million people in Illinois.

Though the poor are chastised for their poverty, the poor in fact are victims who divert attention from the real issue of the extent to which the rich are aided at the expense of the remainder of the population. The poor pay more and receive less.

This is especially true in Illinois where the poor are characterized as free-loaders and parasites to the taxpayers. The truth is that 60% of the state revenues are derived from sales taxes paid most often by the poor.

The poor become the most convenient and visible scapegoats of the economically more affluent segments of the population. At the same time they are subjected to a dubious ethic that suggests that welfare is a privilege rather than a right for all citizens.

Yet America has deemed it an economic value and need to subsidize land, commercial and educational institutions within our society and economy. Before the Johnson Administration retired in January, Secretary of

Agriculture Orvill Freeman testified before the Select Committee on Nutrition and Human Needs of the United States Senate that the national policy is to pay farmers more than $3 billion per year not to produce food or fiber in order to stop our over-production of food. The 7% Investment Tax Credit for businesses was enacted to stimulate business growth. These are only two of the many subsidies presently granted in the nation whose history is one of subsidizing specific industries and institutions in the name of the general welfare.

The Constitution of the United States asserts in its preamble that the paramount purpose of the state is to promote the general welfare of all its citizens. The total American political and social experience can be seen as analogous in some respects to a bank. Thus an American citizen is by definition an investor in the American Bank. He cements this investment by paying taxes, by fighting in wars, by laboring to build the economy and by consuming the products of that economy.

The investment of black people has been costly. It began with the involuntary state of slavery when we were locked out of the definition of citizenship. America's racism defined our status in the Constitution as only 3/5th persons.

In a sense we have never been freed from that classification. Emancipation merely released us to fare for ourselves in a capitalistic system without capital. Then we are humiliated because we are pauperized and contained in a state of municipal servitude called welfare. We are confined to a state of poverty and hunger in a nation of plenty.

Yet it is the case that many black men and women have fought, bled and died in wars from the American Revolution to the undeclared military action we are now engaged in in Viet Nam. Over 187,000 black men fought for their freedom in the Civil War.

But America still spends an average of $954 per second for the war in Viet Nam, while the skirmish against poverty has amounted to less than $55 per person per year.

What we must never forget, however, is that in the early days of this society's development our manpower preceded machine power. Before there were pistons and grease, there were our muscles and sweat. Before there were milking machines, there were fingers extracting that life-giving substance. Before the mechanical cotton picker, there were hands provided by men, women and children who spent their days in terms of endless hours of stoop labor. But it is precisely these people that this system is driving into the hungering crisis.

> The crisis is caused not so much by the transaction from slavery to equality as by a change from an economics of exploitation to an economics of uselessness. With the onset of automation the Negro is moving out of his historical state of oppression into uselessness. Increasingly, he is not so much economically exploited as he is irrelevant. And the Negro's economic anxiety is an anxiety that will spread to others in our society as automation proceeds. (Sidney M. Willhelm & Edwin H. Powell, "Who Needs the Negro?")

The economic system in America has already predetermined the extermination of black people as workers. While automation effects the white community as a vice growing out of improper planning for future phasing out of work programs, it hits the black community as a vengeance virtually removing the black man as a productive economic unit in society. Moreover, where the growth of political power threatens traditional white rural southern interests, blacks are being starved into extinction or into existing from the land. This has been documented by the studies of the Medical Committee on Human Rights, the Tufts University team in the Mississippi Delta project and the Senate Sub-committee on Employment, Manpower and Poverty headed at the time by Senator Robert F. Kennedy.

The truth is that the wealthiest classes have thrown men into competition with matter. Our economy is now contingent upon the fortunes of the defense industries, or the military-industrial complex (a force of critical significance noted by the late President Eisenhower in his farewell address in January, 1961.) The military-industrial complex represents the most powerful single factor in shaping the policy of the nation and economy. Yet it has been all but immune to fiscal accountability and critical examination. Illinois' share of the money is over $1.06 billion.

While Congress and state legislatures quibble over feeding hungry and destitute people, the Defense Department has been reported to regularly spend as high as 200% more than estimated original costs of items of procurement.

Moreover, the Department of Defense holds over $202.5 billion in real and personal property, and over 29 million acres of land, while in a city like Chicago black people are forced to live in dilapidated and deteriorated housing in neighborhoods with 60,000 people or more per square mile.

It appears that the business of defense has steadily widened its sphere of influence from a military-industrial complex including the nation's educational institutions and the labor unions and the political forces.

Though many questioned President Johnson on whether it was possible to have "guns and butter," it is obvious that the construction of military hardware and the destruction of a poor nation with some of those weapons are much more important to the national policy makers than the flesh and blood of brothers and sisters who desire creative action to redeem human lives.

Trapped beneath the burden of the nation's killing programs are 40 million poor people, one-fifth of the population of the world's richest nation. Numerically, there are more poor whites than poor blacks, but percentage-wise there are more black poor than white poor. Obviously the problem of establishing human priorities in a nation so committed to non-human values transcends race.

The Poor People's Campaign was conceived in the mind of Dr. Martin Luther King, Jr., and was carried out through the first phase by his beloved successor, Dr. Ralph David Abernathy, as a way of uncovering the festering sore of America's greed, and the destruction of millions of poor people.

Dr. Abernathy has now called for the Second Phase of the Poor People's Campaign to tell the truth to America about the hunger and the hurt in the land. The rationale for the Poor People's Campaign has not changed in a year. America, listen once again to why we must speak to the nation and the world.

> Someone had to cry out for justice in a land that has placed priority on profits rather than persons.
> Someone had to ring out with clear, moral authority that ten million people went to bed each night suffering physical destruction from malnutrition to acute starvation.
> Someone had to say that not only do we need jobs but that we also need a redefinition of work.
> Someone had to plead for a quality in life that offered wages, but more importantly, fulfillment.
> Someone had to demand that involuntary starvation should be a punishable crime in a land of surplus and waste.
> (Rev. Jesse L. Jackson, "Resurrection City," *Ebony*, Oct., 1968)

America has yet to respond to the Kerner Report on America's racism as the major factor in racial and class disturbances. One year later blacks are still discriminated against and still make less money with more education than whites with less education.

But we cannot allow ourselves to be rendered useless people. Some ideas or definitions may be obvious in this technological whirlwind changing all previous points of reference. But black people are not obsolete for we are somebody; we are God's people.

And the new administration under President Richard Nixon expresses its values in curbing inflation by programming a rise in unemployment by the end of the year of 400,000. Black and other poor people can no longer be psychologically imprisoned with feelings of guilt in a nation whose economy has been managed since the days its slavery policies were determined.

Those who have had to labor in the nastiest and the most menial of jobs have been abused with the label of laziness because they received so little for their efforts and energy. Their blood and sweat built and fed a nation, but they were the last hired, the first fired, and the forgotten in the time of need.

Yet as the technological transitions demand almost immediate change in our conceptions as well as our behavior, it is clear that work must be redefined to fit the needs of this new period. Going to school is work. Education is necessary for the continuation of our technology-oriented society. Thus the student expends his creative energy in his studies and ought to be compensated as he prepares to use his knowledge for the common good in his future work. We have not yet recognized the broad need to subsidize the education of students. Though the numerous scholarship programs have expressed a value of education, they are yet to serve as the model for inducements to study.

At the moment, the Reserve Officer Training Corps (ROTC) program is a major example of using public funds in universities and colleges across the nation to encourage students to finish school. A product of the Defense Department, the ROTC program offers a student a stipend to stay in school in preparation for becoming a professional killer upon graduation. Status as an officer and concrete employment are held up as further inducements for the student. So the best minds of the nation are preparing for military service while they are paid to attend college.

We do not have such a program of inducement to study for other fields. Though we need trained personnel, the nation has yet to set up programs to train doctors, nurses, lawyers, dentists, social workers or teachers. The special programs are aimed at producing another college crop of killers who will become part of the military complex.

The ROTC subsidy, interestingly enough, has not drained away the ambition of brilliant young men. Neither did wealth and subsidies to the rich limit the ambitions and the drives of the Kennedys or the Rockefellers. Nor have the agricultural subsidies to Senator Eastland of Mississippi affected his drive to perform as a politician. Subsidies appear to have had the opposite effect by allowing men to function for their own interests within the American economy and social structure.

The black and the poor, however, have been victimized by being granted only the most difficult and poorly paying chores in the American economy or by being ignored by that economy altogether. Then they are humiliated in their victimized condition by the white propaganda that tells them they are responsible for their condition. Their limited energy, resulting from the hunger and malnutrition forced upon them, distorts their lives while whites withheld the food that they helped raise. Now they are the useless dregs, the unskilled slaves and immigrants of previous generations, that America wants to discard completely. The destruction comes daily in the reminder from the rich of the land that they are living off of privilege rather than right.

The issue is whether the poor, and particularly the black poor, will be considered products or prisoners of this society. As products their potential would become most significant. As prisoners their containment and punishment would be primary. We contend that it is the obligation of this society to see its poor people as products and their economic misfortune as the by-product of a highly advanced technology.

The economic skills of the poor have been limited by displacement brought on by this technology. For example, it is reported in the Joint Economic Committee of the United States Congress hearings that there are at least 500,000 hard core unemployed in the central cities of the nation.

The recognition of the poor as products means that the poor will be nourished and encouraged, not shunted aside and discouraged. When they encounter problems as the result of deficiencies in their training, health or other factors of development, it is up to the society to meet those deficiencies with programs of rehabilitation. This is similar to the response of healing when a society encounters sickness. By contrast we find that the poor are prisoners. Thus caseworkers are not social service persons but are policemen and investigators. The poor are prisoners. The poor are compelled by Administrative edict to submit to means tests before they can receive the basic necessities of life. This places a premium on eligibility rather than on the priority of need. Invasion of the privacy of the poor is considered in the line of duty and the poor seldom see their caseworkers as persons to assist them but as persons who snoop on their private, intimate lives. This makes their homes no longer "their castles" but miniature prisons in which each room becomes a caged-cell block. We propose to end this inhuman and wasteful system and to develop an entirely different concept of persons in need of assistance.

Not prisoners but products of America's social and economic system, the hungry and the poor need to escape from the welfare cycle. Once captured by the welfare cycle, the poor are engulfed by forces bent upon convincing them of their lack of worth, their humiliation and their powerlessness.

Though the need of welfare is economic, the effect captures people psychologically and confines them geographically to the urban and the rural slums of our nation.

Contributing forces include the police, the government, the schools. Police are too busy protecting property of the rich and the white, rather than protecting the citizens in their rights. Political rights of the poor must be guaranteed and protected, thus eliminating voting frauds and the political disenfranchisement. Health and well-being must be protected among all citizens. The police need the authority to arrest slum landlords who violate health standards and building codes. Store owners that abuse the lives of people with tainted meats, bad produce and filthy conditions need to have a healthy fear of being arrested by the police.

The corrupting forces in government have done much to destroy poor people and to contain them in their misery. Racists in the House and Senate of Congress from the southern states control significant committees through chairmanships. They are the nation's legacy of racism at the highest levels of our government. Men like Mendal Rivers, chairman of the House Armed Forces Committee; Wilbur Mills, chairman of the House Ways and Means Committee; Carl Perkins, as chairman of the House Education and Labor Committee control the major policies of this nation in terms of taxation and the use of our economic resources, the military and the wars we fight, and of the school systems and who is employed. Similar control is held in the United States Senate by men such as Richard Russell of Georgia as the chairman of the Senate Armed Forces Committee. The schools have contributed their share to the maintenance of the welfare cycle by teaching irrelevant courses to uneducated youth. They have also been victimized by limited appropriations from the state legislatures and the school boards under the control of those who wanted to perpetuate the dependency of poor people.

The poor and the hungry are deeply scarred by non-economic forces over basically economic matters. They have been psychologically discouraged by the lack of protection for their personal rights and needs. They have been abused by being untaught within the context of the educational system. They have been politically intimidated in terms of their voting rights and their desire for justice. Thus, without the inducement of a living wage in the job market the poor and the hungry have no other place to turn but the welfare market.

Welfare is not even adequate as a concept within the context of our economic and social system. The terms welfare and recipient smack of beggars or parasites intruding on our social structures.

Subsidy, however, is a more meaningful concept that has broad usage across the American scene. Its sole criteria is economic. It has nothing to do with religion or training. Just as the nation subsidizes land and businesses, America ought to subsidize human beings, people who have economic needs.

Subsidy is fuel which allows people to move within the American system. The hungry and the poor need this stimulus to put them in motion. At the same time the other institutions need to move in concert with the poor to correct the ills affecting their lives.

By looking at the welfare area as a geographical place, it is clear that objective standards can be developed as the guidelines for all the supporting institutions. The slums, or the geographic locations of the hungry and the poor, need to be declared disaster areas.

Subjective feelings can be taken away from America's treatment of the poor by dealing concretely with the objective needs of persons in the poverty areas.

Some will ask how to declare an area under disaster. The only answer used previously has been in response to natural crises called "Acts of God." But the hungry and the poor of the nation suffer daily disaster because of acts of men who conspire to put profits over persons and who create injustice out of their own greed.

These disasters contribute to crisis after crisis threatening the very future of our nation. They have been spawned and perpetuated by men and the institutions of America. The American Dilemma must be rechanneled into the American Dream while the hungry and the poor seek for assurances of their stake in society.

The most significant assurance could come by making human subsidy a reality, and a part of the new legal order. In addition, the pursuit of law and order must take serious precedent on the agendas of federal, state and local officials. If housing code violations were illegal and the violators prosecuted vigorously, a new dynamic would be initiated in the slums. New job demands would be immediate in the labor market because housing is in such ill repair. Carpenters, painters, brick masons, truck drivers, *et cetera* would be needed immediately, and those who are unskilled ought to be put to work in on-the-job training programs in construction and rehabilitation of buildings, communities and lives.

Law and order are possible in America. But it is important to understand that order is not the absence of noise, for that is quietness. Order is the presence of justice. And, inherent in order is peace, for there cannot be peace unless the goods of the society are distributed properly. Then law is the form that justice takes guaranteeing that the goods are distributed properly within the community.

The Human Subsidy represents justice to human beings in need. It is respectful of persons created by God and placed on Earth to partake and participate in its abundance. America has the resources and the capacity to provide for each citizen in the drive to eliminate hunger and poverty from the land.

Notes

1. Martin Luther King, Jr., *Where Do We Go From Here: Chaos or Community?* (New York: Harper & Row, Publishers, 1967), p. 3.
2. Press statement made by Martin Luther King, Jr., "The Chicago Plan," Chicago, January 7, 1966, p. 3 (Mimeographed).
3. *Ibid.*
4. St. Clair Drake and Horace Clayton, *Black Metropolis*, Harper Torchbook (New York: Harper & Row, Publishers, 1962), Vol. II, p. 734.
5. W.E.B. DuBois (Editor), "Editorials: Boycotts," *The Crisis: a Record of the Darker Races*, September, 1934, pp. 268-69.
6. W.E.B. DuBois, *Dusk of Dawn*, first published in 1940 (New York: Schocken Books, 1968), pp. 192-220; also by DuBois, *The Souls of Black Folk*, first published in 1903 (New York: The New American Library, 1969), pp. 79-95.
7. Press release from SCLC, "The Quiet Work of SCLC: Operation Breadbasket," Atlanta, Georgia, December 16, 1966 (Mimeographed).
8. Jesse L. Jackson [and David Marshall Wallace], "From October to May: a Report to Rev. C.T. Vivian," Chicago, The Urban Training Center for Christian Mission, May 17, 1966, p. 12 (Mimeographed).
9. Edmund J. Rooney, "New Pressure Campaign Goal–Negro Jobs," *The Chicago Daily News*, February 12, 1966.
10. Compare, for example, "Direct Action: . . . to Dramatize a Plight," by Dorothy Cotton, *The SCLC Story* (Atlanta: The Southern Christian Leadership Conference, 1964), p. 29, and "From the Fullness of the Earth: the Story of Chicago's Operation Breadbasket," by David M. Wallace, *The Register* (Chicago: The Chicago Theological Seminary), November, 1966, pp. 16-20.
11. From "Operation Breadbasket," a brochure distributed by the Southern Christian Leadership Conference, undated [*ca.* 1964].
12. For example, in every company approached, there were no black workers at all in many significant categories of work, especially managerial functions, with the overall average of black workers only about 5% for all companies.
13. From the "Minutes of Operation Breadbasket Steering Committee," Chicago, March 11, 1966 (Mimeographed).
14. Although the Summit Agreement seemed a significant victory at the time, it failed to alter the pattern of segregated housing in Chicago. In retrospect, the main weakness seems to have been neglect of the political realities of Mayor Daley's Chicago.
15. See Appendix I of the original thesis. Copy of Joint Statement from Operation Breadbasket and High-Low.
16. W.E.B. Dubois, *Dusk of Dawn: an Essay Toward an Autobiography of a Race Concept.* Sourcebooks in Negro History. (New York: Schocken Books, 1968).

See also W.E.B. DuBois, "Of Mr. Booker T. Washington and Others," *The Souls of Black Folk*.

17. This Covenant was also included in Appendix II of the original thesis.
18. News Release by Operation Breadbasket, Chicago, March 8, 1967 (Mimeographed).
19. The Guide for Consumer Clubs was also included as Appendix III of the original thesis.
20. See Appendix IV of the original thesis for a copy of the "Directory of Black Businesses," August, 1968.
21. Martin Luther King, Jr., "The President's Report to the Board of Directors of the Southern Christian Leadership Conference," Atlanta, March 21, 1967, pp. 5, 7 (Xerographic copy).
22. See Appendix II of the original thesis for a copy of the "Proposals for A&P's Action," September 23, 1968.
23. See Appendix II of the original thesis for a copy of the "Covenant Between SCLC-Operation Breadbasket and the Chicago Unit, Great A&P Tea Company," October 5, 1968.
24. These Guidelines were also included as Appendix V in the original thesis.
25. This section will deal with the rather rapid expansion of the various program threads, leaving their resolution or current state for a later section.
26. This Paper was also included as Appendix VI of the original thesis.
27. *Ibid.*
28. See Appendix VII of the original thesis for a copy of the "Covenant Between SCLC's Operation Breadbasket and the Chicago Area Districts and the General Office of Walgreen Drug Stores," June 27, 1970.
29. Max Weber, *The Theory of Social and Economic Organization* (New York: Free Press Paperback, 1964), p. 152. The editor of this edition notes the difficulty of finding an English word to translate Weber's term *Herrschaft*. At some points it is translated "authority," in other places as "imperative control," in still others as "imperative coordination." For ease of understanding, "authority" will be used consistently here.
30. *Ibid.*
31. *Ibid.*, p. 151.
32. *Ibid.*, p. 325.
33. *Ibid.*
34. *Ibid.*, p. 328.
35. Weber, *Theory of Social and Economic Organization*, pp. 341-42, and Weber, "Three Types of Legitimate Rule," in *A Sociological Reader on Complex Organizations*, edited by Amitai Etzioni, pp. 9-10.
36. E. Franklin Frazier, *The Negro Church in America*, First Schocken Paperback Edition (New York: Schocken Books, 1966), p. 30.
37. *Ibid.*, p. 34.
38. *Ibid.*, pp. 85-86.
39. Weber, *The Theory of Social and Economic Organization*, p. 330.
40. *Ibid.*

41. This will be discussed in greater detail in considering Weber's category of charismatic authority.
42. Weber, *The Theory of Social and Economic Organization*, p. 331.
43. *Ibid.*
44. *Ibid.*
45. *Ibid.*, p. 332.
46. *Ibid.*, p. 333.
47. *Ibid.*
48. *Ibid.*, p. 334.
49. *Ibid.*
50. *Ibid.*, p. 329.
51. *Ibid.*, p. 330.
52. *Ibid.*, pp. 358-59.
53. *Ibid.*, p. 363.
54. *Ibid.*, p. 359.
55. *Ibid.*
56. *Ibid.*, p. 360.
57. *From Max Weber: Essays in Sociology*, translated and edited by H.H. Gerth and C. Wright Mills, A Galaxie Book (New York: Oxford University Press, 1958), p. 248.
58. Weber, "Three Types of Legitimate Rule," in *A Sociological Reader on Complex Organizations*, edited by Amitai Etzioni, Second Edition (New York: Holt, Rinehart and Winston, Inc., 1969), p. 12.
59. Weber, *Theory of Social and Economic Organization*, p. 360.
60. One possible exception to this should be noted here. Within the first few months of Breadbasket's existence in Chicago, a man with particular photographic and electronic skills joined the staff. However, this person, Jack Finley, was already on the SCLC staff and was reassigned to Operation Breadbasket. It is not clear whether he was "selected" for the staff or whether he made a strong enough case for his skills to "force" his way into the fairly tight Breadbasket staff.
61. Weber, *Theory of Social and Economic Organization*, p. 360.
62. *Ibid.*
63. *Ibid.*, p. 361.
64. *Ibid.*, pp. 361-62.
65. *Ibid.*, p. 362.
66. Weber, *Essays in Sociology*, p. 247.
67. Weber, *The Theory of Social and Economic Organization*, p. 362.
68. *Ibid.*, pp. 363-64.
69. *Ibid.*, p. 364.
70. *Ibid.*, p. 367.
71. *Ibid.*, p. 369.
72. *Ibid.*, p. 370.
73. *Ibid.*
74. *Ibid.*, p. 337.

75. In fact, Weber's definition of "discipline" as a characteristic of rational organization is "the consistently rationalized, methodically trained and exact execution of the received order, in which *all personal criticism is unconditionally suspended* . . ." [italics added], Weber, *Essays in Sociology*, p. 253.

76. W.E.B. DuBois, *Autobiography of W.E.B. DuBois* (New York: International Publishers Co., Inc., 1968), p. 265.

77. W.E.B. DuBois, *Dusk of Dawn* (New York: Schocken Books, 1968), pp. 243-244.

78. W.E.B. DuBois, *Autobiography*, pp. 301, 307.

79. *Ibid.*, pp. 312-14.

Bibliography

American Academy of Arts and Sciences. *Philosophers and Kings: Studies in Leadership*, Vol. 97, No. 3 of *Daedalus*. Cambridge, Massachusetts: The American Academy of Arts and Sciences, Summer, 1968.

Beckhard, Richard. *Organizational Development: Strategies and Models*. Addison-Wesley Series on Organization Development. Reading, Massachusetts: Addison-Wesley Publishing Co., 1969.

Bennis, Warren. *Changing Organizations: Essays on the Development and Evolution of Human Organizations*. Addison-Wesley Series on Organization Development. Reading, Massachusetts: Addison-Wesley Publishing Co., 1969.

Broderick, Francis L., and August Meier, editors. *Negro Protest Thought in the Twentieth Century*. The American Heritage Series. Indianapolis: The Bobbs-Merril Co., Inc., 1965.

Drake, St. Clair, and Horace R. Cayton. *Black Metropolis: a Study of Negro Life in a Northern City*. Harper Torchbooks. 2 Vols. New York: Harper & Row, Publishers, 1962.

DuBois, William Edward Burghardt. *The Autobiography of W.E.B. DuBois*. New World Paperbacks. New York: International Publishers Co., Inc., 1968.

_____. *Dusk of Dawn: an Essay Toward an Autobiography of a Race Concept*. Sourcebooks in Negro History. New York: Schocken Books, 1968.

_____. *The Negro Church: a Social Study*. Atlanta University Publications, No. 8. Atlanta, Georgia: Atlanta University Press, 1903.

Eisenstadt, S.N., ed. *Max Weber On Charisma and Institution Building: Selected Papers*. The Heritage of Sociology Series. Chicago: The University of Chicago Press, 1968.

Etzioni, Amitai. *Modern Organizations*. Foundations of Modern Sociology Series. Englewood Cliffs, New Jersey: Prentice-Hall, Inc., 1964.

_____, ed. *A Sociological Reader on Complex Organizations*, Second Edition. New York: Holt, Rinehart and Winston, Inc., 1969.

Frazier, E. Franklin. *The Negro Church in America*. Sourcebooks in Negro History. New York: Schocken Books, 1966.

Gerth, H.H., and C. Wright Mills, editors. *From Max Weber: Essays in Sociology*. Translated by the editors. A Galaxie Book. New York: Oxford University Press, 1958.

King, Martin Luther, Jr. *Where Do We Go From Here: Chaos or Community?* New York: Harper & Row, Publishers, 1967.

Niebuhr, Reinhold. *Moral Man and Immoral Society*. The Scribner Library. New York: Charles Scribner's Sons, 1960.

_____. *The Nature of Destiny of Man: A Christian Interpretation*. The Scribner Library. 2 Vols. New York: Charles Scribner's Sons, 1964.

Tillich, Paul. *Love, Power, and Justice: Ontological Analyses and Ethical Applications*. A Galaxie Book. New York: Oxford University Press, 1960.

Weber, Max. *The Sociology of Religion*. Translated from the Fourth Edition by Ephraim Fischoff, with an Introduction by Talcott Parsons. Boston: Beacon Press, 1963.

_____. *The Theory of Social and Economic Organization*. Translated by A.M. Henderson and Talcott Parsons, edited and with an Introduction by Talcott Parsons. Free Press Paperback Edition. New York: The Free Press of Macmillan Company, 1964.

About the Authors

Mary Lou Finley received her Ph.D. in Sociology from the University of Chicago and is presently on the faculty of Antioch University Seattle. Her Ph.D. dissertation was a study of the social and medical causes of delays in diagnosing breast cancer and she has lectured and published widely on this and other topics relating to women in society. In 1965 and 1966 she was James Bevel's Administrative Assistant in the Chicago headquarters of the Southern Christian Leadership Conference.

Kathleen Connolly wrote the paper included here when she had just begun the Urban Studies Program at Loyola University. She was active in the civil rights movement in Chicago and had worked with several of the people involved in the Open Housing Conference. She is presently Director of the SAn Francisco Emergency Food Box Program. She has been active in various aspects of urban affairs, including organizing unemployed women and relating churches to urban issues.

John McKnight is Director of Community Studies at the Center for Urban Affairs and Policy Research at Northwestern University. His many publications include *The Future of Low Income Neighborhoods and the People Who Reside There*. He has directed research projects on a wide variety of topics including: Chicago law enforcement determinants of community health, and the effects of the perception of crime upon community responses.

Alvin Pitcher is a long-time Chicago activist. He was administrative assistant to Al Raby (chairman of CCCO) from 1965 to 1967 and secretary of the Agenda Committee of the Chicago Freedom Movement from 1966 to 1967. He was on the staff of Operation Breadbasket from 1966 to 1971 and was an officer of PUSH from 1984 to 1986. From 1952 to 1978 he was on the faculty of the Divinity School of the University of Chicago.

Gary Massoni worked full-time for SCLC and Operation Breadbasket from 1966 to 1970. He is presently with the United Campus Ministry at Oregon

347

State University at Corvallis. A close friend of Jesse Jackson's (they met moving into Seminary housing), Massoni took a leave of absence to be the director of scheduling for the Jesse Jackson for President Campaign in 1987/88.

Index

TITLES IN THE SERIES

Martin Luther King, Jr.

and the

Civil Rights Movement

DAVID J. GARROW, EDITOR

DATE DUE